Soviet and Post-Soviet Politics and Society (SPPS)
ISSN 1614-3515

Founded in 2004 and refereed since 2007, SPPS makes available affordable English-, German-, and Russian-language studies on the history of the countries of the former Soviet bloc from the late Tsarist period to today. It publishes between 5 and 20 volumes per year and focuses on issues in transitions to and from democracy such as economic crisis, identity formation, civil society development, and constitutional reform in CEE and the NIS. SPPS also aims to highlight so far understudied themes in East European studies such as right-wing radicalism, religious life, higher education, or human rights protection. The authors and titles of all previously published volumes are listed at the end of this book. For a full description of the series and reviews of its books, see

www.ibidem-verlag.de/red/spps.

Editorial correspondence & manuscripts should be sent to: Dr. Andreas Umland, c/o DAAD, German Embassy, vul. Bohdana Khmelnitskoho 25, UA-01901 Kyiv, Ukraine. e-mail: umland@stanfordalumni.org

Business correspondence & review copy requests should be sent to: *ibidem* Press, Leuschnerstr. 40, 30457 Hannover, Germany; tel.: +49 511 2622200; fax: +49 511 2622201; spps@ibidem.eu.

Authors, reviewers, referees, and editors for (as well as all other persons sympathetic to) SPPS are invited to join its networks at www.facebook.com/group.php?gid=52638198614 www.linkedin.com/groups?about=&gid=103012 www.xing.com/net/spps-ibidem-verlag/

Recent Volumes

Alexander Sergunin

EXPLAINING RUSSIAN FOREIGN POLICY BEHAVIOR

Theory and Practice

ibidem-Verlag
Stuttgart

Bibliographic information published by the Deutsche Nationalbibliothek
Die Deutsche Nationalbibliothek lists this publication in the Deutsche Nationalbibliografie; detailed bibliographic data are available in the Internet at http://dnb.d-nb.de.

Bibliografische Information der Deutschen Nationalbibliothek
Die Deutsche Nationalbibliothek verzeichnet diese Publikation in der Deutschen Nationalbibliografie; detaillierte bibliografische Daten sind im Internet über http://dnb.d-nb.de abrufbar.

Cover picture: A Knight at the Crossroads. Viktor Vasnetsov, 1878. Oil on canvas. Source: Wikiart.org. Public domain.

ISSN: 1614-3515

ISBN-13: 978-3-8382-0782-7

© *ibidem*-Verlag / *ibidem* Press
Stuttgart, Germany 2016

Table of Contents

Chapter 3.
Threat Perceptions, Foreign Policy,
Military and National Security Doctrines

Chapter 4.
Foreign Policy Decision-Making System

Acknowledgements

A number of generous grants from different organizations made this book possible. First of all, I have to mention a number of grants from St. Petersburg State University (SPSU) (2008–2010) that were devoted to international security (both on the theoretical and practical levels). In 1993, 1996–98 and 2000–2003 I've conducted several research projects on Russian domestic debate on European security and EU-Russia relations which have been sponsored by the Copenhagen Peace Research Institute (COPRI)[1]. In the same periods, the Research Support Scheme, Open Society Institute (Prague) (1996–98), NATO Democratic Institutions Fellowship Program (1997–99), John D. and Catherine T. MacArthur Foundation (2000–01), Finnish Institute of International Relations (UPI) (2000–01, 2004–06), East-West Institute (2000) and International Policy Fellowship (2003–04), Curriculum Development Competition program, Curriculum Resource Center (2007–08), Special Projects Office, Special and Extension Programs (2012) at the Central European University, funded my projects on the Russian and global post-Cold War security discourse and politics.

In the spring 2004 semester I was teaching a course of Russian foreign policy in the Department of Government, Cornell University, Ithaca, NY (as a part of the Fulbright exchange program). The fruitful dialogue with my students and colleagues was very helpful for developing and testing fresh ideas.

In 2003–2004 Prof. Pavel Tsygankov (Moscow State University) led a research project on the Russian post-Soviet IR and the earlier and shorter versions of this study were published both in Russia and the U.S. (Tsygankov and Tsygankov 2005; Sergunin 2003–2004).

Another research project on mapping the post-Cold War International Relations (IR) (both Western and non-Western) was launched by Dr. Arlene Tickner (University of Andes, Columbia) and Prof. Øle Wæver (University of Copenhagen) at the 2004 Montreal International Studies Association (ISA) Convention. Within this project, I was responsible for examining the Russian post-Soviet IR debate.

In 2004, Dr Arkady Moshes from the Finnish Institute of International Relations (UPI) has launched an ambitious research project on the EU-Russia relations with the title "Assessing Russia's European Choice". I was responsible for examining the Russian decision-making mechanism on Europe. The above-mentioned study was followed up by a book project led by Dr. Ted Hopf from the Ohio State University.

---

1   Merged with the Danish Institute for International Studies (DIIS) in 2003.

In 2011–2015, a series of short-term projects on Russian policies in the East and North Europe was conducted with University of Helsinki, Free University Berlin (FUB), University of Tartu and Stockholm University. In 2015 I was a coordinator of a pilot project on German-Russian relations in the context of the Ukrainian crisis (joint project sponsored by the SPSU and FUB). The SPSU-sponsored project on BRICS initiated in 2015 was also helpful in understanding Russia's foreign policies toward key developing countries.

To sum up, this book is both an end-result and follow-up of these projects.

Along with the above-mentioned organizations and projects, I remain indebted to Professor Håkan Wiberg, ex-Director of COPRI, who played a key role in launching and executing the above-mentioned projects by being its principal consultant and by providing me with useful advice at all their stages. I also extend special thanks to Dr. Pertti Joenniemi, former Senior Research Fellow, COPRI / DIIS, for his extensive and insightful comments and suggestions during my work on the projects.

It is a pleasant duty to mention here my gratitude to many colleagues who have helped me with especially useful advice or materials for this book. They include: Dr. Roy Allison, Senior Lecturer, Oxford University (former Head, Russian and CIS program, Royal Institute of International Affairs); Dr. Derek Averre, Research Fellow, The University of Birmingham; Dr. Pavel Baev, Senior Research Fellow, International Peace Research Institute Oslo (PRIO); Vladimir Baranovsky, former Project Leader, Stockholm Peace Research Institute (SIPRI) (until 1998), and currently Deputy Director, Institute of World Economy and International Relations, Russian Academy of Sciences (IMEMO, RAS, Moscow); Dr. Christopfer Browning, (COPRI, Birmingham / Keele / Warwick universities); Professor Barry Buzan, University of Westminster; Dr. Olga Potemkina and Dr. Dmitry Danilov, Institute of Europe, RAS; Prof. Michael Emerson, Senior Research Fellow, Center for European Policy Studies, Brussels; Prof. Mathew Evangelista, Cornell University; Dr. Frank Fischer, Professor of Political Science, Rutgers University; Geir Flikke, Dr. Jakub Godzimirski and Dr. Iver Neumann, research fellows at the Norwegian Institute of International Affairs (NUPI); Prof. Tuomas Forsberg, University of Tampere; Flemming Splidsboel Hansen, Senior Researcher, DIIS; Prof. Lassi Heininen, University of Lapland; Dr. Zlatko Isakovic, Senior Research Fellow, Institute of International Politics and Economics (Belgrade); Dr. Lena Jonson, Senior Research Fellow, Swedish Institute of International Affairs; Prof. Valery Konyshev, St. Petersburg University; Dr. Wojciech Kostecki, Senior Research Fellow, Institute for Political Studies (Warsaw); Dr. Natasha Kuhrt, King's College, London University; Gunnar Lassinantti, ex-Project Leader, Olof Palme International Center (Stockholm); Professor Margot Light, London School of Economics;

Prof. Marina Lebedeva, Moscow State Institute of International Relations (MGIMO); Dr. Raimundas Lopata, ex-Director, Institute of International Relations & Political Science, Vilnius University; Prof. Andrei Makarychev, Nizhny Novgorod Linguistic Universit / University of Tartuy; Dr. Andre Mommen, Department of Sociology, Amsterdam University; Dr. Arkady Moshes, Project Leader, Finnish Institute of International Relations (UPI); Kari Möttlöa, Special Adviser, Finnish Ministry of Foreign Affairs / University of Helsinki; Dr. Hans Mouritzen, Senior Research Fellow, COPRI / DIIS; Dr. Ingmar Oldberg, FOA (National Defense Establishment) / Swedish Institute of International Affairs; Prof. Bob Orttung, George Washington University; Dr. Alexander Pikaev, Senior Research Fellow, IMEMO, RAS; Prof. Mikhail Rykhtik, Nizhny Novgorod State University; Professor Klaus Segbers, Institute for East European Studies, FUB; Dr. Tatyana Shakleina, Senior Research Fellow, Institute of USA & Canada Studies (ISKRAN), RAS, Russia; Professor Jane Sharp, Department of War Studies, King's College (London); Dr. Hanna Smith, Aleksanteri Institute, University of Helsinki; Dr. Stephan Spigeleire, University of Leiden / the Hague Center for Strategic Studies; Dr. Fabrizio Tassinari, Senior Researcher, DIIS; Dr. Arlene Tickner (University of Andes, Columbia); Dr. Dmitry Trenin, Moscow Carnegie Center; Professor Ivan Tyulin, ex-First Vice-Rector, and Dr. Andrei Zagorsky, ex-Vice-Rector, Moscow State Institute of International Relations (MGIMO); Dr. Christian Wellmann, former Deputy Director, Schleswig-Holstein Institute for Peace Research; Prof. Øle Wæver, University of Copenhagen; Irina Y. Zhinkina, Senior Research Fellow, ISKRAN, RAS.

I am thankful to a number of research centers and institutions—the Department of International Relations Theory & History, SPSU; Department of Political Science, St. Petersburg campus, Higher School of Economics; Department of International Relations & Political Science, Institute of International Relations & World History, Nizhny Novgorod State University; Nizhny Novgorod Linguistic University, Russia; COPRI / DIIS, Denmark; Department of Government, Cornell University; SIPRI and Department of Political Science, Stockholm University, Sweden; International Institute for Strategic Studies, London, UK, and the Department of Politics, School of Sociology, Politics & Anthropology, La Trobe University, Melbourne, Australia, which provided me with excellent research environments and warm hospitality. Without their liberal support and help this work was not possible.

Alexander Sergunin
St. Petersburg State University, Russia
December 2015

Acronyms

ACV	Armored combat vehicle
ASEAN	Association of South-East Asian Nations
BA	Bachelor of Arts
BALTCOM	Baltic Communication System
BASREC	Baltic Sea Region Energy Cooperation
BEAC	Barents Euro-Arctic Council
BMD	Ballistic missile defense
BPS	Baltic Pipeline System
BRICS	Brazil, Russia, India, China, South Africa
CBSS	Council of the Baltic Sea States
CERI	Center for International Studies, Paris
CES	Common Economic Space
CFDP	Council on Foreign and Defense Policy
CFE	Treaty on Conventional Armed Forces in Europe
CFM	Committee on Financial Monitoring
CIS	Commonwealth of Independent States
COPRI	Copenhagen Peace Research Institute
CPRF	Communist Party of the Russian Federation
CPSU	Communist Party of the Soviet Union
CRM	Conflict Resolution and Mediation
CSCE	Conference for Security and Cooperation in Europe
CSTO	Collective Security Treaty Organization
DAAD	German Academic Exchange Program
DC	Decile coefficient
DIIS	Danish Institute for International Studies
DPR	Donetsk People's Republic
EaP	Eastern Partnership
EBRD	European Bank for Reconstruction & Development
ECTS	European Credit Transfer System
ECU	European Currency Unit
EEZ	Exclusive economic zone
EEU	Eurasian Economic Union
ENP	European Neighborhood Policy
EST	European Security Treaty
EU	European Union
FEZ	Free economic zone
FIS	Foreign Intelligence Service
FOI	National Defense Establishment (Sweden)
FSS	Federal Security Service

FTA	Free Trade Area
FUB	Free University Berlin
G-7	Group of Seven
G-20	Group of Twenty
GATT	General Agreement on Tariffs and Trade
GRU	Glavnoe Razvedavatel'noe Upravlenie – the Main Intelligence Directorate of the General Staff
JHA	Justice and Home Affairs
IAN	International Affairs Network
ICTs	Information and communication technologies
IFRI	French Institute for International Studies, Paris
IISS	International Institute for Strategic Studies, London
IMEMO	Institute of World Economy & International Relations
IMF	International Monetary Fund
INTAS	International Technical Assistance (to the CIS countries), EU program
INTERREG	EU's program on interregional co-operation
IR	International Relations
ISA	International Studies Association
ISAF	International Security Assistance Force
ISKRAN	Institute of USA & Canada Studies, RAS
KOR	Kaliningrad Defense District
LDPR	Liberal Democratic Party of Russia
LPR	Lughansk People's Republic
MA	Master of Arts
MED	Ministry for Economic Development
MFA	Ministry of Foreign Affairs
MGIMO	Moscow State Institute of International Relations
MGU	Moscow State University
MNEPR	Multilateral Nuclear Environmental Program in the Russian Federation
MoD	Ministry of Defense
NAFTA	North American Free Trade Area
NATO	North Atlantic Treaty Organization
NDA	Northern Dimension Area
NDEP	Northern Dimension Environmental Partnership
NDI	Northern Dimension Initiative
NEGP	North European Gas Pipeline
NEP	New Economic Policy
NGO	Non-governmental organization
NIS	New Independent States
NPP	Nuclear power plant
NPT	New Political Thinking

NRC	NATO-Russia Council
NSS	National Security Strategy
NUPI	Norwegian Institute of International Affairs
OECD	Organization for Economic Cooperation & Development
OSCE	Organization for Security and Cooperation in Europe
PCA	Partnership and Co-operation Agreement
PfP	Partnership for Peace (NATO program)
PHARE	Poland and Hungary, Aid for the Reconstruction of Economies
PIR-Center	Center for Russian Political Research
PR	Public relations
PRC	People's Republic of China
PRIO	Peace Research Institute Oslo
PTT	Power transition theory
RAAS	Russian Association of American Studies
RAND	Research & Development Corporation
RAS	Russian Academy of Science
RAU	Russian-American University
RFPF	Russian Foreign Policy Foundation
RISA	Russian International Studies Association
RISS	Russian Institute for Strategic Studies
ROC	Russian Orthodox Church
RPSA	Russian Political Science Association
RUSI	Royal United Services Institute
SCO	Shanghai Cooperation Organization
SEZ	Special economic zone
SIPRI	Stockholm Peace Research Institute
SPSA	Soviet Political Science Association
SPSU	St. Petersburg State University
START	U.S.-Soviet Strategic Arms Reduction Treaty
TACIS	Technical Assistance to the Commonwealth of Independent States
TAPRI	Tampere Peace Research Institute
TEMPUS	Trans-European Mobility Program for University Studies
TLE	Treaty-limited equipment
UK	United Kingdom
UN	United Nations
UNESCO	United Nations Education, Science & Culture Organization
UNIDO	United Nations Industrial Development Organization
UNSC	United Nations Security Council
UPI	Finnish Institute of International Relations
US	United States
USSR	Union of Soviet Socialist Republics
WEU	West European Union
WTO	World Trade Organization

Introduction

Russia in search of itself:
a post-Soviet identity discourse

It became a common-place for the Western scholars and politicians to ascertain that post-Cold war Russia's foreign policy behavior is often unpredictable, irrational, anti-Western, aggressive / expansionist and even irredentist (Carafano 2015; Cox 2014; Gaddy and O'Hanlon 2015; Granholm et al. 2014; Gressel 2015; Lukas 2009; Mankoff 2009; Snetkov 2015; Stoner and McFaul 2015). Moscow's harsh reaction to NATO's 1999 Kosovo intervention (including Russian commandos' surprise move from Bosnia to the Pristina airport) and the Georgian 2008 offensive in South Ossetia, Crimea's takeover and Donbass rebels' support by Russia in 2014, Moscow's unexpected intervention to the Syrian civil war and air strikes against the Islamic State in 2015 are some examples of such a behavior.

Foreign policy analysts differ by their specific explanations of the Kremlin's foreign policies over the last quarter of the century (see the first chapter). However, many of them tend to see a clear connection between Russia's "unpredictable" and "aggressive" behavior and its ongoing search for a new national identity. Russia is still at the stage of nation-building. It never existed within the current borders as an independent state or had such economy, system of government, administrative and societal organization.

Shaping of a new identity always has two dimensions—domestic and international. The domestic dimension implies creating internal cohesion, reaching a national consensus on the fundamental principles of government and values, sharing some common cultural and spiritual features. Self-perception is also important. Internally, a nation perceives itself as a united entity, as a bounded community. In this case people treat other people as members of the same community. The international dimension suggests self-assessment in relation to people belonging to a different community rather than to the same one. Understanding differences between nations and uniqueness of its own nation is also crucial for the formation of an identity. As Richter rightly comments, 'National identity serves as the crucial organizing principle justifying and providing coherence to the state's domestic order, yet the boundaries defining this identity can be formulated only with reference to the external environment' (Richter 1996, 74).

As the humankind's history demonstrates, international impulses were often even more significant than domestic factors. For many countries, national debate on foreign relations has been an easiest way to form an identity of its own. They looked at the outer world as at the mirror to see what images they have got. The trouble is that there could be some aberrations and the external dimension of national identity can be formed on the nationalistic or even chauvinistic basis which most likely would have negative implications both for a nation and its neighbors.

Since the Russian foreign policy discourse definitely aims, among other things, at forming of a new national identity, it is important to examine whether this debate is immune from nationalism and xenophobia or not, whether it facilitates the birth of a new type of identity based on the democratic principles or can regress to authoritarianism and totalitarianism. This is also important in terms of civilizational orientations: whether Russia will choose European / Western orientation or the Asian / Eastern one? Or perhaps Russia would prefer a civilization of its own, as some Russian theorists claim? Self-perception and self-identification of the country is also crucial for becoming a reputable and authoritative actor on the international arena. If Russia to solve (or starts to solve) an identity 'puzzle' it could define properly its national interests, foreign policy priorities and formulate sound national security, military and foreign policy doctrines. It also would become more predictable and responsible international partner which could be able to contribute to the creation of a stable and secure systems both on the regional and global levels.

As far as the 'geographic dimension' of the Russian identity discourse is concerned Europe takes a unique position in Russian mentality and particularly in security thinking. For centuries Europe was a source of both cultural inspiration and security threat, advanced technologies and innovations which destroyed Russian traditions and values. In modern times, major wars and aggressions against Russia came from Europe ranging from the Polish invasion in the beginning of the 17th century to the Nazi aggression of 1941.

Some Russian historians date the origins of the Western offensive even by earlier times. They note that from the beginning of the 13th century Russians were mainly concerned with the German expansion to the Baltic lands. The German crusaders captured the Russian forts on the Dvina, and pushed into Russia before being defeated by Prince Alexander Nevsky in the 'Battle on the Ice' of Lake Chudskoe (Peipus) in 1242.

In addition to strategic-military dimensions, the German-Russian rivalry turned out very soon into the religious confrontation between Catholicism and Orthodoxy. This, however, did not prevent Orthodox Russians to support Catholic Poles and Lithuanians at the famous battle of Grünwald in 1410 resulted in the crushing defeat of the Teutonic Knights.

Even in the 20th century, Russia (and the Soviet Union) retained its perception of East Europe as a front-line against Western expansion either in the form of German *Drang nach Osten* or NATO 'aggressive plans.' Moscow's diplomacy, military doctrines and armed forces posture in the area were subordinated to the objectives of the global confrontation with the West.

It should be noted that civilizational or identity 'flavor' has always been present in the Russian debate on Europe.

Since the time of Peter the Great Russian elites looked at Europe with both hope and apprehension. They wanted to be Europeans by their habits and mode of life (sometimes even by language—for one and half century French was a main language spoken by the Russian aristocracy), but, at the same time, they had to assert their 'Russianness' in order to keep their national identity and links to the Russian people. Russia was always eager to be a part of Europe not only in geographic sense but also in terms of civilization. However, Europe with rare exception was reluctant to acknowledge Russia's 'Europeanness'. Russia's century-dated efforts to form a system of European alliances where Moscow could act on the equal footing with other great powers were a story of failure. Even within the framework of the *Entente Cordiale* Moscow has not been treated by Britain and France as a really equal partner. The West's reluctance to admit post-Communist Russia into major security and economic Euro-Atlantic institutions such as NATO and the EU convinced Kremlin that the old practice continued.

This contradiction between Russia's eagerness to be European and the West's unwillingness to recognize Moscow as a part of Europe has received much attention in Russian philosophy and social sciences and led to the split among the Russian political and intellectual elites. Since the mid-19th century controversy between the Slavophiles and Westerners could be traced as a main dividing line between different Russian foreign policy schools. While the Westerners are unreservedly in favor of Russia's joining Europe at any price—even at the expense of national interests and sovereignty, the Slavophiles believe that Russia forms the civilization of its own. According to the Slavophiles, Russia is neither Europe nor Asia and should retain its own identity. If Russians themselves would respect their country and traditions, then foreigners (including Europeans) would do the same (see chapter 2).

The entire Russian policy towards Europe over the two last centuries can be roughly described as a pendulum swing between the two above extremes. Periods of Europe-oriented Russian policy (Alexander I and its participation in the anti-Napoleonic coalition, *Entente Cordiale,* Litvinov's 'collective security' strategy in the mid-1930s, Gorbachev's Common European House concept, Kozyrev's early course) have been succeeded by the more nationalistic or globalist (the Soviet period) patterns. As the post-Cold War history shows, it is safe to assume that the 'pendulum model' will be effective in a foreseeable future as well.

With the collapse of the USSR and the disappearance of most dangerous threats from the West, the Russian policy makers suddenly found themselves in a new strategic and geopolitical situation. According to a majority of Russian theorists of the early 1990s which belonged to different foreign policy schools, main external threats to Russian security should originate—in the foreseeable future—from the South or East rather than West (Arbatov 1994, 71; Lukin 1994, 110; Vladislavlev and Karaganov 1992, 35; Zhirinovskiy 1993).

Under these circumstances, quite animated discussions on Russia's national interests have been started by the Russian political, military and intellectual elites. Do any constant Russian interests exist? Or should they be completely re-defined? What place in the set of the Russian foreign policy priorities should different regions take? For example, some analysts suggested that, from security point of view, Europe was no longer as important for Moscow as it was during the Soviet times (Fadeev and Razuvayev, 1994: 114; Baranovsky, 1996: 167). Others argued that the area will retain its traditional meaning as a border zone or bridge between the East and the West (Uspensky and Komissarov, 1993: 83; Institute of Europe, 1995: 21–23; Sergunin, 1996b: 112–115). Some Russian theorists underlined that given the changing nature of world power (economic power now matters more than military might) Europe became one of the global poles and, for this reason, Russia should pay more attention to economic cooperation with the EU (Pichugin, 1996: 93; Pierre and Trenin, 1997: 16–18; Trenin, 1997: 117–118; Zagorski, 1996: 67; Zagorski and Lucas, 1993: 77–107). Other analysts believed that the region was becoming strategically important again as NATO and the EU were moving to the Central and East European countries. To their minds, Russia and its allies were vulnerable for potential Western encroachments again as in the times of German crusaders or Hitler's *Blitzkrieg* (Gromov, 1995: 9–13;

Lyasko, 1995: 2; Trynkov, 1995: 65–68; *Nezavisimaya Gazeta,* 11 April 1996). With the resumption of Europe-Russia tensions in the wake of the Ukrainian crisis this theme became popular again (Guschin et al 2015; Krutikov 2014; Markov 2014; Sergunin 2014b; Tauscher 2015; Trenin 2015). At the same time, some Russian foreign policy schools insist on the need to pay more attention to the consolidation of the post-Soviet space under the Russian leadership (Bolgova 2015; Lukyanov and Krastev 2015; Michel 2014) and / or develop closer relations with the BRICS countries (Lukyanov 2011 and 2014; Okuneva 2012; Panova 2013; Simha 2013; Stuenkel 2014).

Similarly, an animated discussion is taking place with regard to the Russian threat perceptions and national security doctrines. What are the domestic and international determinants of Russian foreign policy? Which security threats are more vital—internal or external? What type of security—'hard security' or 'soft security'—is more important? What kind of threats (if any) is posed by the recent international developments? How should the post-Cold War dynamics be reflected in a national security, military and foreign policy doctrines? Does Russia need such doctrines at all? Whether the national security, foreign policy and military doctrines play an important role in shaping Russia's European strategy or they are empty declarations? It should be noted that the study of the doctrinal component of the Russian foreign policy and security discourses is particularly helpful in understanding how theories and concepts produced by the foreign policy schools are translated into the language of practical politics.

In addition to changes in the geopolitical landscape, there was a revolution in the paradigmatic basis of Russian post-Communist foreign policy and security thinking. The Marxist paradigm collapsed and Russian theorists started the search for new ones. The former theoretical and methodological uniformity has been succeeded by pluralism. On the one hand, this environment has been susceptible for the rise of new foreign policy schools and approaches. On the other hand, a number of unexpected problems emerged. Some Russian analysts borrowed Western theories without any critical evaluation or taking into account the situation in the Russian scholarship and politics. Others converted into anti-Communists and anti-Marxists with the same energy and vigor as they took stand on the Marxists principles before. Meanwhile, achievements and strongest points of the Soviet school of International Relations (IR) have been forgotten. The general economic decline in the country in the 1990s and the 'brain drain' from the Russian academia to the commercial sector, government and foreign countries were also detrimental to the quality of the Russian security discourse.

In dealing with the 'paradigmatic revolution' and its implications for both Russian IR theory and foreign policy a student of Russian post-Communist foreign policy thinking confronts one more set of research questions. Is it possible to produce any categorization of the Russian foreign policy schools or not? Which criterion (criteria) should be used? Whether these schools are genuine Russian production or have been copied from the Western samples? In which direction does the Russian foreign policy debate move—further polarization of views or their convergence, reaching a sort of a foreign policy consensus? Is such a consensus possible in principle? If yes, what can unite and divide different currents of Russian security thought? What is the mainstream of the present-day Russian security thinking? Is a dialogue between the Russian and non-Russian (Western, Eastern) discourses—modern and post-modern problematiques—possible or not?

An important aspect of the problem is how the above discourse affected the decision-making process. The radical changes in the Russian decision-making system posed a number of questions which are also far from thorough exploration. What is the constitutional framework for Russia's foreign policy-making? Whether it matters or, in reality, different—unwritten—rules of the game exist? Who are the key figures in policy-making? Where are the core and the periphery of the decision-making system? What are the particular procedures? Whether there is some competition between the government agencies or not? If yes, how are their activities coordinated? Whether implementation system works properly or decisions simply remain on paper? Does some rivalry between political appointees and bureaucracy exist or not?

The study of the decision-making system not only provides the analyst with knowledge of the behind-the-scenes process but also encourages him to question why democratization of the above system has not been completed. Why is there still no effective parliamentary control over Russian foreign and security policies which could be comparable with the Western, democratic, standards? Why were the President and Parliament often unable to establish working relationship? What are the sources of conflict and areas of contention? Whether the Russian leadership succeeded in establishing civilian control over the military and intelligence community or not? In addressing these questions, a student of Russian foreign and security policies has to link this particular problem to the broader context of Russian domestic politics and highlight the difficulties in creating of an effective foreign policy decision-making mechanism in a period of transition.

The post-Communist era brought about not only changes in the decision-making procedures but also some new political actors. Numerous pressure groups, NGOs and regional elites claimed their rights to take part in formulation of Moscow's international strategy and the federal government was unable to ignore these claims any longer. What kind of interest groups and regional elites has been involved in shaping Russia's foreign and security policies? Did they really affect Moscow's international course? If yes, whether their impact was negative or positive? A more theoretical question may be raised: whether their participation in foreign policy making can be interpreted as a sign of an emerging civil society in Russia or it is just an evidence of parochial politics in this country?

It should be noted that the lack of reliable sources limits the scope for profound analysis of the current decision-making system. Moreover, this system and regulations are extremely unstable in post-Communist Russia. Foreign policy legislation, procedures and key actors change so fast that it is very difficult to define by whom, when and why a decision has been taken, what can be expected in the near future and so on.

The above questions form the core of a broad research agenda which, however, can be reduced to the four main issues:

1. Which IR theories are applicable to explaining Russia's present-day foreign policy?

2. What are the main foreign policy schools in post-Communist Russia and what sort of theories do they produce?

3. How did the Russian threat perceptions and national security doctrines evolve in the post-Soviet period?

4. How does the Russian foreign policy decision-making system operate?

Sources. Despite the fact that a student of contemporary politics always feels a lack of sources (especially reliable ones) some of them are available. The data for this research were drawn primarily from eight main categories of sources:

Documents of international and intergovernmental organizations (CIS, BRICS, Shanghai Cooperation Organization (SCO), EU, Council of Europe, OSCE, NATO, Nordic Council, Council of the Baltic Sea States (CBSS), Barents-Euro-Arctic Council (BEAC), etc.). These publications are helpful in reconstructing the international context in which Russian foreign and security policies have been shaped and operated. They shed light on three levels of Russia's foreign policy—sub-regional, regional and global. It should be noted, however, that these documents reflect the end-product of the debate rather than the Russian foreign policy and security discourses as such.

Russian government documents and publications. There are several categories of such materials:

(*a*) Presidential and prime ministerial decrees and other documents which regulate various aspects of Russian foreign and security policies and activities of executive agencies in these areas. This sub-group of sources is crucial for studying decision-making process at the top level of the Russian foreign policy machinery albeit it provides little information on the behind-the-scene activities.

(*b*) Publications of certain government agencies involved in Russia's foreign policy making and implementing such as the Ministry of Foreign Affairs (MFA), the Ministry of Defense (MOD), the Security Council and so on. They assist in understanding which particular role the executive bodies play in taking decisions. They also shed light on interdepartmental differences and competition.

(*c*) Parliamentary publications and documents. Laws and resolutions on foreign and national security policy which the Russian legislature passes from time to time help to examine both legal framework and conceptual basis of international policy making.

Both houses of the Russian Parliament (the Federal Assembly)—the State Duma, the lower one, and the Council of the Federation, the upper house of the legislature (as well as the Supreme Soviet, their predecessor)—publish bulletins on the regular basis where plenary and committee debates are covered.

Documents of the party factions as well as interviews with the leaders of the legislature (speakers, committee chairmen, leaders of party factions, prominent foreign policy experts, etc.) are also of significant interest.

Some drafts of legislative acts as well as background materials are available. This is important because a student of Russian politics can realize how the legislature operates and how decisions within this body are taken.

Parliamentary documents are particularly valuable for discovering links between various foreign policy schools, political parties and groups in the Parliament. Since the legislature is more open than the executive branch of the government sometimes it is easier to investigate different undercurrents in Russian foreign policy making on the basis of the parliamentary rather than executive sources.

3. Publications of political parties and organizations. Parties used to publish their political platforms (including foreign policy sections) on the occasion of either parliamentary or presidential elections. Sometimes it is done via policy-oriented journals. The party leaders used to publish books or pamphlets where they elaborate their views on topical foreign policy issues. Parties also encourage publishing of expert assessments and analytical papers on various issues. Almost each party has a newspaper or journal of its own. For example, Our Home Russia sponsored a be-weekly edition *Nash Dom i Otechestvo* (Our Home and Fatherland). Communists published *Pravda* (Truth) and *Den* (Day). Social Democrats were grouping around the journal *Svobodnaya Mysl'* (Free Thought) while the Slavophiles favored to *Nash Sovremennik* (Our Contemporary) and *Molodaya Gvardiya* (Young Guard). The Liberal Democratic Party printed up a huge number of its publications—*Liberal* (The Liberal), *Pravda Zhirinovskogo* (Zhirinovskiy's Truth), *Sokol Zhirinovskogo* (Zhirinovskiy's Falcon) and so on.

4. Publications of the Russian think tanks. Numerous think thanks—both those working on government and independent—have been established in the post-Soviet period. They mainly provided decision-makers with expertise and some of them took part in policy making itself. Most of the Russian think tanks are not concerned about theory and quite pragmatic in terms of combination of principles of different IR schools. A majority of Russian 'brain trusts' claim non-party or independent status. However, they are connected to one of the political groups or government in one way or another. For example, the Council on Foreign and Defense Policy led by Sergei Karaganov and the Fund 'Politics' led by Vyacheslav Nikonov had very close relations with the government agencies. RAU (Russian-American University) Corporation cooperated with the Communist Party. The Gorbachev Fund was close to the Social Democrats.

There is also a number of foreign think tanks and foundations which established their branches or networks in Russia—Moscow Carnegie Center, Heritage Foundation, McArthur Foundation, Open Society Institute (Soros Foundation), Eurasia, Moscow Research Foundation (in fact, this was a branch of the Ford Foundation), Konrad Adenauer Foundation, Friedrich Ebert Foundation, Naumann Foundation and so on. They tried to establish links between the Russian and Western political and intellectual elites as well as to form a pro-Western elite in Russia *via* exchange programs, grants, joint research projects, seminars and publications.

Some of these institutions were closed because they have been considered as 'foreign agents'.

Think tanks publish bulletins, occasional papers, books and proceedings of the conferences sponsored by them. Some of them run journals. For instance, the Gorbachev Fund sponsored *Svobodnaya Mysl'* while the Moscow Carnegie Center published *Pro et Contra* (in addition to occasional papers and monographs). Think tanks' publications are important for examining how the link between the academia and decision-makers (the government and political parties) is created and how the leadership is provided with foreign policy expertise.

5. *Books and monographs* produced by the Russian scholars belonging to various IR schools. This is one of the most important categories of sources for this research because the book-size work provides a researcher with rather complete and systematized information on an author and views of the school which he / her represents. Since the book format allows it, an author has sufficient space to develop his / her argumentation and describe his / her theory at length. Not only theory itself but also the author's way of reasoning, research methods and technique, system of arguments, intellectual precursors and empirical basis can be examined.

Along with the writings of the Russian theorists a number of review works produced by both Russian and foreign authors are helpful as well. Some provide a student of the Russian foreign policy discourse with a systematized outlook of different foreign policy schools, including their categorization, history, basic doctrines, comparison with other schools, evaluation of their impact on policy making and so on (Baranovsky 1997; Dunlop 1993; Malcolm 1994; Malcolm et al. 1996; Sergunin 2003, 2004, 2005, 2007a and 2009; Tsygankov and Tsygankov 2005).

Other scholars describe Russia's foreign policy making, including the role of formal and informal actors (Blackwill and Karaganov 1994; Clunan 2009; Crow 1993; Donaldson and Nogee 2009; Gvosdev and Marsh 2013; Malcolm et al. 1996; Sergunin 2007b and 2008).

The third group of works examines Moscow's policies in specific regions—Europe (Baranovsky 1997; Blackwill and Karaganov 1994; Dawisha and Parrot 1994; Dunlop 1993; Engelbrekt and Nygren 2010; Institute of Europe, 1995; Kolobov and Makarychev 1998; Mouritzen 1998; Roberts 2013; Zagorski and Lucas 1993), relations with the U.S. (Blackwill and Karaganov 1994; Goodby and Morel 1993; Roberts 2013; Stent 2014), post-Soviet space (Bolgova 2015; Lukyanov and Krastev 2015;

Michel 2014), Middle East and Asia Pacific (Blackwill and Karaganov 1994).

However, few works cover the whole range of the above research questions providing a comprehensive analysis of the problem (Baranovsky 1997; Kanet 2010; Legvold 2007; Malcolm 1994; Malcolm et al. 1996; Mankoff 2009; Smith 2005; Tsygankov 2012 and 2016).

6. *Working and occasional papers.* Research papers on Russian foreign policies published by various Russian, European and US research institutes and universities, such as the RAS institutes—Institute of Europe, Institute for the USA and Canada Studies, Institute of World Economy and International Relations; Moscow State Institute of International Relations (MGIMO), Russian Institute of Strategic Studies, Moscow; School of International Relations, St. Petersburg University; Nizhny Novgorod State University, Nizhny Novgorod Linguistic University; Copenhagen Peace Research Institute / Danish Institute of International Studies (DIIS), Copenhagen; the Stockholm International Peace Research Institute (SIPRI); Department of Peace Research, Uppsala University, Swedish Defense Establishment (FOI), Sweden; Norwegian Institute of Foreign Affairs (NUPI), Oslo; Peace Research Institute Oslo; Tampere Peace Research Institute (TAPRI), Finland; French Institute for International Studies (IFRI), the Center for International Studies (CERI), Institute for Strategic Studies, Paris; Institute of Eastern Europe, Free University Berlin; the International Institute for Strategic Studies (IISS), Royal Institute of International Affairs, London; Brookings Institution, Carnegie Endowment for International Peace, Georgetown Center for Strategic and International Studies, Heritage Foundation, Washington, DC; East-West Institute, New York; Harvard University, Cambridge, Mass.; RAND, Santa Monica and others.

7. *Periodicals and journals.* Articles and essays published by the Russian and foreign IR theorists and foreign policy and security experts in journals and newspapers also augmented the data-base for this research. This category covers a more wide range of foreign policy schools than book-size publications because the representatives of these schools sometimes have no opportunity, time or capability to write and publish book-format works. Journal and newspaper publications are also more sensitive to the changes both in the political conjuncture and theories. However, they used to be less profound and analytical and more empirical and policy-relevant than books and monographs. One should be careful as far as this category of sources is concerned. Seriousness of the

author, his / her data-base, real authority and impact on the Russian security discourse should be double-checked.

The following journals have been most helpful for this research: *Alternatives, Conflict and Co-operation, Diplomaticheskiy Vestnik, The Economist, European Journal of International Relations, European Security, Europe-Asia Studies, Foreign Affairs, Foreign Policy, International Affairs (London), International Affairs (Moscow), International Organization, International Relations, International Security, The International Spectator, Journal of Peace Research, Military Review, Millennium, Mirovaya Ekonomika i Mezhdunarodnye Otnosheniya, NATO's Sixteen Nations, Orbis, Perspectives, Polis, Political Science Quarterly, Pro et Contra, Review of International Affairs, RUSI Journal, Security Dialogue, Survival, Svobodnaya Mysl, World Affairs*, etc.

Among newspapers the following editions can be mentioned: *The Baltic Independent, The Guardian, International Herald Tribune, Izvestiya, Krasnaya Zvezda, Le Mond, Moscow News, Nash Dom i Otechestvo, New York Times, Nezavisimaya Gazeta, Nezavisimoe Voennoe Obozrenie, Novaya Gazeta, Pravda, Rossiyskaya Gazeta, Russia Direct, The Times, Washington Post*, etc.

8. Interviews with experts, scholars, governmental officials, and legislators involved in making and study of security policy were valuable sources as well. Similar to the previous category, these sources can be subjective. Nonetheless, they are particularly helpful in understanding of motivation of Russian foreign policy makers and relations between various political groups and schools.

As mentioned above, it is very difficult to deal with such a fragmented and sometimes contradictory data-base. Numerous problems, such as comparability, reliability, systematization, classification and interpretation of sources, inevitably emerge at some point. To solve these problems the scholar must examine different accounts, carefully compare them with each other, verify their authenticity and information value. Methods such as classification and systematization, which are based on identification of homogenous groups of sources as well of similarities and dissimilarities between them, bring an analytical order into research efforts and help in organizing sources for comparative procedures. It is also important to select sources which properly represent different schools of thought (in other words, they should be exemplary, typical) and reflect their major principles. Finally, preference should be given to original rather than secondary sources in order to reduce the risk of error and create an adequate image of the object.

These research tools can serve as more or less reliable safeguards against misinterpretations and help to overcome the limitations of the sources and compile substantial and sufficient data for the study.

Structure of the book

The structure of this book is determined by the research questions posed above. Following the introductory section where the research agenda is defined, sources and the structure of the book are described, it is divided into three chapters.

Chapter 1 demonstrates that most popular Western theories that aims to explain Moscow's foreign policy behavior often do not hold much explanatory power. In contrast with the power transition theory, this book argues that Russia is neither a status quo state aiming at keeping the main international system rules intact nor a revisionist one that aspires to radically change those rules. Rather, Russia is a reformist state which is unsatisfied with the existing rules of the "game" but it does not want to change them radically. It only wants to adapt these rules to new global realities and make them more acceptable for all the members of the world community. That's why the concepts of "peaceful coexistence" and "soft power" are better designed to describe Russia's post-Soviet international policies.

The "status panic" theory is applied in this chapter to explain Russia's seemingly "irrational" behavior. The collapse of the USSR, which is perceived by current Russian leadership as the greatest geopolitical disaster of the 20th century, and the concomitant loss of super power status have left Russia with an agonizingly uncertain status. While Russia's nuclear arsenal still makes it qualify for top tier, its performance in almost any other area leaves it among states which were, until recently, inferior to it. This relatively sudden development has arguably resulted in a kind of status inconsistency or even "status panic", from which post-Soviet Russia is still struggling to emerge. This chapter discusses Russia's post-Soviet international course from a status perspective. It will focus on the status aims—political privileges and prestige—and instruments to elevate Russia's standing in relation to other world players.

Chapter 2 examines different Russian foreign policy schools that emerged during the post-Communist period. Sources of change in Russian foreign policy and security thinking, such as geopolitical cataclysms in the post-Cold War and post-Soviet era, collapse of the Marxist IR paradigm and opening up of the Russian security discourse for the dialogue with the outer world, etc., are studied. A new categorization of Russian foreign policy schools is introduced. Major schools, such as 'Atlanticism', 'Eurasianism', 'derzhavniki', realism, geopolitics, neo-Communism, social democracy, environmentalism and post-positivism, are described. The causes and parameters of the emerging foreign policy consensus are examined. This chapter also aims at finding out what ideas that circulated among the academics and experts have been picked up by the decision-makers. The chapter demonstrates that the foreign policy discourse is a way of searching for both a proper international course and Russia's new national identity.

Chapter 3 analyses the evolution of the Russian threat perceptions and national security doctrines in the post-Communist period. Basic pro-visions of the laws and concepts such as the laws on security of 1992 and 2010, foreign policy concepts of 1993, 2000, 2008 and 2013, military doc-trines of 1993, 2000, 2010 and 2014 and national security concepts and strategies of 1997, 2000, 2009 and 2015 are reviewed and their implica-tions for the country's foreign policies are investigated. The study shows that there were fundamental changes in Russia's threat perceptions. The most recent documents underline that there is no immediate external threat to Moscow and that internal rather than external processes chal-lenge the country's security.

Chapter 4 describes the Russian security policy decision-making sys-tem. It is both documentary and analytical in nature and presents data on constitutional powers of the President and Parliament, organization of the foreign policy machinery and its evolution—over the last two and half decades, decision-making procedures, functions of and relations between different governmental agencies, coordination of these bodies' activities, sources and areas of tension between the executive and legislative branches, impact of interest groups, NGOs and regional elites on policy making, organization of foreign policy expertise and so on. The author argues that, although the current decision-making mechanism is far from perfection, it has dynamically evolved from the state of chaos and unpre-dictability to a system with clear purposes, established procedures, proper division of labor and coordination. However, the problems with the lack of transparency and democratic control over the Russian foreign policy deci-sion-making remain to be solved.

The concluding section presents some broad conclusions related to the past, present and foreseeable future of Russian foreign policies.

Chapter 1.
Theorizing Russian Foreign Policy

Russian foreign policy has always been an "uncomfortable" or exceptional case for IR theorists. Theories which they have tried to apply to the study of Moscow's international course in the post-Cold war era worked poorly or did not work at all. Scholars, who want to apply Western theories to Russian foreign policy, often have to justify this against claims that Russia is *sui generis* and that empirical knowledge of Russia's history, culture and current policies are far more important to understand Moscow's international behavior than any theoretical sophistication. However, as we know from the history of science, it is useless and counterproductive to contrapose theory to empirical knowledge. Ideally, they should go hand in hand, and support each other. As some European experts on Russian foreign policy rightly note, "Without theoretical reflection research on Russian foreign policy risks to remain a branch of area studies that relies on descriptive approaches but at the same time is full of hidden commitments to dubious theoretical assumptions" (Forsberg et al. 2014, 262). To continue this way of reasoning, without theoretical foundations, research often lacks either the critical edge or credibility.

In this chapter, the most popular theoretical interpretations of the Kremlin's post-Soviet foreign policy are critically reviewed and some alternative explanations are suggested.

Power transition theory

The realist / neo-realist *power transition theory* (PTT) developed by A.F.K. Organski (1958) and his followers (Wittkopf 1997; Tammen 2000) is the most popular IR theory among the Western experts on Russia's foreign policy. This theory aims at explaining the causes of international conflicts and wars by the rise of emerging powers that are discontent with international rules established by the dominant powers. According to this theory, all states can be classified to one of two categories—either *status quo* or *revisionist*. Powerful and influential nations such as the U.S. who have benefited from the previously established world order fall under the category of *status quo* states while nations dissatisfied with their place on the international spectrum are often considered *revisionist* states. The PTT was based on the assumption that the revisionist state aims at either a radical change of old rules or imposing new rules on other international actors.

According to the PTT school, Putin's Russia is a typical revisionist state. For example, the experts from the U.S.-based Heritage Foundation believe that Russia poses four distinct, but related problems for the U.S. and other international actors: First, Putin's regime challenges core democratic values by combining a lack of respect for political, civil, and economic rights with a dysfunctional economy. Second and most dangerous for the West, Russia poses a series of worldwide strategic and diplomatic challenges, including buildup of its nuclear arsenal and military. Third, Russia poses threats to discrete U.S. allies and friendly regimes around the world, such as the Baltic States, Poland, Finland, Sweden, Georgia and Ukraine. Fourth, Russia's cooperation with "rogue" states (Iran, Syria, North Korea) and its increasing tendency to play a spoiler role pose another set of threats (Carafano 2015, 1).

The followers of the "revisionist" school believe that, in security affairs, Russia maintains a zero-sum view of the world. Absolute security is the goal, which if successful would mean absolute insecurity for everyone else. The belief in the military instrument is strong, and Russia has focused on rebuilding its military capability in the last decade. Use of force against smaller neighbors and illegal annexation is a part of the policy (Granholm et al. 2014, 10, 25).

In explaining the sources of Russia's foreign policy behavior, the "revisionist" school tends to reject any wrongdoings on the part of the West. The developments such as the NATO campaign in Kosovo in 1999 (and subsequent Kosovo's secession from Serbia), the U.S. missile defense program in Eastern Europe, U.S.- and EU-supported efforts to "promote democracy and good governance" in post-Soviet nations (which is called by the Kremlin a series of "color revolutions"), and above all the eastward expansion of NATO are not considered threatening Russia's security and a legitimate ground for Moscow's counter-reaction. This school accuses the Kremlin of having the aspirations to exercise a neo-imperial control over its neighbors and believing that those neighbors have no corresponding right to determine their own destiny. What the Russian regime could not tolerate, the protagonists of this school maintain, is quite simple: any independent sources of power on its borders or inside them that could resist the regime's will (Carafano 2015, 3).

The moderate version of the "revisionist" school tries to explain the radical change in Moscow's foreign policy behavior paradigm by the failure (or incomplete nature) of democratic reforms in post-Soviet Russia.

These reforms derailed from a "proper" way and degenerated to a state / oligarchic capitalism model based on natural resources exports, centralism and dominance of kleptocratic bureaucracy. Such a regime has been reluctant to be integrated on globalized terms and it can only survive by maintaining a strict domestic control and generating an image of Russia's "hostile encirclement"—mainly for internal consumption (Granholm et al. 2014, 10, 26–29). At the same time, high revenues from oil exports in the 2000s made affordable for the Putin and Medvedev regimes to have both "butter and guns", i.e. to raise living standards for common Russians and launch military modernization programs. In turn, this created an illusion among the Russian leaders that Moscow could allow itself to conduct a more assertive international course and even to dream about the returning the great power status.

The extreme version of this school prefers to see Russia as an "incorrigible spoiler" or even a "rogue" who is in principle unable to assimilate / internalize democratic values and play by established international rules. For the supporters of this sub-school, the entire Western neo-liberal course on engaging post-Soviet Russia in democratic transformation and international cooperation was doomed to failure. As one neoconservative analyst observes, "Since at least the 17th century, Russia has been torn—and has oscillated—between viewing itself as a basically Western nation or as a great and imperial power that embodies values apart from those of the West and has historical license to control its neighbors in the name of increasing its power and advancing its concept of civilization" (Carafano 2015, 3). For this sub-school, the rise of the Putin regime is simply another moment in Russian history when the pendulum has swung away from the West.

The proponents of the "revisionist" interpretation of the present-day Russian foreign policy differ by their views on how serious the Russian threats to international security are and whether Moscow's revisionist ambitions are of short- or long-term character. Some Western analysts believe that Russia is serious about playing a more assertive role in world politics, returning a great power status and becoming one of the power poles in the international relations system (Granholm et al. 2014, 15). They point to the factors such as Russia's size and geopolitical centrality of its territory, its energy resources, its nuclear arsenal, the modern portion of its conventional armed forces, and above all its willingness to attack, subvert, and play the role of a spoiler. This sub-school underlines that Moscow is actively reshaping old (CIS, Collective Security Treaty Organization (CSTO), SCO, etc.) and building new alliances (Eurasian

Economic Union (EEU), BRICS) trying to challenge the West both on the regional and global levels.

This grouping acknowledges the fact that Russia has shown that it is a force to be reckoned with in the international system. It admits that the Ukrainian crisis has acted as a catalyst and speeds up the process of transformation of the international order. The present-day international system is most likely only at the beginning of a long process of structural changes that will have an impact on the local, regional and even the global level. Among other things, Moscow's policies challenge regional cooperation around the world, the design of the European security architecture, the level of defense expenditures, the robustness of energy policies, and great power relationships in Europe, Asia and the Americas.

This sub-school also notes that the Ukrainian crisis has triggered intense identity-searching on what it means to be Russian, Ukrainian, European and what a globalised world stands for. As one scholar dramatically emphasizes, "We may have a new ideological rivalry brewing, where the global liberal world order stands against an authoritarian, state-capitalistic model" (Granholm et al. 2014, 15).

However, the dominant sub-school within the "revisionist camp" is the grouping which believes Russia is "a declining power with feet of clay" (Carafano 2015, 4). The analysts from this grouping point out that Russia is economically weak and dependant on oil exports which is now not that profitable as before the 2014 oil price crisis. Today's Russia has no wide ideological appeal comparable to the Communist ideology. As for Moscow's international partners, nations such as China may also resent the Western international order, but they can be considered at best as ambivalent allies for Russia. They challenge the order not for Russia's benefit, but for their own. Russia does not direct or control them, or even inspire them ideologically.

This sub-school notes that comparisons between the Soviet Union and contemporary Russia are misleading, no matter how much the Putin regime promotes them to justify its own rule or to project an image of equality with the U.S. and other power poles. However, despite the fact that Russia is far weaker than the USSR it does not mean that the West should ignore Moscow's geopolitical ambitions. The proponents of this sub-school admit that Russia can be a problem that will be with the West for a very long time, although its urgency will wane.

The "revisionist" school's proponents also differ by their recommendations on how to deal with a "resurgent" Russia. One group of experts suggests a "new containment" policy that could include measures, such as economic, financial and political sanctions against Russia and specific Russian officials, businessmen and companies; increasing NATO's military presence and activities in East European countries; deployment of the U.S. / NATO ballistic missile defense (BMD) system in Europe; enhanced cooperation with non-NATO states such as Finland and Sweden; suspension of Russia's membership in or its expulsion from international institutions, such the G-8, Council of Europe, Interpol, etc. as well as revision of Russia's status and actions in other international organizations, etc. (Granholm et al. 2014, 57–64, 78–79). Some experts recommend the West to give up the elite-centered Russia policy approach in favor of an approach that focuses on the public and on civil society.

There is also difference of opinion between the U.S. and European experts with regard to the details of the "new containment" policies. For example, the European analysts are quite skeptical about the role that the U.S. should play in the Ukrainian crisis and about its policy on sanctions against Russia. They believe that Washington does not see political or economic co-operation with Moscow as important, especially since Europe in general has become much less important to the U.S. that is now focused on Asia. They also fear that current U.S. policy is driven by the domestic weakness of the Obama administration. According to these experts, the OSCE is toothless and NATO is both exclusive in its membership and a bête noire (an object of fear or alarm) for Russia, so none of the existing institutions are up to the task. For this reason, they believe the EU and / or its key member-states (Germany and France) should take a lead in dealing with "resurgent" Russia (Meister 2014, 10).

Another version of the "revisionist" sub-school admits that containment probably was a reasonable approach to the USSR because it was large and very threatening. Putin's Russia is by no means near the power that the Soviet Union was in the late 1940s, when containment was launched. Calling for the West to apply containment policy to the present-day Russia gives the Putin regime more credit than it deserves. This sub-school recommends a policy of constrainment rather than a policy of containment. According the Heritage Foundation's experts, the constrainment approach should be "to defend its allies and interests and to respond to destructive Russian actions with policies that raise Russian costs going forward and thus incentivize Russia to choose other, more desirable actions" (Carafano 2015, 7).

These costs can be of reputational, rhetorical, economic, financial, and military character. The protagonists of the constrainment approach believe that the West is vastly better equipped to bear costs than Russia because it has a larger and more flexible economy and political system. In any long-run competition, Russia will be at a profound disadvantage to the West. However, when the proponents of the constrainment approach come to policy recommendations, the latter are basically similar to what the "containment" sub-school suggests (cf. Carafano 2015, 13–34).

The alternative version of the PTT school believes that contemporary Russia is a status quo-oriented rather than revisionist power (Kühn 2015). According to this grouping, even Moscow's policies towards Ukraine are basically consistent with Moscow's continuous orientation since the break-up of the Soviet Union. The Russian national interest, which drives that orientation, is to preserve Russian influence in the post-Soviet states and to prevent NATO from enlarging eastwards. While Moscow's interest has remained the same over time, the strategy for achieving that end has changed. However, Western policy analysts have not followed the twists and turns in Russian strategy carefully enough.

This PTT sub-school believes that Moscow prefers to keep status quo not only in Europe but also globally. For example, the Kremlin is rather reluctant to launch a serious UN reform. Particularly, with Russia and other 'former' great powers among the permanent members of the UN Security Council (UNSC), any reforms seem unlikely for the foreseeable future. While Russia might see an expanded UNSC in its interest, its veto power is not up for negotiation. Other members of the permanent five, such as the UK and France, are probably also in favor of status quo (Granholm et al. 2014, 14).

According to the adherents of the "status-quo" school, the source of the problem is that the post-Cold War European security order failed to include Russia on equal terms (Charap and Shapiro 2014a and 2014b). For much of the quarter century since the Soviet Union's collapse, the U.S. and its allies had unchallenged authority in shaping the approach to post–Cold War regional security and the structures that would lie at its core. This put the focus on the expansion of NATO and the EU which was perceived by Russia with apprehension. As the Euro-Atlantic institutions absorbed the nations of the former Warsaw Pact in Central and Eastern Europe and began exploration of closer ties to the post-Soviet states, Moscow hardened its position against expansion and set a redline at the former Soviet borders. The Russian-Georgian "mini-war" in August 2008 was a clear sign of that line.

And when Ukraine, following the dismissal of its former president Viktor Yanukovych in February 2014, signaled its willingness to link its future to the EU and NATO, Moscow reacted with the use of force, taking over Crimea and supporting rebels in the country's south-east. Preventing Ukraine from going West has been a central issue in the conflict and is at the core of its geopolitical dimension (Collins 2015, 3; Sergunin 2013, 86).

According to the "status quo" PTT sub-school, the Ukrainian conflict also has a major geoeconomic dimension. Since 2009 Brussels undertook a project to construct its relations with its new neighbors on the basis of arrangements it defined as an Eastern Partnership (EaP). These arrangements included new trading regimes as well as provisions promising greater openness for the movement of people and a number of commitments to political reform by aspiring partners (Joint Declaration of the Prague Eastern Partnership Summit 2009; Makarychev and Sergunin 2013a, 320; Sergunin 2013). Most significantly for the relations among the states concerned, in particular Ukraine, these new arrangements promised to upset the economic status quo and threatened the web of economic ties Russia had with Ukraine, including the free trade area regime. Ukrainians' interest in closer relations with the EU also appeared to challenge openly Moscow's efforts to build a EEU to offset the integration projects driven by the EU. The EaP amplified the threat to Russia's economic interests and geoeconomic objectives and was seen to alter significantly the status quo of trade arrangements between Ukraine and Russia and between Ukraine and the EU, to Russia's disadvantage (Collins 2015, 3; Sergunin 2013, 24–25 and 2014b, 82–85).

The "status quo" sub-school believes that re-engagement with Russia—not immediately but over the mid-term—is inevitable, because Russia is too important for European and global security and because the current strategy of punishment lacks the most important part to a successful strategy: a clear objective (Charap and Shapiro 2014a and 2014b; Kühn 2015). Even though the economic sanctions are having a serious negative impact on the Russian economy, it is not clear what the objective of the sanctions is. Is it the unlikely scenario of Russia moving out of Ukraine (including Crimea)? Is it regime change? And what then? Who can say whether the next Russian leader will be more cooperative and not less rational? The Western politicians and academics have failed to answer these questions.

According to the "status quo" school, if the West comes to the conclusion that reengagement is critical for a variety of reasons, it will have to answer the question of how to deal with Russia's power concerns. On a less abstract level that would mean talking about NATO's open-door policy, addressing the status and security of non-aligned post-Soviet states such as Ukraine, Moldova, Georgia, or Azerbaijan, debating additional security measures for U.S. allies, and figuring out stabilizing measures in the realm of arms control (especially the future of the U.S. / NATO BMD system in Europe), which address an asymmetric NATO–Russian relationship (Collins 2015; Kühn 2015, 8). Engaging on these issues neither means that the West will have to share Russia's worldview, nor that it should act accordingly. But for a start, it would be good to at least try to understand Russia.

No matter how plausible explanations of Russia's foreign policy behavior suggested by the PTT proponents are, they, however, are unable to capture the complexity of the object under study, deconstruct Moscow's motivation and produce a proper theory unraveling the Kremlin's international course in the post-Cold war era.

- First of all, it should be noted that the PTT was mainly designed for the Cold War period when the bipolar international relations system was in place. The two superpowers—the U.S. and USSR—were the status quo actors who were interested in maintaining a power balance in the world. With the collapse of the Soviet Union, the whole international system has radically changed and it is still in making, without a stable and clear structure. The PTT can still probably work in some cases even in the present-day world, but it is hardly applicable to explaining not only Russia's foreign policy but also other key actors' international behavior.

- For example, in contrast with the Cold war era, the U.S. can hardly be treated as a status quo actor. In the 1990s, when the U.S. has remained the only superpower and enjoyed a "unipolar moment", Washington tried to radically reshape the world order to its benefit (Haass 2008). On the contrary, Russia, which was rather weak in the 1990s and tried to keep at least its status of a regional power (with some attributes of a great power such as nuclear weapons and the seat in the UNSC), could be considered a status quo rather than a revisionist state. In the 2000s, when the trend towards a multipolar international relations system has been revealed, the U.S., Russia and other key international actors (the EU, China, Japan, India, etc.) were actively seeking new roles in an emerging world order.

- In fact, none of the key global or regional players can be considered as purely status quo or revisionist power. For example, on the global level, the U.S. would like to maintain its status of a sole superpower but Washington is unable to do that because of the lack of resources and resistance from other world's power centers. At the same time, Washington often behaves as a revisionist power on the regional level by intervening local conflicts, shifting regional military-strategic balances and ousting undemocratic and anti-Western regimes. The same is applicable to Russia which is interested in keeping status quo and promoting international cooperation in East Europe, Arctic and Asia Pacific but, at the same time, is quite assertive in Ukraine, Trans-Caucasus and the Middle East. Beijing is willing to cooperate with Russia and other BRICS countries but it is quite aggressive in South China Sea and economically expansionist in Central Asia, Africa and—most recently—in the Arctic.

To sum up, in an increasingly multipolar world, a new global order is gradually emerging, the order which cannot be explained with the help of the PTT because this theory was designed for the Cold War-type hierarchical (bipolar) system which has already gone a quarter of the century ago.

One more problem with the PTT is that it ignores the existence of a third type of states—the reformist one. Similar to the revisionist powers this kind of states is unsatisfied with the existing rules of the 'game' but they do not want to change them radically; rather they aim at reforming them to adapt them to the new realities and make them more comfortable for all the members of world or regional community. Such states prefer to act on the basis of existing rules and norms rather than challenge them. All changes (reforms) should be made gradually, through negotiations and to the benefit of all the parties involved. One can distinguish between more or less assertive reformist actors but even most assertive ones hardly can be seen as revisionist states.

The concept of a reformist state is relatively new theme in the IR literature. Scholars prefer to call such states 'pluralist', 'non-aligned', etc., and usually associate these terms with emerging powers (such as the BRICS countries) (De Coning 2014; Odgaard 2012). The emerging powers agree to play by existing rules but want to make them more just and adequate to the changing realities. They do not accept a dominant state (states) imposing rules on the rest of the world and favor a multipolar world model (Nadkarni and Noonan 2013).

It is safe to assume that Russia perfectly falls into the category of reformist rather than revisionist or status quo states. On the one hand, Moscow is unsatisfied with the West's geopolitical and geoeconomic dominance in the world. However, on the other hand, Russia does not want to destroy completely the existing "rules of the game" which are based on the UN legal and institutional systems. Rather, Moscow prefers to change global political and economic systems peacefully, within the international law framework.

For example, along with other emerging economies Russia is discontent with the global economic and financial systems which, the Kremlin (and other BRICS countries) believes, was established to the benefit of the "club" of highly developed countries ("OECD club"). It is not incidentally that BRICS has institutionally consolidated itself in the context of the global financial crisis of 2008–2010: its member states strongly believed that the West should be blamed for a 'short-sided' and 'reckless' financial policies that led to the crisis and that they should act together in this critical situation. Their decision to establish a $100 billion development bank to finance infrastructure projects and a $100 billion reserve fund to steady their currency markets has aimed at creating safeguards against new global crises and making them less dependent on economic and financial rules imposed on the world by the wealthiest nations (Russia Says BRICS Development Bank Ready to Launch 2014).

As a reformist state Russia shares other emerging powers' belief that the structure of global institutions is inadequate to the 21st century realities, while the plans to reform these institutions remain just on paper (Stuenkel 2014). Existing political structures were built around the bipolar world of the Cold War and have remained virtually unchanged since then. Moscow believes that emerging powers rightly question the legitimacy of the existing system and want a global political structure that reflects the multi-polar world order that is gradually taking shape nowadays. That's, for example, why the BRICS and many G-20 nations favor the UN system reform because the current system is seen as a relic of the 1945 balance of power. However, Russia calls on these countries to understand that it is uneasy to implement such a reform and that all the structural and procedural changes should be made gradually and in a cautious way. Moscow and emerging powers underline that the proposed UN reform should not undermine the role of this organization. On the contrary, one of the main priorities of the proposed reform is "to preserve and strengthen the UN Security Council's role as a body bearing the primary responsibility for maintaining international peace and security" (Russian Foreign Ministry 2013, 5).

For Moscow and its partners from BRICS and G-20 nations, it is clear that current global problems demand entirely new approaches. They believe that the West has monopolized the global debate and by doing this it impedes a search for fresh ideas and effective solutions that could result from a more inclusive discussion. Russia and its friends among the developing countries were especially unhappy about the frequent use of military force by the U.S. and its NATO allies in the post-Cold war era. For example, the Russian strategic document on BRICS underlines the need "to prevent the use of the UN, first of all the Security Council, to cover up the course towards removing undesirable regimes and imposing unilateral solutions to conflict situations, including those based on the use of force" (Russian Foreign Ministry 2013, 5).

Furthermore, Russia has found it difficult to find a stable identity and increase its influence on the world stage within existing institutions, and it has been looking for ways to strengthen its geopolitical positions by forming a new global politico-economic structure. The fact that they represent different parts of the world lends even more weight to their aspirations. Following the collapse of the Soviet Union, Russia was reduced to the level of regional power. According to Lukyanov, "The notion of multipolarity has shaped Russian foreign policy horizon since mid-90s, when it became clear that Russian integration into Western system as an equal partner was not an option" (Lukyanov 2010). The concepts of G-20, BRICS, RIC (Russia, India, China), SCO offered Russia a way to reassert its global aspirations and to draw attention to its economic progress. Moreover, these institutions allowed Russia to do this in a non-confrontational way albeit the U.S. remains unconvinced that these groupings are not directed against anyone and still sees them (especially BRICS) as a threat to its power.

Russia also believes that the non-Western, inclusive institutions can be helpful in promoting international security cooperation, more specifically in areas such as conflict resolution, non-proliferation of weapons of mass destruction, combating international terrorism, drug trafficking, piracy, money laundering, illegal migration, etc. (Okuneva 2012; Panova 2013; Russian Foreign Ministry 2013, 6–7).

To conclude, the concept of reformist power compliments the PTT, makes it more adequate to the current realities and better characterizes the nature of Russia's foreign policies in the post-Soviet era.

Peaceful coexistence concept

One of the remarkable changes in the Russian foreign policy philosophy, which took place even prior to the Ukrainian crisis, was the return of the famous peaceful coexistence concept.

The concept "peaceful coexistence" is deeply rooted in Russian foreign policy thinking. The concept dates back to the post-civil war debates in Bolshevik's Russia. When the civil war has been over and the hopes for the world revolution have gone, the Bolsheviks found themselves isolated in a hostile world, and with an economy which had collapsed. To the strains imposed on the economy by the World War I, were added that of the civil war of 1918–21, also known as the period of 'War Communism', which meant placing economic resources at the disposal of the new state in the fight against the enemies of the revolution.

In 1921 the Communist party leadership had turned to the so-called New Economic Policy (NEP), which legalized a certain revival of capitalism within limits determined by the state, in order to alleviate the desperate economic and political domestic situation. Vladimir Lenin recognized that the fight to secure peaceful coexistence (or "cohabitation", the term which he initially preferred) would also bring much needed relief, not only to the regime but also to the working people. There was also the recognition that Soviet Russia was cut off from much needed capital and technology from the advanced countries, this was a problem, it was hoped, that peaceful coexistence would soon redress. As Lenin noted, "A durable peace would be such a relief to the working people of Russia that they would undoubtedly agree to certain concessions being granted. The granting of concessions under reasonable terms is desirable also for us, as one of the means of attracting into Russia, during the period of coexistence side by side of socialist and capitalist states, the technical aid of countries which are more advanced in this respect" (Lenin 1970a, 197).

More generally, the development by Lenin of the policy of peaceful coexistence arose logically from his theory of world revolution. According to this theory, a socialist revolution was possible in one country because of the uneven development of the world. Therefore it was necessary to work out the relations of such a country to the others, which still remained capitalist. Leninism recognized that there would be a period of coexistence between capitalist and socialist states, and that it was in the interest of the working class in each country to avoid military confrontation, and that therefore socialism should pursue a policy based on peaceful coexistence (Chubarian 1976; Griffiths 1964; Horak 1964; Jacobson 1994; Kubálková and Cruickshank 1978; Lerner 1964; Light 1988, 27–45; Tsygankov 2012, 97–117, 155–171).

The aim of Lenin's policy of peaceful coexistence was to reduce the possibility of military confrontation between Soviet Russia and the "capitalist camp", to make it harder for "war-mongering capitalist governments" to start wars against the Soviet state. In so far as capitalism exists, such a policy would be imposed on any rational socialist government. Lenin sought to find a way to deal with the contradiction between the two systems, in response not only to the failure of the world revolution to successfully fight for state power in the other countries, but also to the inevitability of a period of coexistence.

According to Lenin, the efforts to ensure military peace, however, did not rule out a different kind of war. As Lenin noted in the debates about trading concessions, "Concessions did not mean peace with capitalism, but war in a new sphere. The war of guns and tanks yields place to economic warfare" (Lenin 1970b, 78).

The first international presentation of Lenin's peaceful coexistence policy took place at the April 1922 International Economic Conference in Genoa. The Soviet delegation led by the Peoples Commissar for Foreign Affairs Georgy Chicherin tried to demonstrate Moscow's non-aggressive intentions and overcome the negative image of the new Soviet state created by the Bolsheviks' "export of revolution" policies. As Chossudovsky (1972) noted, Chicherin presented three key principles of peaceful coexistence:

1. It is the recognition of the difference in property systems in capitalist and socialist countries which lies at the heart of the coexistence question (…)

2. The principal objective of foreign policy and diplomacy in East-West relations is the settlement of all questions at issue without recourse to force, *i.e.* by negotiation.

3. War is *not* inevitable.

In the interwar period (the 1920–30s), Moscow remained loyal to the peaceful coexistence strategy: it managed to attract Western investment and technologies to modernize the Soviet economy, join the League of Nations and even engage in a dialogue with some European countries on creation of a collective security system aimed against Nazi Germany (Chubarian 1976; Tsygankov 2012, 97–117, 155–171). Despite the fact that such a strategy was unable to prevent a new world war, its legacy was quite useful for the postwar peace-building and world-ordering, including the establishment of the UN system and development of international law.

At the 20th Congress of the Communist Party of the Soviet Union (CPSU) (1956) the then Soviet leader Nikita Khrushchev elevated the peaceful coexistence concept up to the status of the USSR's official doctrine. In addition to the Leninist concept and UN Charter's principles, the revised version drew heavily on the more recent Indian idea of *Pancha*

Chila, or "Five Principles," which included principles such as coexistence, respect for the territorial and integral sovereignty of others, nonaggression, noninterference in the internal affairs of others and the recognition of the equality of others (De Coning et al. 2014, 100–112).

Peaceful coexistence was subsequently included to the CPSU's Third Program (CPSU 1961, Chapter VIII), its new version of 1986 (CPSU 1986, Part 3, Chapter III) and written into the 1977 Soviet Constitution (Konstitutsiya 1977, Chapter 4, Art. 28 and 29). The latter two documents included an expanded list of principles such as sovereign equality; mutual renunciation of the use or threat of force; inviolability of frontiers; territorial integrity of states; peaceful settlement of disputes; non-intervention in internal affairs; respect for human rights and fundamental freedoms; the equal rights of peoples and their right to decide their own destiny; cooperation among nations; arms control and disarmament; and fulfillment in good faith of obligations arising from the generally recognized principles and rules of international law, and from the international treaties signed by the Soviet Union (CPSU 1986, Part 3, Chapter III; Konstitutsiya 1977, Chapter 4, Art. 29).

The peaceful coexistence concept has not only survived but even been strengthened in the Gorbachev era (see next chapter). The situation, however, has changed in the post-Soviet period. In contrast with its central position in Soviet foreign policy thinking, peaceful coexistence concept was largely absent from the Russian political lexicon under the Yeltsin and early Putin regimes. Even if the doctrine's principles still existed in Russia's post-Soviet thinking and international strategies, the term itself was viewed mainly as an historical phenomenon. It carried such strong Marxist-Leninist connotations that many Russian audiences almost automatically associated it with the Soviet time.

However, by mid-2000s the concept was in use again. Initially, some Russian analysts, referring to coming of a "cold peace" in the U.S.-Russia relations under the Bush Jr. administration, used the term in ironic sense. For example, already in 2006 the Russian prominent foreign policy expert Sergey Karaganov sarcastically asked whether Moscow and Washington would be "going back to peaceful coexistence?" implying that two countries based their foreign policies on fundamentally different principles (Karaganov 2006).

Moscow's renewed interest in the peaceful coexistence concept can be explained by several reasons.

First and foremost, at some point, the Kremlin realized that previous models of Russia's relations with the West, such as comprehensive security (late Gorbachev's era); Russia is the West's 'younger partner' (Kozyrev's era); cooperative security (late Yeltsin's and early Putin's periods); strategic (or just) partnership (second Putin's and Medvedev' administrations), did not work. The return to the old, time-tested and— seemingly—reliable foreign policy concept was seen as a logical step in a search for a proper doctrinal basis for Moscow's international strategy.

Furthermore, since mid-2000s there was Moscow's growing dissatisfaction with the West's reluctance to respect Russia's global and regional interests and treat her as an equal partner. Putin's Munich speech of 2007 marked the moment when the Kremlin started to redesign its foreign policy in a more assertive way (Putin 2007).

Over time, the Russian-Western controversies on international issues were augmented by the fundamental differences on interpretation of core values, such as democracy, rule of law, human and minority rights, freedom of speech, independent mass media, etc. (Makarychev and Sergunin 2013a; Sergunin 2014a). The West became increasingly critical of the Putin regime accusing it of authoritarianism and human rights violations. Similar to the Cold war era, both the West and Russia tended to believe that they belonged, if not to antagonistic, but to rather different socio-political systems. Under these circumstances, the Kremlin viewed the coexistence principle as a proper approach to dealing with its Western partners.

Interestingly, there was a Western / NATO analogy of the peaceful coexistence concept in the post-Cold war era—a cooperative security doctrine. NATO's 2010 Lisbon Strategic Concept (NATO 2010) even elevated "cooperative security" to one of the alliance's core tasks on a par with "collective security" and "crisis management" and prepared the bloc for the adoption in April 2011 of a partnership policy document entitled "Active Engagement in Cooperative Security: A More Efficient and Flexible Partnership Policy" (NATO 2011). As Flockhart (2014, 18) notes, NATO's cooperative security strategy sought to use partnerships as a geopolitical tool for sustaining essential features of the liberal order, as well as trying to change that order in a way that will make it more acceptable to emerging powers that did not share the liberal values underpinning it. According to former U.S. Secretary of State Hilary Clinton, such a policy "reflects the world as it is—not as it used to be", a world in which America "will lead by inducing greater cooperation among a greater number of actors and reducing competition, tilting the balance away from a multipolar world and toward a multi-partner world" (Clinton 2009).

NATO's cooperative security strategy with regard to Russia was based on the assumption that Brussels and Moscow could have both divergent and convergent views on regional and global security problems but it should not prevent them from a dialogue. Politically, there were a number of areas of friction between NATO and Russia. For example, Moscow remained deeply unhappy about NATO's plans to build BMD in Europe or accept new members, including the post-Soviet states such as Georgia, Moldova and Ukraine. NATO and Russia also disagreed on the question of increased transparency on military issues such as military exercises and sub-strategic nuclear weapons.

Those tensions were often exaggerated by mass media. On a practical level, however, the cooperative trend prevailed in the pre-Ukrainian crisis period. Because of the shared interest in stabilizing Afghanistan, Russia has offered reliable and affordable transit routes for supplies in and out of the country for the NATO-led International Security Assistance Force (ISAF) mission (2001–2014). Through the NATO-Russia Council (NRC), the partners have trained thousands of counter-narcotics officials from the Central Asian states, Afghanistan and Pakistan—officials who have been instrumental in making seizures of drugs which would otherwise have ended up in Russia and Europe. Together, NATO and Russia are helping to supply the Afghan army with helicopters, a crucial capability, especially when ISAF ended in December 2014. Beyond that, NATO and Russia have agreed around twenty core areas of cooperation, including the fight against terrorism, counter-piracy and disaster relief (Flockhart 2014, 44). In each area there were concrete projects underway, for example, the development of technology to detect explosives in public areas, or to track together aircraft that might be under the control of terrorists in the airspace bordering NATO and Russia. Although most of these projects were frozen in the aftermath of the Ukrainian crisis, they were instrumental in accumulating cooperative experiences and conducive to embedding the coexistence principle in the NATO-Russian relations.

It should be also noted that, above all, the coexistence concept quite nicely fits a reformist state's political philosophy and can be applicable to the explanation of foreign policy behavior of many reformist powers, including Russia. The peaceful coexistence concept acknowledges the rights of other states to have different socio-economic and political systems as well as diverging views on international problems. This concept calls for non-interference to domestic affairs, solving conflicts peacefully, on the basis of international law, preference of soft rather than hard power foreign policy instruments—exactly what the reformist philosophy stands for.

For these reasons, not only Russia but also other reformist states prefer to use the peaceful coexistence concept. In this sense, they speak the same language and understand each other very well. Some influential international actors like, for instance, China, never stopped to use this term. For example, commenting on the August 1999 Bishkek Declaration of the Shanghai Five then Chinese President Jiang Zemin underlined that protection of fundamental international principles, such as respect to national sovereignty, territorial integrity, non-interference to domestic affairs, equality, peaceful coexistence, the UN's leading role in world affairs, etc., should be an important priority for those who oppose the "neo-interventionism" of the U.S. and NATO (Stroitel'stvo 1999).

From the Kremlin's point of view, the peaceful coexistence concept helped to overcome shortcomings of previous policies, reconcile extremes and integrate different approaches to a single and clear strategy on the international arena.

It should be noted, however, that Russia's present-day interpretation of the coexistence concept is different from its Soviet original. The differences between the two versions can be described in the following way.

The Soviet and post-Soviet peaceful coexistence concepts have different ideological underpinnings: the Soviet version was based on the Marxist-Leninist ideology while the current version has no a clear ideological fundament (the so-called national idea has not yet been shaped to date). Moreover, their ideological principles can collide with each other when, for example, the Putin regime suggests conservatism as a basis for Russia's present-day national idea (Sergunin 2014a). Conservatism, with its emphasis on traditional values and protection of national interests and national sovereignty, definitely opposes to the revolutionary, progressive and cosmopolitan spirit of Marxism-Leninism.

Furthermore, strategic goals and the roles of the coexistence concept in Soviet and Russian foreign policies are different. In the Soviet era, the coexistence concept was a strategy for the transitional period when two antagonistic social systems had to (reluctantly) cohabit. However, it did not replace fundamental theoretical concepts of Marxism-Leninism, such as the world revolutionary process, class struggle principle, abolition of exploitation of man by man and private property. The peaceful coexistence's strategic aim was still an elimination of the world capitalism and world-wide victory of socialism (Chubarian 1976; Light 1988). The fight against world imperialism should be continued but by other means and in other spheres. Competition in the field of economy and high tech as well as "ideological warfare" should take place instead of an open military confrontation.

Currently, Moscow has no such revolutionary / radical objectives. The present-day coexistence concept is of more defensive rather than offensive character. Moscow has no intention to destroy the dominant capitalist system. Rather, Russia wants to be integrated to this system but on equal terms. The Kremlin does not aim to imposing its values or model on other nations; it wants only to be treated with respect and on the mutually beneficial basis.

There are also completely different geopolitical contexts. In the Cold war era, the USSR was a superpower, a leader of the socialist world. Moscow has conducted its peaceful coexistence policy on the basis of strategic parity with another superpower—the U.S. Post-Soviet Russia has lost its superpower status and now it tries to secure its "normal great power" standing. Moscow does not lead any powerful coalition or alliance comparable to the Warsaw Pact. In the wake of the Ukrainian crisis it found itself in semi-isolation. Geopolitically, Russia is in a situation which is to some extent similar to the position of the post-revolutionary / post-civil war Soviet Russia, the moment when the Lenin-Chicherin peaceful coexistence doctrine was born. Of course, for present-day Russia, the peaceful coexistence policy is not a survival strategy as it was in the case of early Soviet Russia; but still it characterizes the course of an actor whose international standing is rather weak and needed to be improved.

The current interpretation of Russia's peaceful coexistence concept can be summarized in the following way:

- Similar to the old concept's version, the Kremlin believes that countries with different socio-economic and political systems can coexist peacefully. However, in contrast with the Marxist-Leninist interpretation, now the coexisting systems belong to the same type of social formation rather than they are of antagonistic nature.

- At the same time, Moscow does not accept the dominance of one or group of states; instead, it favors a multipolar world model (the concept which now prevails over the Russian foreign policy discourse) where Russia can find its legitimate and rightful place.

- The soft power instruments are preferable while military power is a last resort, an exceptional tool which should be used when other means are exhausted.

- In spite of numerous divergences with the West, Russia has a broad cooperative agenda with the U.S., EU and NATO that includes WMD non-proliferation; arms control and disarmament; conflict prevention and resolution; fighting international terrorism and transnational crime; environment protection and climate change mitigation; civil protection; outer space and world ocean research; humanitarian and cultural cooperation, etc.

- The coexistence concept is mostly designed for Russia's relations with the West / developed countries. Moscow's relations with the CIS, BRICS and developing countries are based on other theoretical / conceptual principles ranging from the moderate version of Eurasianism to various interpretations of the partnership model.

It should be noted that the coexistence concept is not yet a part of Russia's active political vocabulary; many Russian academics and politicians are quite allergic to the Leninist / Soviet type of the peaceful coexistence doctrine. But implicitly the concept has already returned to the Russian foreign policy discourse.

Soft power concept

The new / old Russian foreign policy philosophy of "coexistence" and reformism has paved a way to the search of international strategies that are alternative to hard power policies. The soft power concept coined by Joseph Nye (2004) was seen by the Kremlin as relevant to the new foreign policy.

Looking retrospectively at the history of the soft power concept in Russia, it became attractive to the country's leadership as early as Vladimir Putin's second presidency in 2004–2008. The concept emerged in the context of the Kremlin's more active policies in the so-called "near abroad" (i.e. in the post-Soviet space) in particular, as Moscow was seeking to consolidate its power among its perceived compatriots. The "Russian World" concept that covered Russian speakers living abroad was introduced as part and parcel of the first version of a soft security strategy. The series of "color" revolutions in Georgia in 2003, Ukraine in 2004 and Kyrgyzstan in 2005 was also conducive to the launch of the Russian soft power debate.

With the help of the soft power concept, the Kremlin aimed to foster economic, political and socio-cultural integration in the post-Soviet space. Its previous policies in the area were mostly elite-oriented. In practical terms, this meant securing local regimes' positions (often) at the expense of Russia's security and economic interests. It appeared, however, that the pro-Russian regimes lost their power in some CIS countries (e.g. Viktor Yanukovych in Ukraine), while their successors often opted for playing an anti-Russian card to consolidate their power. Currently, even in the most stable and traditionally pro-Russian countries such as Kazakhstan and Belarus, popular support for integration with Russia is not sufficiently strong. Thus, by applying soft power techniques Russia hopes to improve its international image and increase its attractiveness to both elites and societies in the CIS countries.

There has also been the need to improve Russia's international image—not only in CIS countries, but also worldwide—which seriously suffered after the "five-day war" with Georgia in August 2008 and public protests against alleged fraud during the 2011 parliamentary and 2012 presidential elections. The Kremlin launched a massive propaganda campaign to downplay Russia's image of an "aggressive" and "undemocratic" country with the aim of making it more attractive to international partners. This goal was viewed as especially important for Moscow's relations with the EU. The latter, on the one hand, was seen as a key international actor as well as Russia's major trade partner and a source of investment and know-how. On the other hand, the EU was Russia's major critic in areas such as human rights, the lack of progress in legal and administrative reforms, and in fighting corruption (Makarychev and Sergunin 2013a). For example, the soft power concept rose in prominence in the Russian political vocabulary during the pre-election debates of 2012, including the so-called "programmatic" articles by Vladimir Putin (2012a). In these articles, Putin promised to make Russia an attractive and reliable international partner, open to cooperation with foreign countries.

Moreover, there was a need to revisit the foreign policy concept after the 2012 presidential election. As stated in President Putin's decree of 7 May 2012 (issued immediately after his inauguration), the basic goals of the previous concept had not been achieved (Putin 2012b). According to Putin, one of the factors that prevented Russia from taking 'solid and respected positions in the international community'—the task which was set in the 2008 Foreign Policy Concept (Medvedev 2008)—was its negligence of soft power instruments.

The Kremlin acknowledged the fact that Russia was lagging behind other major international actors who had already developed and begun to implement their soft power doctrines. According to Konstantin Kosachev (ex-director of *Rossotrudnichestvo*, the Russian governmental agency responsible for relations with the CIS and compatriots living abroad), Russia has preserved its hard power parity with other key international players but it is lagging behind them in terms of soft power (Kosachev 2012b). As explained in the 2013 Russian Foreign Policy Concept, soft power is used by some international actors in a rather destructive and illegitimate way (Putin 2013a). Russian experts often refer to the US, which they see as preferring to use soft power as an addition to military / coercive instruments rather than as its only foreign policy method (Konyshev and Sergunin 2012; Kubyshkin and Tzvetkova 2013). Many Russian experts are also increasingly persuaded by Nye's idea of smart power where "in a smart power strategy, hard and soft [power] reinforce each other" (Nye 2013). These analysts argue that while Russia should copy American "best practices", it should also aim to develop a more effective model of soft power strategy (Kosachev 2012a; Kubyshkin and Sergunin 2012; Kubyshkin and Tzvetkova 2013; Lukyanov 2009; Tsygankov 2013a and 2013b).

Upon his 2012 re-election, President Putin called on Russian foreign policy makers to think about the use of non-traditional foreign policy instruments, including soft power tools (Putin, 2012c). Russia's need for soft power capabilities was also acknowledged in the new Russian Foreign Policy Concept of February 2013, which was elevated to the status of official Kremlin strategy. The rise of the Kremlin's interest in the soft power concept coincided with serious changes in Russia's foreign policy philosophy (which were described earlier).

It should be noted that the Russian political leadership and academic community have interpreted the soft power concept differently from Nye's original version. According to Nye, soft power is one of the three possible ways to exercise power and accomplish an actor's goals—coercion, payment or attraction—and he associates soft power with the latter method.

However, as Nye emphasizes, powers such as China or Russia, who proclaimed their adherence to the soft power concept for various reasons, fail to become attractive to targeted international audiences. According to Nye, one of the basic mistakes made by China and Russia is that they did not realize that "the development of soft power need not be a zero-sum game. All countries can gain from finding each other attractive" (Nye 2013). Many Chinese and Russian soft power initiatives often pursue overtly pragmatic, interest-based goals rather than aim to take into account international partners' interests and, for this reason, are met with suspicion or even hostility.

Russian political leaders have largely interpreted the soft power concept in a very instrumental and pragmatic way. Initially, it was perceived by Moscow as an instrument of policy towards its compatriots in post-Soviet countries. For example, in 2008 the Russian Foreign Minister Sergei Lavrov (2008) commented:

> Nowadays the growing role is played by the so-called "soft power"—an ability to affect the environment through civilizational, humanitarian, cultural, foreign policy and other forms of attractiveness. I believe that the whole grammar of our diverse links with compatriots should be constructed precisely with account of these factors.

With the start of Putin's third presidential term in 2012, the Kremlin moved to a broader—but still instrumentalist—understanding of soft power. Its soft power strategy is now seen as a set of foreign policy "technologies" that help to achieve Moscow's goals with regards to particular states and—more generally—strengthen Russian positions worldwide (not only in the CIS). For instance, the Russian Foreign Policy Concept of 2013 underlined:

> Soft power has become an indispensable component of contemporary international politics, which is a complex set of instruments for resolving foreign policy tasks backed by potential of civil society, information and communication, humanitarian and other methods and technologies, alternative to a classical diplomacy (Putin 2013a).

The promotion of Russia's positive image abroad is considered to be an important priority in its soft power strategy. As the above doctrine emphasizes, this should be done through the development of "effective means of information influence on public opinion abroad" as well as through strengthening the positions of the Russian language and culture abroad, *inter alia* with support of compatriots (Putin 2013a).

Some prominent Russian analysts link the concept of soft power to a new, broader, reading of security (Gronskaya and Makarychev 2010; Rusakova 2010; Sergunin and Karabeshkin 2015; Tsygankov 2013a and 2013b). These analysts believe that in the post-Cold War era "security" includes not only hard (military), but also soft (non-military) dimensions, including economic, political, societal, environmental, human and information strands. By the same token, they maintain that power in international relations is gradually changing its nature; it is now less coercive and softer. For these Russian theorists, the hard power strategy is associated with military power while soft power is linked to non-military attributes such as a viable economy, political strength, a healthy society, sustainable ecology, attractive culture and efficient public diplomacy (Konyshev and Sergunin 2014; Lukyanov 2009; Troitsky 2011). In other words, this Russian IR school suggests a different and broader understanding of the soft power concept than Nye's definition. In fact, it includes all non-military instruments and resources available for international actors. However, it also contradicts Nye's definition because he excludes coercion as well as economically driven influence ('payment' in his terminology) from soft power.

It should be noted that along with the significant deviation of Russia's interpretation of soft power from Nye's definition, there is also a lack of clarity and uniformity in the terminology used by Russian academics and politicians. For example, there are several overlapping concepts, such as "NGO-diplomacy" (non-governmental organizations' international activities), "popular diplomacy" (people-to-people international contacts), "public diplomacy" (Russia's policies that are addressed to the civil society of foreign countries rather than to their governments) and the "humanitarian dimension" of foreign policy (similar to the notion of public diplomacy). These are all commonly used in Russia when referring to soft power (Sergunin and Karabeshkin 2015).

Although Russian experts differ in their reading of these concepts, the general trend in Russian mainstream thinking is to see "soft power" as an integrative term that encompasses all the above-mentioned notions.

To sum up, radical shifts in Russia's foreign policy philosophy have made the soft power concept both desirable and palatable to Kremlin strategists. The analysis will now focus on what soft power potential is available for Russia and how effectively it has been used by Moscow.

According to Nye, soft power is, first and foremost, an ability to be attractive. To quote Nye (2004, 11), the soft power of a country rests primarily on three resources: "its culture (in places where it is attractive to others), its political values (when it lives up to them at home and abroad), and its foreign policies (when they are seen as legitimate and having moral authority)". As mentioned above, Russian theorists believe that there are also economic dimensions to soft power, albeit these can also effectively serve as hard power instruments.

The Russian political class believes that the country possesses huge soft power potential but it is often misused or used ineffectively. It is worth mentioning that Russian soft power strategists view the Soviet experience of international propaganda and positive image-making as useful. As noted by Feodor Lukyanov (2013), this experience proved quite efficient and can be re-installed quite easily if staffed with sufficient resources. The former head of *Rossotrudnichestvo*, Konstantin Kosachev, acknowledged that his agency was a logical successor of "the traditions and practical skills which [had] emerged yet in the old Soviet times" (Kosachev 2012b). According to Kosachev (2012b), the Soviet Union actively utilized soft power techniques and, for this reason, its international reputation was very high. In practical terms, a re-launching of the system of "friendship societies" with foreign countries has been proposed, as well as the organization of the Festival of Youth and Students in 2017.

Prior to the Ukrainian crisis, the international consulting company Ernst & Young ranked Russia third among the emerging markets and tenth among the top global soft powers (Ernst & Young 2012, 10 and 14). Moscow emphasized the economic aspects of its soft power in its policies in the post-Soviet space while it relied mostly on cultural and political instruments in the 'far abroad' (which did not exclude the use of some economic leverage, such as relatively cheap energy supplies). For example, Moscow tried to promote itself as an attractive economic power (the source of investment, a reliable energy supplier, a promising market for foreign consumer goods and labor force, etc.) in the post-Soviet space in order to develop the Customs Union and the Eurasian Economic Union projects. Prior to the Ukrainian crisis, Moscow managed to convince the EU countries that it could be a reliable economic partner rather than a source of severe socio-economic problems (e.g. illegal migration or smuggling) for its European neighbors. With the introduction of the Baltic Pipeline System in 2001 and the Nord Stream gas pipeline in 2011, Russia reinforced its position as the main energy supplier for Europe.

The "cultural component" of Russia's soft power is based on the attractiveness of Russian "high" culture throughout the world and in neighboring countries. For example, the Russian Ministry of Culture sponsors the Golden Mask annual theatre festival, which presents Russia's most prominent performers to the Baltic public. Cultural exchanges between Russia and other post-Soviet states have tended to grow as well. The Russian higher education system is still attractive for students from the former Soviet republics because the best Russian universities in Moscow, St Petersburg and some other provincial cities are still able to provide foreign students with good training in the 'hard' sciences as well as the humanities.

Russian diasporas in the post-Soviet states are viewed by the Kremlin as a channel for projecting soft power. For example, in relation to the Baltic States, Moscow possesses a unique resource with the Russian speaking population constituting about a third of the overall population in Latvia and Estonia. These communities are relatively consolidated (despite some internal controversies). They often feel discriminated against by the local regimes and do 'not identify themselves with new statehood' (Lukyanov 2009), but still appreciate a number of advantages provided by the Baltic States' independence. In general, the Russian-speaking minorities in the post-Soviet countries view Moscow as a natural protector and have a rather positive attitude to Russia and Russian culture.

In the pre-Crimean era, Moscow made great strides in improving its bilateral relations with many European countries. In addition to Russia's friendly relations with Finland in the post-Second World War period, Moscow sought to improve its relations with Lithuania and Sweden as well as to 'repair' its complicated bilateral ties with Denmark (because of the 2002 Chechen Congress in Copenhagen), Estonia (after the 2007 "Bronze Soldier" conflict), Latvia and Poland (both of which have had numerous historical conflicts with Russia). Dmitry Medvedev's 2009 European Security Treaty (EST) proposal aimed to strengthen the regional security system (Sergunin 2010).

The Russian CBSS presidency program for 2012–2013 was specially designed to promote a sub-regional soft power agenda, including trade, investment, ecology, cross-border cooperation, people-to-people contacts and cultural initiatives. Moscow's ambition was not only to promote universal values (such as the prevention of radicalism and extremism as well as the protection of children's rights in the region), but to export what were perceived to be Russian traditions of inter-ethic and inter-religious tolerance and multiculturalism (Ministry of Foreign Affairs of the Russian Federation 2012, 7). This is viewed as a specific Russian soft power resource. The active strengthening of people-to-people contacts and the facilitation of visa regimes in the region could be considered by the regional public to be a source of attractiveness originating in Russia's foreign policy. The Ukrainian crisis, however, has undermined Russia's soft power efforts in Europe and other regions.

The process of soft power's institutionalization in Russia started even before the term itself became part of the official vocabulary. In 2007, the *Russkiy Mir* (Russian World) Foundation was established by a presidential decree (although with NGO status). The Foundation's main function is to promote the Russian language, culture and education system abroad. The ideological background and authorship of the title "Russian World" is often ascribed to Pyotr Shedrovitsky. He argued that "during the 20th century as a result of tectonic historical shifts, world wars, and revolutions, the *Russian World* as a network structure of large and small communities thinking in and speaking the Russian language emerged" (Shedrovitsky 2000).

The *Russian world,* based on cultural and communication resources of the Russian language, is then interpreted as soft power capital that can be utilized for agenda-setting (images of the future) and strengthening the sustainability of Russia's statehood ("the more people and communities need Russia, the more sustainable it is"). For example, the *Russkiy Mir* nominates the best teachers and students of the Russian language and culture for the position of "Professor of the *Russkiy Mir"* and "Student of the *Russkiy Mir".* It also has fellowship and internship programs for foreign scholars and students to be hosted in Russia. The Foundation organizes various conferences, competitions and olympiads on a regular basis.

In 2008, the *Rossotrudnichestvo,* Federal Agency for the CIS (Compatriots Abroad and International Humanitarian Cooperation) was established with nearly the same mission as *Russkiy Mir* but with governmental status under the Foreign Ministry. As then President Medvedev put it, the agency was to become "the key instrument of the so-called soft power" (Government of the Russian Federation 2012). Today the agency has representative offices in almost all European countries, the US, Canada and major Asian, African and Latin American states. In addition to these two main institutions, a number of (often state-affiliated) NGOs, such as the Gorchakov Foundation for Public Diplomacy, Andrei Pervozvanny Fund, International Foundations for Working with Diasporas Abroad "Rossiyane", International Council of Russian Compatriots, Library 'Russian-language Literature Abroad' and International Association of Twin Cities partake in soft power activities.

Historically, the City of Moscow was a pioneer in pursuing its "foreign policy" in the post-Soviet space. In 1999, the Moscow Foundation for Support of Compatriots (named after Yuri Dolgorukiy) was established by the decree of then Mayor Yuri Luzhkov (later it was transformed into the Moscow Foundation for International Cooperation). The Foundation had a scholarship program for Russian-speaking students, mostly targeting compatriots in the CIS and the Baltic countries. For example, Russian businesses invested in a network of the Houses of Moscow which should serve as "centers of culture and business cooperation". Currently, there are six houses—in Bishkek, Minsk, Riga, Sofia, Sukhumi and Yerevan. In 2010, following Luzhkov's resignation, the Foundation was reorganized into two separate units under the control of the Department of Foreign

Economic and International Relations: the Moscow Center for International Cooperation and the Moscow House of Compatriots.

The growing activism in the sphere of soft power policy is also demonstrated by the Russian northwestern regions, which "specialize" in developing twinning and humanitarian contacts to contribute to the support of compatriots abroad. For example, St Petersburg, the Leningrad Oblast, Kaliningrad and Karelia are traditionally active in twinning with neighboring foreign towns and various European regions (Joenniemi and Sergunin 2012). Programs of cooperation with compatriots have recently been launched by some of these regions.

The Russian higher education system has gradually built up its soft power potential. It is becoming internationalized *via* the introduction of the Bologna Process and has increased the state quota for foreign students to be trained in Russian universities. The frameworks for academic exchanges are diversifying. The state-funded "slots" for study in Russian universities are distributed through Russian embassies, with 70–100 "slots" for each country annually. A number of leading universities (such as Moscow State University, St. Petersburg State University and the Higher School of Economics) organize student enrolment independently through competitions. The leading regional universities, such as Kant Baltic Federal University (Kaliningrad), St. Petersburg-based universities, Kuban State University, Voronezh State University and Siberian and Far Eastern universities, have numerous collaboration programs with partner universities in neighboring countries, including joint undergraduate and graduate programs and research projects.

The Russian academic community is also quite active in using professional associations to increase its soft power capabilities. For example, Russia's northwestern universities play a prominent role in the Baltic Sea Region University Network and promote academic exchanges in the region. As stressed by then Prime Minister Putin (2012a), "we should increase our educational and cultural presence in the world by several times, and increase it on the order in those countries, where a part of population is speaking or understanding Russian language".

Finally, one should not forget the role played by the Russian Orthodox Church in soft power strategies. For example, the Russian Orthodoxy played the role of both a "back channel" and an informal mediator between Russia, Georgia and Ukraine during the crisis years. Experts agree that its international presence increased after the election of Kirill as a Patriarch, but are split over its perception abroad. As one Latvian expert wrote, "religious freedom, highly regarded in the West, offers some degree of legitimacy to the international activities of the Russian Orthodox Church" (Kudors 2010, 3). According to Lukyanov, this is one of the main assets of Russia's soft power, but "foreign counteragents are frightened by it even more than by traditional leverages" (Lukyanov 2009). To overcome such accusations, some Russian experts suggest positioning the Orthodox Church as a transnational organization (Tezisy 2012, 51).

Post-Soviet countries are quite suspicious about Moscow's soft power policies in this region. Both the policy-oriented and research literature is replete with critical assessments of Russian soft power efforts, especially in the post-Soviet space. According to one account, "unlike the traditional definition of soft power, Russia's soft power does not display emphasis on legitimacy and moral authority.... It serves to divide rather than unite and to arouse apprehension rather than provide comfort" (Grygas 2012). For example, the Baltic States' complaint list includes "creation, maintenance and support of Kremlin-friendly networks of influence in the cultural, economic and political sectors", dissemination of biased information, local agenda-setting through the Russian state-controlled media, and making compatriots primarily loyal to the Kremlin. Western experts believe that Russia's main objective is to undermine the statehood of post-Soviet states and enhance the sphere of its influence. Another interpretation sees Moscow as "seeking to exploit the Western concept of 'soft power' ... reframing it as a euphemism for coercive policy and economic arm-twisting" (Minzarari 2012).

Some Russian experts, in fact, echo this observation by saying that the concept of "soft power" has two meanings: narrow, linked primarily to attractiveness; and broad, the ability to change the policy preferences of others (Troitsky 2011). The second meaning, in practical terms, is very close to the notion of "hard power".

If we look at specific areas of Russia's soft power policies, foreign experts have been fairly critical of Moscow's economic policies. For example, Russia's energy potential has often been perceived as an "energy weapon"—i.e. a hard rather than soft power instrument.

As for the "cultural dimension" of Russia's soft power policies, Russian "high" culture has proved difficult to instrumentalize for practical purposes. In part, Russia's rich cultural traditions are often overshadowed by negative perceptions of current political developments in this country (Troitski 2011). Moreover, in contrast with "high" culture, contemporary Russian popular culture, lifestyle and media products seem to be less attractive for foreigners, even for Russia's compatriots. The (excessive) presence of Russia-made entertainment and news in the local media is often viewed as a threat to constructing a "true" national or European identity.

It is often claimed that ethnic minorities in post-Soviet countries live in a Russian "information space", which allegedly undermines their loyalty to their states of domicile. In general, one may find that attitudes of Russian compatriots towards Russia are quite ambiguous. On the one hand, they express certain affinity with Russia and even with the ruling political regime (e.g. vast majority of the Russian citizens residing in Estonia voted for Putin in 2012). On the other hand, when they are able to make a choice about where to get education and / or where to migrate, they prefer Europe or North America to Russia.

The role of compatriots in Russia's soft power strategy has been subject to criticism as well. As identified by a Polish expert, "Russian policy in this regard seems to contradict the concept of soft power: instead of winning people over who do not share Russia's foreign principles and goals, the country seeks to mobilize those who already agree with them" (Ćwiek-Karpowicz 2012). Besides, soft power is often perceived by local political elites as creating a Russian "fifth column" that works against independent statehood. Statements made about the need to consolidate Russian compatriots abroad (which can be realistically achieved only in the Baltic States) exacerbate existential fears even more (Conley et al. 2011).

With the start of the Ukrainian crisis, the hostile attitude of the Baltic States to Moscow's efforts to develop cooperation with compatriots has significantly increased. The allegations that "we are the next on Russia's list" and that the "Donbass scenario" can be repeated in the Baltic States have become widespread in the Baltic media.

At the same time, some Russian experts believe that Moscow's ability to use compatriots as a soft power instrument is often over-estimated, since the size of Russian communities in the post-Soviet states is decreasing, while their cultural and political orientations are getting more diverse, complicating the task of their consolidation. As one Russian analyst argues:

> [T]hey [Russian communities] are unlikely to be the resource, the instrument of the Russian soft power, rather, they might be its target, provided that under soft power we understand not a set of political spinning technologies but the development of strong ties with our compatriots based on business, scientific cooperation, interaction in the field of education and culture and, of course, political support. (Smirnov 2012)

Regarding the attractiveness of the Russian political values, as many foreign experts maintain, Russia struggles to harmonize its traditional values with internationally recognized democratic values and standards. As argued by Kosachev (2012a), on the one hand, "freedom, democracy, rule of law, social stability and respect for human rights have become 'a consumer basket' of the modern world". On the other hand, "there are differences in their [values] *individual manifestation* due to national, historical and other specifics" (Kosachev 2012a; emphasis in original).

To put it differently, Moscow finds it a challenge to persuade others that it shares universal values and that it is ready to disseminate them throughout the world. Equally, Russia is unable to make its domestic socio-economic and political model attractive and sell it to other nations. Even Kosachev (2012a) admits that Russia cannot export its specific model since "it has not developed any such model yet".

Moscow is also short of efficient foreign policy tools in the soft power domain. None of Russia's large-scale foreign policy initiatives (including the EST draft and the Russian CBSS presidency program) gained solid international support. The Kremlin sometimes does not take into account "local peculiarities" in its soft power activities. For example, the three Baltic republics suffer from an "inferiority complex" because their local statehood and identities are still in their formative phase. The very process of state- and identity-building is often based on the negative 'othering' of Russia. In this context, any Russian soft power efforts are interpreted as attempts to breach Baltic sovereignty, identities and security. Besides, Russia is repeatedly blamed for having a 'hidden plan' to reintegrate the Baltic States into its sphere of influence.

To continue the analysis of Russian soft power's shortcomings, it should be noted that Moscow's instruments in this field are predominantly "statist"—i.e. government-based and controlled. Harnessing the potential of NGOs is not a priority for Russia. Those NGOs that are 'officially' allowed to participate in soft power activities are, in reality, semi-governmental and perceived by "target audiences" in the post-Soviet countries accordingly. From Nye's point of view, Russia's neglect of civil society's role in soft power politics is a serious mistake.

According to Nye (2013), much of America's soft power is produced by civil society—from universities and foundations to cinema and popular culture—rather than by the government. Moscow often tends to forget what Nye (2004, 17) wrote about the interaction between the government and non-governmental sectors in the soft power sphere: governments should 'make sure that their own actions and policies reinforce rather than undercut their soft power'. On a number of occasions the Kremlin has undercut the activities of Russian regions, municipalities, private companies, universities and NGOs that aimed to promote cooperation with international partners in the economic and humanitarian spheres.

The lack of transparency (and its natural "satellite"—corruption) is another grave shortcoming of Russia's soft power policies. Moscow's soft power initiatives are often oriented either to the relatively narrow circles of local political elites or to certain (pro-Kremlin) parts of Russian communities in post-Soviet countries who are ironically called "professional compatriots". As one expert notes,

> Lithuania is lucky with the main Russian problem of corruption. That's why the major part of Russian projects aimed at strengthening attractiveness among the former republics of the USSR is sinking in the backwater of corruption, and Lithuania can feel quieter (BaltInfo 2012).

Duplication is another problem for Russian soft power policies in the post-Soviet space. For example, there is no clear division of labor between the *Rossotrudnichestvo* and *Russkiy Mir*. As a result, their partners in foreign countries are often puzzled by the rather chaotic and competing activities of these two leading Russian soft power agencies.

To conclude, there was no accident in the Kremlin's turn to the soft power concept over the last decade. A number of powerful factors, such as the need to redesign its foreign policy doctrine in line with the present-day standards, to improve its international image and strengthen Russia's world-wide authority (especially in the post-Soviet space),—encouraged Moscow to familiarize itself with this concept. Since the late 2000s it has been deeply embedded in Russia's both foreign policy discourse and machinery.

In contrast with some wide-spread stereotypes, I argue that Moscow did not limit itself to simple copying the soft power concept. The Russian understanding of soft power strongly deviates from either the 'classic' one (Nye-based) or suggested by other Western academics and practitioners. The Russian interpretation of soft power is rather instrumentalist, pragmatic and interest-centric. The Russian Foreign Policy Concept of 2013 defines the soft power as a 'set of instruments' which is helpful in achieving foreign policy aims by means of civil society institutions, ITs and communication, humanitarian and other methods that are different from classical diplomacy (Putin 2013a). President Putin was even more pragmatic and instrumentalist by defining the soft power as a mere foreign policy tool or technology that helps either to lobby Moscow's interests in foreign countries or improve Russia's international image (Putin 2012a; Putin 2012b).

The lack of a well-defined terminology, the use of overlapping concepts is another remarkable feature of the Russian scholarship on soft power. To make further theoretical progress the Russian academia should further develop its conceptual apparatus and reach a consensus on basic terms related to the soft power problematique.

It should be also noted that such a strategy represents a combination of ideational and material motives. On the one hand, the Kremlin sees soft power as an important instrument in returning and maintaining Russia's status of a great power as well as in shaping the future world order and making the West (particularly the U.S.) abide by the rules of that order. On the other hand, Moscow—in a quite pragmatic way—views the soft power strategy as an efficient tool in promoting its national interests in foreign countries, coalition-building and counter-balancing the West in the global geopolitical game (Sergunin and Karabeshkin 2015).

I tend to agree with other authors' assessment that presently, the Russian soft power has a rather contradictory performance: On the one hand, Russia possesses huge soft power resources of economic, societal, political and cultural nature. On the other hand, Moscow is often unable to use these resources in a proper and coherent way. As Nye (2013) pointed out, "...for China and Russia to succeed, they will need to match words and deeds in their policies, be self-critical, and unleash the full talents of their civil societies".

Is Russia able to effectively implement its soft power strategy? Unlike other experts who often succumb to temptation to give straightforward and simple (sometimes simplistic) answers to this important question, I'd prefer a more sophisticated approach. In general, my answer is 'yes' because numerous evidences of Russia's soft power diplomacy's effectiveness can be found, especially in the post-Soviet countries. However, it goes without saying that numerous shortcomings (especially the lack of coordination between various governmental bodies responsible for the soft power policies and between the government and NGOs) as well as international crises, including the Georgian and Ukrainian ones, make the Russian soft power policies less efficient and sometime undercut the Kremlin's strategies in the neighboring regions. It is still a long way to go to bring Moscow's soft power strategy to widely-accepted standards and make Russia a really attractive international partner.

One more difficult question for Moscow is how to combine soft and hard (military) power arsenals in its future foreign and security policies and how to develop a "smart power" concept of its own? This is not a purely theoretical question; rather, it is the very practical one. As a series of "colored revolutions" in the post-Soviet space and Arab East demonstrated, soft security challenges can be quickly transformed into hard security threats to the ruling regimes. The Kremlin does not hide the fact that one of its main strategic aims for the foreseeable future is to prevent any internal or external threat to the existing political regime. The Russian leaders point out that soft power methods are preferable ones, but, at the same time, they underline that they would not hesitate to use coercive instruments against their opponents—domestic or foreign—if an existential threat to emerge.

Status theory(ies)

This theory (or—more exactly—group of theories) is particularly useful in explaining Russia's seemingly "irrational", "unpredictable", "emotional" and "voluntaristic" behavior. The rationalist IR theories, including PTT, soft power and peaceful coexistence concepts, are often unable to explain why Moscow acts contrary to its alleged national interests. For example, Russia did not want an increased NATO's military presence on its Western borders but the Ukrainian crisis, which was partially provoked by Moscow itself, finally resulted in NATO's military build-up in East Europe. In the post-Cold war era, Russia did not want to alienate Ukraine from itself and aimed to keeping friendly relations with this country regardless the nature of political regimes in Kiev. However, it failed to establish good relations with the post-Yanukovych regime preferring to take over Crimea and support the Donbass rebels while Ukraine became clearly anti-Russian and pro-Western. Russia is in a difficult economic situation now because of the dramatic fall of oil prices and Western sanctions but despite the limited economic and financial resources the Kremlin continues the massive program of rearmament of the Russian armed forces and its costly military intervention in the Syrian conflict. These are few examples of Russia's seemingly "irrational" and "self-damaging" behavior on the international arena that cannot be explained by "classical" IR theories.

The status theories try to deal with non-rational factors that shape the state's foreign policies, focusing on drivers, such as self-esteem, reputation, resentment, anger, shame, sympathy, honor, dignity, glory and other emotional / psychological categories which often confront each other and make a country's international course chaotic and unpredictable. No surprise that the status theories were borrowed by IR from disciplines such as social psychology and social anthropology.

For example, in the late 1960s and in the 1970s there emerged a body of IR scholarship devoted to the relationship between conflict and status consistency / inconsistency. This group of scholars tried to find a link between status inconsistency (the case when a certain state believed that it is treated by other state(s) in a way which is inconsistent with its (often self-perceived) status) and violent conflict (war) (East 1972; Midlarsky 1969; von Riekhoff 1973; Wallace 1973). This type of research was later continued by works on the roles of status deficit and concerns in initiation of various regional conflicts (Gochman, 1980; Volgy and Mayhall, 1995). Some scholars tried to overcome a pure empiricism of status-related studies and made efforts to produce IR-based status theories (for example, a methodology of network-based measures of international status suggested by Renshon (2013)).

A body of academic literature that examined the role of status in world politics from different IR paradigms has emerged in the 2000s. It should be noted that, in dealing with status-related issues, traditional IR paradigms, such as neo-realism and neo-liberalism, tended to focus on material interests of survival and economic gain seeing status primarily as a function of states' military and economic capabilities. As for the post-positivist schools, initially the status concept was not a priority analytical category for their research agenda as well. For example, social constructivism preferred to emphasize the importance of identity and norms for state behavior rather than status or prestige concerns (Onuf 2013). However, constructivism with its emphasis on identities, norms, inter-subjective relations has paved the way to theoretical approaches that focused on psychological aspects of foreign policy making and behavior (Shannon and Kowert 2012).

The application of status theories to post-Cold War Russian foreign policy started from the discussions on whether Russia's primary goal has been to restore and strengthen its position as a great power in world politics or to acquire some material gains and ensure its security (Kanet 2007 and 2010; Larson Shevchenko 2010; Neumann 2005 and 2007; Trenin 2011; Tsygankov 2005). Unsurprisingly, these discussions were especially animated during the Putin presidency when Moscow's foreign policy has turned particularly assertive with the Kremlin becoming even more sensitive to defend its interests, as well as its status in the international arena. The collapse of the USSR, which is perceived by President Putin as the greatest geopolitical disaster of the 20th century, and the concomitant loss of superpower status have left Russia with an agonizingly uncertain status. While Russia's nuclear arsenal still made it qualify for top tier, its performance in almost any other area left it among states which were, until recently, inferior to it. This relatively sudden development has arguably resulted in a kind of status inconsistency or even "status panic", from which post-Soviet Russia is still struggling to emerge (Forsberg et al. 2014; Hansen and Sergunin 2014, 94; Morozov 2009; Sergunin 2014b, 87–88; Smith 2014).

As Richard Pipes (2009) notes, Moscow's craving a great power status assumes obsessive forms, particularly because "Russians suspect deep in their hearts that their claim to this status is dubious—that they are not really a great power in economic, political or military terms". According to the U.S. scholar, "this obsession compensates for the inferiority complex that a majority of Russians feel when they compare themselves with genuine great powers, notably the United States".

According to Hanna Smith (2014), Russia since 1991 can be viewed as a status underachiever in that it has not consistently been recognized as a great power internationally, while at the same time greatpowerness has been assumed, for historic and geopolitical reasons, as given for the population and political elites of Russia. This gap between greatpowerness as a part of self-identity and the actual status of a state in international politics can lead to mutual misperceptions and misunderstandings and, eventually, to dangerous tensions.

Andrei Tsygankov (2012 and 2014) emphasizes the role of emotions in Russia's relations with the West. He believes that "sibling rivalry" can be a useful metaphor for describing Russia-West relations, but he points out that "family quarrels" may be particularly difficult to resolve or contain. According to Tsygankov (2014, 353), the sibling rivalry perspective suggests that sharing power / status may not be sufficient to solve current problems in Russia-West relations—what required is a process of extending to Russia a social recognition and including it as an equal participant in various economic, political, and security projects. The family quarrel metaphor implies that Russia and the West are culturally interdependent and may only progress in their relationships if they learn to respect each other's values.

Russia's tough position in the Ukrainian conflict, its determinedness to display political and military power, including the Syrian case, were additional incentives to IR theorists to apply different analytical approaches to the study of Moscow's international behavior. For some (neo-realist) scholars this is simply a sign of the recurring struggle for power and security in the international anarchy (Mearsheimer 2014; Sergunin 2014b), but for others (constructivists and post-structuralists) the assertive turn in

Russia's foreign policy has more to do with identity and domestic politics. According to this view, Russia's current behavior is essentially driven by its fear of loss of great power status (Casula 2010; Clunan 2009; Forsberg et al. 2014; Malinova 2014; Morozov 2009; Smith 2014; Tsygankov 2016, 251–255).

Even prior to the Ukrainian crisis many scholars have suggested that status concerns have become more important than pure security and economic questions on Russia's foreign policy agenda (Heller 2013; Smith 2014). Others remind us that this has been the case for centuries. In view of Richard Sakwa (2008), the historical "Russia Problem" is not about the security dilemma but about how Russia is able to receive the status and respect from the West that it expects. Similarly, Iver Neumann (2005) argues that Russia's main current problem in Europe may not be a question of security as such but Russia's status in relation to other European powers.

Status questions have become particularly visible in Russia's relations with the West. The lack of genuine recognition of Russia's great power status and equality with other Western great powers is often seen as a primary reason why Russia has turned away from cooperating with the West on a number of issues (Morozov 2009; Tsygankov 2012, 2014 and 2016, 15–22, 251–255; Stent 2014; Smith 2014). Typically, status concerns are seen as leading to suboptimal decision-making, because foreign policy becomes driven by emotions rather than rational interests. For some analysts, Russia's unpredictable and confrontational behavior is based on a psychological complex defined by its obsession to being a great power (Casula 2010; Malinova 2014; Morozov 2009; Pipes 2009; Smith 2005 and 2014). For others, Russia's emphasis on status is a rather natural reaction to Western disregard for it after the end of the Cold War (Forsberg et al. 2014; Hansen and Sergunin 2014, 94; Heller 2013; Larson and Shevchenko 2010; Sergunin 2014b; Tsygankov 2012, 2014 and 2016, 251–255).

The realist IR paradigm regarded a state's position in the international status hierarchy as based on military power, especially as demonstrated in war. A further implication of realism is that the concentration of power helps to determine a state's foreign policy. Against this notion, other IR schools (e.g., the English School) have pointed out that having the recognized status of great power with certain special rights and duties has always required approval from the other great powers and other states in the international community (Larson and Shevchenko 2010, 69; Tsygankov 2014, 353). Having superior military capabilities does not necessarily bring with it superior status, acceptance, or respect.

For example, hosting the Olympic Games has traditionally been an indicator of rising power status, as illustrated by Russian President Vladimir Putin's remark that being awarded the 2014 Winter Olympics was a "judgment of our country" (Delany and O'Flynn 2007).

As far as status-seeking strategies are concerned a state that wants to improve its standing may try to pass into a higher-status group of states, compete with the dominant group, or achieve preeminence in a different domain. The choice of one type of strategy over another depends on the openness of the status hierarchy as well as the values of the status-seeker and established powers (Larson and Shevchenko 2010, 71).

If the boundaries of higher-status group of states are permeable, a lower-status state may conform to the norms of an elite group to gain acceptance, pursuing a *strategy of mobility*. Since the end of the Cold War, Russia has adopted liberal democratic reforms and capitalism (at least at the declaratory level) to be admitted into the West-led economic and political institutions such as IMF, WTO, Council of Europe, G-7, etc. After being admitted into elite clubs, states may continue to pursue status but within the context of the club's rules. However, Russia often failed to play by rules of these institutions and was either excluded from them (G-7) or criticized / punished (WTO, Council of Europe).

If elite group boundaries are impermeable to new members (for instance, EU and NATO for Russia), the lower-status states may strive for equal or superior status through a *strategy of competition* (Larson and Shevchenko 2010, 72). Status-seekers may also turn to competition when they regard the higher-status group's position as illegitimate or unstable. For example, Moscow made great efforts to portray NATO as an "aggressive power", "war-mongering organization" in the case of the alliance's military interventions in the Balkans in the 1990s. The Kremlin has also challenged NATO eastward expansion's legitimacy pointing out that with the dissolution of the Warsaw Pact the military threat to Europe from the East has gone.

The competition strategy may aim to equal or outdo the dominant states and / or organizations in the area on which their claim to superior status rests. In international relations, where status is in large part based on military and economic power, competition often entails traditional geopolitical rivalry, such as competition over spheres of influence or arms racing. For example, Moscow's fierce reactions to a series of "color revolutions" in the post-Soviet states (including the Ukrainian ones of 2004 and 2013–14) can be explained by its desire to protect Russia's "traditional sphere of influence".

The competition strategies may also be manifested in spoiler behavior, as in Russia's opposition in the 1990s and early 2000s to U.S. intervention in the Balkans and Iraq, as well as its efforts to eliminate the U.S. military presence in Central Asia, despite having an interest in U.S. defeat of the Taliban in Afghanistan. As Richard Pipes sarcastically noted, "When the Kremlin says 'no' to Western initiatives, Russians feel that they are indeed a world power" (Pipes 2009).

When the international status hierarchy is perceived as legitimate or stable, status-seekers may look for prestige in a different area altogether, exercising *creativity strategy*. This may be done by (1) reevaluating the meaning of a negative characteristic, or (2) finding a new dimension on which their group is superior (Larson and Shevchenko 2010, 73). The strategy of both reevaluating a negative attribute and identifying a different dimension is illustrated by Russia's Eurasianist and neoconservative schools that celebrate Russia's collectivism, spiritualism, traditionalism, and Orthodox Christianity in contrast to the West's spiritually impoverished individualism, materialism and liberal moral norms (Laruelle 2008; Sergunin 2014a; Shlapentokh 2007).

In contrast to the competition strategy, social creativity does not try to change the hierarchy of status in the international system but rather tries to achieve preeminence on a different ranking system. Indicators that a state is pursuing the creativity strategy include advocacy of new international norms, regimes, institutions, or a developmental model. In contrast to the mobility strategy, the essence of the creativity strategy is the attempt to stake out a distinctive position, emphasizing the state's unique values or contributions.

Often social creativity is accompanied by high-profile diplomacy, with charismatic leaders who take a prominent role on the world stage. For example, the Soviet leader Mikhail Gorbachev tried to achieve greatness for the Soviet Union as the moral and political leader of a new international order shaped on principles of the New Political Thinking (NPT) such as mutual security, non-offensive defense, and the Common European Home (see next chapter). In 2013, President Putin gained some international prestige by suggesting an original plan of Bashar Assad's chemical weapon destruction in exchange for the West's non-interference to the Syrian civil war.

Russia's efforts to create alternative institutions, such as CIS, Customs Union, EEU, CSTO, SCO, BRICS, etc., and develop new international norms and rules within them can be explained in the context of Moscow's creativity strategy to gain a higher prestige and authority in the world.

As some analysts summarize (Forsberg et al. 2014, 263; Hansen and Sergunin 2014, 94), there remain some fundamental research questions to be addressed by status theories:

1. What are the status markers in contemporary international politics? Are they shared or contested by the key international actors?

2. What are the status aims—e.g., political privileges and prestige—pursued by international players?

3. What determines the extent to which political, security and business elites pursue social status as an intrinsic goal that goes beyond their material gains and interests?

4. When can external status recognition (for example, access to a prestigious club of states or international organization) dampen a state's quest for material capabilities or deferential treatment?

5. What are the instruments used by international actors to elevate their standing in relation to other world players?

6. When and to what extent can internal status verification (a domestic consensus on a state's high rank and prestige), substitute for external verification (other states' perceptions of a state's international reputation)? And when do such self-assured discourses about a state's presumed position rather fuel the desire for more external verification, higher international status position and possible angry reactions to alleged disrespect?

7. To what extent can different kinds of domestic political and social institutions as well as a specific decision-making system dampen the foreign policy impact of wide-spread domestic anger about 'foreign disrespect'?

8. Is status-seeking always detrimental to international peace and stability or may the desire for greater status motivate rising powers to take on more responsibility for maintaining world order?

These questions form a future research agenda for Russian foreign policy studies from the status theory's perspective.

* * *

To sum up the review of different IR theories applicable to explaining Russia's present-day international course, these theories are complimentary rather than mutually exclusive. The specific theories should be used depending on the research objectives and context. Such a multidisciplinary approach provides a reliable theoretical basis to study the complex and multifaceted problem represented by Moscow's post-Soviet foreign policy.

Chapter 2.
Russian Foreign Policy Schools

The end of the Cold War, the breakdown of the USSR, the re-emergence of Russia as a separate, independent entity, and the challenges of the globalizing world have compelled Russia to redefine its national interests and make significant adjustments in the spheres of both foreign policy and the conceptual basis of its international strategy. In turn, this has led to a fierce debate on foreign policy priorities among scholars, experts and practitioners. This debate is far from ending. Neither a coherent international strategy nor a solid theoretical basis for it has yet been found.

There are three main objectives with this chapter:

- *First,* to distinguish and depict the main *foreign policy schools* in the country.

- *Second,* to outline the *problematique* of the Russian IR discourse that includes issues such as changes in the post-Cold War international relations system; an emerging world order; globalization and global governance; international security and arms control regime; Russia's place in the globalizing world and specific priorities of its international strategy.

- *Third,* to examine an institutional dimension of the Russian post-Soviet IR: where and by whom IR is studied and taught; what the division of labor between different organizations is; what the institutional problems are, etc.?

The Soviet legacy

The Russian IR theory of the early 1990s was heavily affected by the Soviet legacy in terms of concepts, theories and methodological approaches.

The classical Soviet IR theory drew heavily upon the Marxist-Leninist-Stalinist teaching. The key elements of this theory included the following principles:

- The world was undergoing a global social revolution that was manifested in various forms—socialist and bourgeois—democratic revolutions, worker and national-liberation movements. The main historical mission of the Soviet Union and its allies from the socialist camp was to facilitate such a revolutionary process by various means from financial assistance to anti-capitalist forces to propaganda and even military interventions (as a last resort) (Arbatov 1970; Light 1988).

- Class struggle was a driving force of the global revolutionary change. Proletariat / worker class was a progressive force because it represented a more advanced socio-economic system and, for this reason, it was a natural leader of the society on latter's way to socialism (Light 1988; Sanakoev and Kapchenko 1977). On the contrary, the capitalist class exemplified a reactionary force and should be deprived from power (depending on a specific situation by peaceful / parliamentary or coercive / military means).

- In the post-World War II period, the class struggle was mainly manifested by the Cold War-type of confrontation between socialism and capitalism that should sooner or later result in an ultimate victory of socialism / communism (Arbatov 1970; Chubarian 1976).

- As a part of the globalist IR paradigm the Soviet IR theory emphasized the overall structure of the international system. In their analysis of international relations Soviet theorists departed from the assumption that the global context within which states and other entities interact was really important. They assumed that to understand the foreign policy behavior of states required not only internal factors shaping their external policies. One must first find out how the structure of the international relations system conditioned certain actors to behave in certain ways. Soviet IR specialists also believed that it was very important to view international relations from a historical perspective. It is only through an examination of history the current international environment can be understood. For the Soviet IR theory, the rise of capitalism, its development, changes, and expansion was the defining characteristic of the international system. A world capitalist system conditioned the behavior and even creation of all states and other international actors. Contrary to the Western IR paradigms of realism and liberalism, that saw states as a given and independent variables, Soviet theorists viewed states as dependent variables. The particular focus of global-centric analysis was on how some states, classes, or elites created and used mechanisms of domination by which they managed to benefit from this capitalist system at the expense of others. Soviet IR specialists were typically concerned with the development and function of dependency relations among industrialized states and the poor, underdeveloped countries. They saw this North-South disparity (and divide) as a major source of world instability and revolutionary movement. In addition, the Soviet IR theory emphasized more than other schools the critical importance of economic factors in functioning of the international system

- The Soviet IR theory differed from the Western IR schools by their vision of key units of analysis. Contrary to state-centric paradigms the Soviet IR theory assumed that states are not unitary actors. Classes from across national boundaries, as capitalists, for example, may co-operate internationally to maintain a political and economic environment hospitable to investment by multinational corporations. Workers from different countries have also demonstrated their solidarity on numerous occasions. Where realists saw anarchy, Soviet IR specialists noted a hierarchy of classes and states in which the weak were subordinated to the strong. For these reasons, for them the key (and primary) units of analysis were classes, races and gender rather than nation-state which was viewed as a secondary / dependent actor (Arbatov 1970; Sanakoev and Kapchenko 1977).

By mid-1970-early 1980s, the Soviet IR theory has undergone a rather unusual change. Despite its controversies with realism which was seen as a major rival among the Western IR paradigms the Soviet IR has tacitly incorporated a number of postulates of structural realism (neo-realism). In contrast with traditionalism which made emphasis on classes as a key international actor and class interests, the new Soviet IR paid more attention to realist-type categories such as state, state / national interests, 'balance of forces' (power balance) and 'spheres of influence'. At the same time, Soviet scholars denied an anarchical / chaotic nature of international relations. Similar to neo-realists Soviet scholars made great strides in developing system approach to world politics (Antyukhina-Moskovchenko 1988; Gantman 1984; Kukulka 1980; Pozdnyakov 1976). System analysis, rational choice approach, modeling, simulation and game theory have become popular research methods among the Soviet IR specialists. As a result of these conceptual changes Soviet foreign policy became less indoctrinated / messianic and more pragmatic with regard to the capitalist, socialist and developing countries.

The Gorbachev era has brought about new radical changes in the Soviet IR. There was a shift from the neo-realist-like approach to a combination of liberalism and globalism (with a prevalence of the latter). This—sometime strange—mixture of traditional Marxism with West-oriented concepts has got a name of a New Political Thinking. The key principles of NPT included:

- The prevalence of 'all-humankind' / planetary interests over national interests (Gorbachev 1987; Gromyko and Lomeiko 1984).

- The end of confrontation between socialism and capitalism (Mshvenieradze 1987).

- Concentration of international efforts on solving global problems and mutually beneficial collaborative projects (Globalnye Problemy 1987).

- Creation of an efficient world-wide mechanism of interdependency that could prevent potential conflicts (Gorbachev 1987; Mshvenieradze 1987).

- Complex and multidimensional understanding of international security that included not only politico-military but also economic, societal, environmental, cultural and other dimensions (Gromyko and Lomeiko 1984).

- Overcoming of political divisions in various parts of the world, including Europe ('common house Europe' concept, reunification of Germany, Soviet troop withdrawal from Central and Eastern Europe).

- Promotion of arms control and disarmament, conversion of the defense industry and the military infrastructure (Petropvsky 1982; Pharamazyan 1982; Politika Sily ili Sila Razuma 1989).

Despite the innovative and far-reaching character of some Soviet / neo-Marxist IR theories in the 1970–1980s (including NPT) they still faced numerous problems of both theoretical and practical nature. *First,* an ideological indoctrination was still characteristic to the Soviet IR. The latter viewed the world through the simplistic lenses of either the class struggle principle or 'planetary values' and did not allow any views that could clash with the official doctrines. In turn, this inevitably led to scholastics and self-isolation from the world IR. *Second,* both the traditionalist Marxist IR theory and NPT ignored the very existence of national interest; instead, they developed the concepts of either state or class interest or 'all-humankind interest'. These concepts were either too narrow-focused or abstract and simply did not fit into the post-Cold War political context. *Third,* the Soviet IR basically existed at the macro-level ('grand theories') while mezo- and micro-level theories and research methods were lacking. This made difficult translation of general / abstract IR theories into foreign policy practice. *Finally,* old Soviet theories were unable both to explain the end of the Cold War and provide Moscow with a new vision of an emerging world order.

The Post-Soviet IR: adapting to change

It took a while for the Russian post-Soviet IR to move from a paradigmatic uniformity, Marxist-Leninist concepts and self-isolation to ideological pluralism and joining the world IR discourse. Several factors have impeded this process.

First, after the collapse of Marxism, which had served as an official theoretical basis for the social sciences, a sort of theoretical vacuum has emerged. For some time, Russian academics simply did not dare to touch on theoretical problems because they were too sensitive for them. They were unable or did not want to fill the above vacuum with some new theories of their own or theories borrowed from abroad. Because of a long-term isolation from world social sciences many Russian IR specialists were simply unfamiliar with Western theories or treated them as a hostile / unacceptable political philosophy.

Second, there was a sort of institutional inertia in the post-Soviet academia because most of professors who taught IR or related disciplines were trained in the Soviet period and in a pro-Marxist spirit. This generation of Russian scholars was simply unable or did not want to grasp new theoretical approaches, research methods and problematique. At the same time, these professors were assigned with a task to establish IR and political science departments in the Russian universities in the early 1990s. In many universities (especially in the periphery) departments of international relations and political science were mainly formed on the basis of the former departments of Marxist-Leninist philosophy, scientific communism and the Communist party history.

One more institutional aspect of the problem was that before the collapse of the USSR IR was taught only in the two elitist Soviet universities that trained future diplomats—Moscow State Institute of International Relations (MGIMO) and Institute of International Relations (Kiev State University, Ukraine). IR itself was seen as an empirical / historical rather than theoretical discipline.[2] University curricula were full of empirical / applied disciplines such as IR history, area studies, diplomatic and consular services, diplomatic protocol, foreign languages, etc., which were seen as an

---

2   The MGIMO (where a couple of disciplines on system and foreign policy analysis were taught) was the only exception from the rule.

integral component of diplomats' professional training. That's why when in 1994 a new federal educational standard for the IR training program was approved by the Russian Ministry of Education (similar to the Western universities it was designed in a way to train not only diplomats but also specialists in IR in a broader sense) and several Russian universities (St. Petersburg State University, Nizhny Novgorod State University, Kazan State University, Urals State University, Tomsk State University, Far Eastern University, etc.) decided to introduce this program they faced a problem of qualified teachers' staff. The faculty had to develop both courses and curricula almost from the scratch and this, of course, affected the quality of training in a negative way. The institutional / curriculum change lasted until late 1990s and early 2000s.

Third, Russian teachers' poor foreign language skills and the lack of regular international academic contacts have also impeded the development of the field in the early 1990s. Few Russian IR specialists were experienced in studying or making research abroad. It was typical for the Soviet / Russian scholars to make research or write Ph.D. theses without visiting a country (or countries) of interest. That's why various academic exchange programs between Russia and foreign countries (that were booming in the 1990s) were really important for internationalizing Russian scholars and opening up the local academia for international cooperation. International donor organizations such as the Soros Foundation (and its various derivatives), MacArthur Foundation, Ford Foundation, Fulbright Program, Kennan Institute, Carnegie Endowment, East-West Institute (all are from the U.S.); British Council; DAAD, Volkswagen Foundation, Friedrich-Ebert-Stiftung, and Konrad Adenauer Foundation (Germany), etc., were crucial for the development of a new-type Russian IR community.

Fourth, Russian scholars had to respond to the real challenges posed by the post-Cold War international environment and meet the immediate needs that confronted the newly born Russian diplomacy. This environment was more favorable to applied rather than theoretical studies.

Fifth, the development of the Russian post-Communist IR theory in the 1990s was hindered not only by the prevalence of applied research but also by the inclination of the world politics discourse to ideological rather than academic / theoretical approaches. Various political parties and groupings pressed Russian foreign policy experts to produce policy-oriented rather than objective / independent research. For this reason, both the Russian academia and expert community were highly politicized and deeply involved in power struggle of the 1990s.

Sixth, with the rise of numerous "think tanks" and a more or less independent mass media the demand for foreign policy experts in these spheres has dramatically increased. Many gifted scholars have moved from the academia over to analytical centers, newspapers / journals and TV channels or tried to combine these new jobs with their old ones. This has made international studies more popular but their quality and standards of expertise have become worse (Tyulin 1997, 188). Again, theoretical issues remained ignored.

Finally, the chronic economic crisis and changes in public attitudes to science have had a most negative impact on the state of the field in Russia. The state and society as a whole have lost interest in science and higher education (at least for a while) and the prestige of these fields have declined accordingly. Salaries have fallen dramatically and social security has almost been destroyed. Scholars have migrated from the academia either abroad or to other sectors (private business, politics, think tanks, mass media). According to the then Russian Deputy Prime-Minister Vladimir Bulgak, in 1991–97 15,200 Russian scientists have taken up foreign citizenship and another 5,000 worked in foreign countries on a contractual basis (these figures included specialists in natural sciences) *(Roisiyikaya gazeta,* 10 January 1998, 2). The situation has started to slowly change in a positive direction about ten years ago when universities managed to attract more students on the commercial basis and the government decided to channel a part (not really significant) of Russia's income from oil and gas exports to the higher education system.[3] Still, the Russian higher education system is less attractive than other sectors (private business, public service, mass media, etc.) in terms of salary, opportunities for professional career and prestige. It continues to experience the lack of finance, skilled personnel and government's attention and care.

In sum, these factors have prevented rather than facilitated the development of IR theories in post-Communist Russia. Moreover, they have been conducive to the ideologization of the Russian foreign policy debate.

---

3   Together with housing, health care system and agriculture higher education became one of the four 'national priority' programs funded from the federal budget.

Mapping post-Soviet IR:
institutional dimension and topics for research

Theoretical pluralism in the post-Communist Russian scholarship has been accompanied by the quantitative growth of research and training centers dealing with IR. Four main categories of centers can be identified: university departments and centers; the Russian Academy of Sciences; ministerial institutes and research centers; and independent think tanks.

Universities. Compared to other sectors of the expert community the Russian higher education system found itself in a better situation. Despite the lack of finance and governmental support Russia's leading universities, such as, for example, the MGIMO, Moscow State University, St. Petersburg University, etc., not only survived but also broadened the scope of research and improved curricula and training programs. There can be at least two explanations of this phenomenon. *First,* professors and researchers became free in choosing theoretical approaches and teaching methods. This created a fruitful atmosphere for developing IR in terms of both research and teaching. *Second,* universities learnt fast how to make fund-raising and earn money. University administrators succeeded in searching Russian and foreign grants, establishing good contacts with wealthy sponsors and attracting promising candidates for undergraduate, graduate and post-graduate programs who are ready to pay for training. As mentioned, some prominent Western foundations and donors have initiated sponsorship programs to assist Russian international studies. Many of them established offices in Moscow and some regional centers. *Third,* in the 1990s Moscow allowed peripheral universities to establish IR training programs of their own. This, in turn, has resulted in mushrooming training centers around Russia. More than 30 universities have now IR and area studies training programs.

The whole Russian higher education system (including international studies) has been radically changed. Several "generations" of the IR federal educational standard have been developed by the Ministry of Education over the last 25 years. In contrast with the Soviet-era curricula, new training programs included more theoretical disciplines. Along with historical, diplomatic and linguistic components, new curricula now have political science, economic, legal and cultural studies disciplines and are closer to international standards. Since 2003, when Russia has pledged to join the Bologna process, a new round of reforms is underway in the higher education system (including the IR programs). This reform aims at harmonizing European and Russian university systems by introducing in Russia a two-level system (bachelor and masters degrees), ECTS (European Credit Transfer System), more variable curricula, less centralized quality assurance system, diploma supplement and so on.

As mentioned, geography of the Russian IR became more diverse over the last 25 years. However, most of the university centers of international studies are still based in Moscow. For example, in the post-Soviet period the MGIMO focused its research on the following topics: IR theory (Alexeeva 2001; Bogaturov, Kosolapov, Khrustalev 2002; Ilyin 1995; Khrustalev 1991; Kokoshin and Bogaturov 2005; Lebedeva 2000 and 2003 / 2006; Lebedeva and Tsygankov 2001; Torkunov 1997, 1999, 2001, 2005; Tyulin 1991 and 1994); national, regional and global security (Bogaturov 1997; Davydov 1993; Kulagin 2006; Torkunov 1995, 1997, 1999, 2001, 2005; Zagorski 1993); globalization / regionalization dichotomy (Antiglobalizm i Global'noe Upravlenie 2006; Bogaturov 2010; Busygina 2006; Melville 1997; Voskresensky 2002); conflict resolution (Lebedeva 1997); foreign services of different countries (Lapin 2002; Popov 2004; Selyaninov 1998; Torkunov 1997, 1999, 2001; Torkunov and Mal'gin 2012; Zonova 2003 and 2004); diplomatic history (Bogaturov 2000; Akhtamzyan 1994; Narinsky 1995; Nezhinsky et al. 1995); international law (Kolosov, Krivtchikova et al. 1994); international economy, eco-diplomacy and techno-diplomacy (Gertchikova 1994 / 1995) and international information (Vlassov and Vasiliev 1997: 62–63, 74–90).

Along with departments (such as departments of diplomacy, international relations and foreign policy, political science, European and American history, oriental studies, global economics, international economic relations and foreign economic operations, international information and journalism, international law, constitutional law and so on) the Center for International Studies (established in 1974) conducts interdisciplinary studies of world politics with special emphasis on international relations system, regional stability and security, conflict resolution and Russian policy towards specific regions (including Europe) (Grabovski 2005; Khrustalev 1992; Solodovnik 1995; Zagorski 1994; Zagorski and Zlobin 1992).

Moscow State University aims at examining international relations history (the Department of Modern and Current History); IR theory (Department of Sociology of International Relations, Department of Comparative Polititics) (Fel'dman 1998; Gadzhiev 1997; Kokoshin and Bogaturov 2005; Lebedeva and Tsygankov 2001; Manykin 2001 and 2009; Panarin 1997 and 2003; Tsygankov 1995, 1996, 1998, 2002, 2007; Tsygankov and Tsygankov 2005, 2006); international law and constitutional law of foreign countries (Faculty of Law); global economics (Economic Faculty); international information and mass media (Faculty of Journalism).

Some other Moscow-based universities also run research projects on IR history and theory, international law, world economy and integration, area studies (including Europe)—Russian University of Peoples' Friendship (Blishenko 1990; Blishenko and Fisenko 1998), Moscow State Pedagogic University, Russian State University of Humanities (Libert and Logunov 2005), Russian Academy of Public Service (Bakushev 1997), Higher School of Economics, Moscow State University of Commerce, and Russian Academy of Economics.

Among the non-Moscow-based universities the St. Petersburg State University should be mentioned first and foremost. The Department of Modern and Current History is traditionally involved in studies of diplomatic history. The International Relations Faculty (established in 1994) targets at examining not only IR history but also IR theory, political thought history, international security, area studies and Russian foreign policies (Barygin 2007; Katsy 2007; Khudolei 2004 and 2006; Konyshev 2001, 2004, 2006; Konyshev and Sergunin 2013; Mezhevich 2002; Morozov 2002, 2005, 2006 and 2009). A number of units of the Political Science Faculty (departments of political science theory and international politics) (Achkasov and Lantsov 2011; Lantsov and Achkasov 2007) and Faculty of Economics (e.g., the Department of World Economics) (Lomagin 2001; Sutyrin and Lomagin 2001) study international relations system and international organization.

A number of other St. Petersburg-based universities such as St. Petersburg Pedagogical University, European University (Proskuryakova 2005), St. Petersburg University of Economics and Finance, St. Petersburg University of Technology, North-West Public Service Academy, etc., deal with international relations and world economy.

Many other peripheral universities are also quite active in international studies. Diplomatic history studies are strong in universities such as the Ivanovo State University (Bisk 2001), Nizhny Novgorod State University (Khokhlysheva 1999; Kolobov 2001) and Urals State University. IR theory is represented by centers such as the Nizhny Novgorod State University (Baluev 2001, 2002 and 2003; Khokhlysheva 2005; Kolobov et al. 2004; Safronova 2001), Nizhny Novgorod Linguistic University (Makarychev and Sergunin 1999; Malhotra and Sergunin 1998; Sergunin 2003 and 2004), Ural Federal University (Mikhailenko 1998) and Irkutsk State University (Novikov 1996). Security studies and conflict resolution are well-established in the Nizhny Novgorod State University (Baluev 2001 and

2002, Khokhlysheva 2000 and 2002; Kolobov 2005; Kolobov et al. 1992, 1997, 2005; Kolobov and Yasenev 2001), Nizhny Novgorod State Linguistic University (Makarychev, Sergunin 1993, 1997, 1998, 2003, 2005) and the Voronezh State University (Glukhova 1997). The globalization / regionalization processes are thoroughly discussed in the Nizhny Novgorod State Linguistic University, Ural Federal University (Mikhailenko 2008), Volgograd State University and Ulyanovsk University of Technology (Magomedov 2000; Makarychev 2000, 2002 and 2003; Sergunin 1999b, 2001, 2005). European studies are developed by the Ivanovo State University (Polyviannyi 2003), Mari State University (Fominykh, Yarygin), Nizhny Novgorod State University (Branitski 2006; Branitski and Kamenskaya 2003), Nizhny Novgorod State Linguistic University (Emerson 2007; Joenniemi and Sergunin 2003; Makarychev 2005 and 2006; Sergunin 1993), Voronezh State University (Artemov 1999), Ural Federal University (Goldthau and Onokhine 2003).

It should be noted that rapid growth of peripheral centers not only brought to an end Moscow's monopoly on international studies but also provided the Russian IR scholarship with regional perspectives and added theoretical polyphony. Moreover, this process has contributed into training personnel for the local diplomatic and international business structures which are developing now rather dynamically in the regions. *Inter alia* it provided regional political, security and economic elites with expertise in world politics and made them more independent (from the federal center) in the foreign policy sphere. Therefore, peripheral IR has implicitly facilitated the process of democratization and decentralization of Russia's foreign and security policies in the post-Communist era.

The Russian Academy of Sciences (RAS). As compared with universities the RAS was less successful in adapting its research, financial and administrative structures to the post-Soviet realities. There are several factors that impeded IR development in the RAS system. *First,* the Academy is more dependent on the government in terms of finance. It has less opportunities for launching commercial projects. Low salaries, the lack of resources and opportunities for professional career provoked a real 'exodus' of foreign policy experts from the RAS in the 1990s.

Second, foreign foundations and private sponsors are less generous in case of academic institutions; they prefer to deal with higher education institutes, independent think tanks and NGOs because they are less conservative, more dynamic and influential in terms of affecting society and foreign policy making.

Third, similar to the academia in general, the RAS has experienced a competition from other segments of the expert community—universities, consulting firms, NGOs, mass media and, especially, public service.

The RAS lost many talented scholars even before the economic decline caused by the market reforms of the early 1990s. Under late Gorbachev and early Yeltsin many leading researchers left the RAS for high-ranking positions in the government, politics, higher education system and mass media.

Nonetheless, the RAS managed to keep some skilled personnel to develop international studies. The RAS institutes—the Institute of Europe (Borko 2000 and 2003; Butorina et al. 2003; Butorina and Borko 2006; Deryabin 2000; Potemkina 2002; Zhurkin 1998), IMEMO (Baranovsky 2002), Institute for the USA & Canada Studies (ISKRAN) (Davydov 1993; Troitsky 2004), Institute for Far Eastern Studies, Institute of Oriental Studies and Institute for Slavic Studies (Arbatova 1999)—are particularly good in area studies because many of them are organized in accordance with geographic principle.

The Institute of General History (Nezhinsky et al. 1995) and IMEMO (Kamenskaya et al. 2007) are traditionally good in diplomatic history studies.

IMEMO, Institute of Sociology, Institute of Government and Law, Institute of Ethnology and Anthropology develop conflict prevention and resolution studies (Kudryavtsev 1994 and 1995; Stepanov 2014; Vorkunova 2008 and 2012).

Unfortunately, the RAS pays little attention to IR theory as such. Few RAS scholars from ISKRAN (Shakleina 2002a and 2002b), IMEMO (Bogaturov et al. 2002; Delyagin 2006; Kosolapov 1992 and 1999; Delyagin 2006; Gadzhiev 1997) and Institute of Europe (Razuvaev 1993a; Sorokin 1995) published theoretical works. Universities still retain their priority in this particular field.

Ministerial centers and institutes. Since the Soviet time many Russian foreign policy, economic, security and defense ministries / agencies have got think tanks and training institutions of their own. For example, MGIMO has got 'dual loyalty' being subordinated to both the Ministry of Higher Education and Foreign Ministry. In addition to MGIMO which trains students for the Russian foreign service, there is a Diplomatic Academy which trains or re-trains mid-career diplomats. Along with departments (for instance, the Department of Foreign Policy Studies), there are several purely research units such as the Center for Methodology of International Studies and Center for Global Problems that are involved in international studies as well. The Foreign Ministry itself has got a Department of Historical and Archival Studies which is in charge with handling ministry's archives and publication of documents.

Similar to the Foreign Ministry, the Defense Ministry (MoD), Federal Security Service (FSS) and Foreign Intelligence Service (FIS) have got both educational and research institutes such as the General Staff Academy, Military University, FSS and FIS academies. These institutions mainly focus on studying national and international security policies.[4] They are also rather active in examining the role of the military and intelligence agencies in shaping and implementing world politics. In addition, they take part in debates on Russian national security doctrine and organization. Prior to its merge with the General Staff Academy, the Institute of Military History focused on studying and publishing archival documents.

The Presidential Administration and the Cabinet of Ministers run a number of specialized higher education institutions which basically train personnel for the federal and regional public services. Some of them, such as the Russian Academy of Public Service[5] (and its regional branches), Public Economy Academy, and Academy of Finance conduct research projects on international relations, world economy and international law.

The Russian Institute for Strategic Studies (RISS) is the most authoritative organization among the state-run research institutes dealing with international studies. In accordance with the 1992 presidential decree, the RISS is a state research organization which should provide the governmental bodies with analytical information and recommendations related to national security. The RISS was established by Yevgeny M. Kozhokin, a former member of the Supreme Soviet and chairman of the sub-committee on defense and security. Initially, the Institute operated under the FIS auspices but in 2009 it was subordinated to the Presidential Administration. The RISS has a staff of over 70 research fellows and several regional representative offices (St. Petersburg, Kaliningrad, Nizhny Novgorod, etc.). It is mainly financed from the state budget but it also managed to get grants from NATO and other foreign donors. The Institute maintains close relationships not only with the Presidential Administration, but also with the Foreign and Defense Ministries, security services and the Parliament (State Duma and Council of Federation).

The priority areas of research for the RISS include: national security and Russia's strategic interests in different regions of the world; develop-

---

4   See, for example, Adarchev 1998.
5   Merged with the Academy of National Economy.

ments in the CIS countries; European security system; Russia-NATO and Russia-EU relations; disarmament and global stability; non-proliferation of weapons of mass destruction; and peacekeeping operations (Antonenko 1996, 42; http://en.riss.ru/category/analysis/).

The RISS produces an academic journal (*Problems of National Strategy*), books, reports, analytical reviews, expert evaluations, analytical memoranda and papers. The Institute periodically holds international conferences on national and global security, arms control and disarmament.

Because of their official status and proximity to the governmental agencies these institutes have a unique opportunity to influence Russian foreign policy decision making. Some of them (e.g., the Diplomatic Academy, General Staff Academy and the RISS) are really influential. This, however, makes them more policy-oriented and less academic. Obviously, to contribute to the Russian IR debate in a positive way these institutions need more coordination and cooperation with the university and RAS centers.

Independent research centers. The rise of public policy centers is an important characteristic of the Russian political and intellectual life in the post-Communist era. Most of them have been created for purely political purposes such as monitoring, providing expertise and prognoses, servicing election campaigns, human rights protection and so on. For this reason, few of them have been oriented to fundamental research.

Some of these centers aim at affecting foreign policy making. The Council on Foreign and Defense Policy (CFDP) which was established by Sergei Karaganov (then Deputy Director of the Institute of Europe) is the biggest and most influential one. The Council was established in February 1992 as an independent non-governmental organization. The Council is directed by an Assembly of some 50 prominent figures in government, business, academia, and the mass media. For example, retired top-ranking governmental officials, businessmen and journalists, such as former Foreign Minister and Secretary of the Security Council Igor S. Ivanov; First Deputy Defense Minister N.V. Mikhailov; Secretary of the Security Council Yuri Baturin; First Deputy of Chief of the General Staff Valery L. Manilov; Deputy Director of the FIS G.A. Rapota; Deputy Director of the FSS A.E. Safonov; President of the Russian Union of Industrialists and Entrepreneurs Arkady I. Volsky; President of the Russian Bank Association S.E. Yegorov; Director of RISS Kozhokin; Deputy Chairman of the Duma Defense Committee Alexei Arbatov; Chairman of the Duma Foreign Affairs Committee Vladimir Lukin; Editor-in-Chief of newspaper 'Nezavisimaya gazeta' Vitaly T. Tretyakov'; President of the NTV company Igor E. Malashenko, etc., were among them. The Council has a small permanent staff of some ten and a number of part-time staff for specific projects. The CFDP is led now by famous Russian journalist Fyodor Lukyanov.

The Council's activities include publication of occasional reports and policy papers; regular meetings and informal discussions among policy analysts and decision-makers; conferences, seminars, and discussion groups; research projects; educational campaigns in mass media; consulting and training for technical and social assistance programs (Antonenko 1996, 40; http://svop.ru/проекты/). According to the Council's charter, the CFDP does not conduct projects at the request of the government structures but chooses the topic of research on its own initiative and based on the decisions of the Assembly and the Board.

Although the Council claims that it is not an analytical think tank, but it unites the leading Russian specialists in foreign and defense policies and aims at providing decision-makers with recommendations on the following topics: Russian national interests; threat assessment; developing and evaluating new strategic concepts; regional and global security; ethnic and religious conflicts; arms control; conversion and so on.

The CFDP assisted in establishing the Valdai Discussion Club in 2004. According to the Club's websitr, its goal is to promote dialogue between Russian and international intellectual elite, and to make an independent, unbiased scientific analysis of political, economic and social events in Russia and the rest of the world. Over 900 representatives of the international scholarly community from 62 countries have taken part in the Club's work. The Club runs several research projects on international politics and regularly publishes policy papers and reports. The Valdai's research programs include security and war studies; contemporary state: changing institutions and leadership; globalization and regionalization; general state of the world economy and global governance; global alternatives to the liberal model of social and political development; Eurasia (http://valdaiclub.com/programmes/description/).

The Russian Foreign Policy Foundation (RFPF) is another influential non-governmental actor in the decision-making process. The Foundation was established in 1992 on the initiative of the Foreign Ministry by the Diplomatic Academy, *International Affairs* magazine, and several powerful Russian banks (Incombank, Avtovazbank, Menatep) and companies (KAMAZ, LUKoil and others). From the very beginning the RFPF was designed for bringing together the Russian foreign policy and business communities as well as harmonizing their interests (Antonenko 1996: 45).

For this reason, it paid more attention to practical rather than research activities.

However, its research program is also quite impressive. The Foundation holds several conferences a year and publishes their proceedings. The RFPF was very active in establishing contacts with Russian regions, such as Kaliningrad, Karelia, Krasnodar, Novosibirsk, the Russian Far East and other members of the Russian Federation that conduct intensive foreign policies. The RFPF even established regional offices in Krasnodar and Novosibirsk.

Among other policy-oriented independent centers the Foundation 'Political Studies', the Foundation 'Politics', Russian Foreign Policy Foundation (RFPF), Russian Public Policy Center, RAU (Russian-American University) Corporation, Center for Ethno-political and Regional Studies, Center for National Security and International Relations, Institute for Defense Studies and others should be mentioned.

The second group of think tanks tries to combine both applied and fundamental research. Over the last 25 years it included various organizations that ranged from representative offices of foreign think tanks (the Moscow Carnegie Center, East-West Institute), expert institutions (the Moscow Public Research Foundation, which incorporated the Center for Strategic Assessments; the Center for Russian Political Research (PIR-Center) (Orlov 2002); the Center for International Research and Programs (Leshukov 1999), the Baltic Research Center (Sodruzhestvo Nezavisimykh Gosudarstv 2002) (both from St. Petersburg), Nizhny Novgorod Center for Socio-Economic Expertise, etc.) to public policy centers (the Gorbachev Foundation (Federalism i Publichnaya Sfera v Rossii i Kanade 2001), 'Strategy' Foundation (St. Petersburg) (Gorny 2004; Proskuryakova 2005), etc.).

It should be noted that in contrast with well-established democracies, in Russia think tanks and public policy centers are relatively few in terms of numbers, centrally-located (mostly in Moscow and St. Petersburg) and less influential (in terms of decision-making). It is still a weaker element of the foreign policy making community.

Professional associations. Professional associations are an important constitutive element of a well-established IR community. They help to coordinate research activities and inform specialists on newest developments in the academia. Prior to the collapse of the USSR the Soviet Political Science Association directed by Georgy Shakhnazarov was in charge with co-ordination of international studies. The Russian Political Science Association has been established as a successor of the SPSA in 1991.

However, it became very soon a fighting arena between the former 'scientific Communists' and the new generation of political scientists. As a result, the work of the RPSA was stalled for a while.

Nonetheless the need for a specialized international studies association which could play a coordinating role was felt by the majority of Russian academics. Some professional associations covering area studies tried to take lead. For example, the Russian European Studies Association was established by the RAS in 1990.

In the 1990s, the two Russian capitals—Moscow and St. Petersburg—competed in establishing a professional international studies association. In 1996, with the help of the European Office of the International Affairs Network (American organization) the Faculty of International Relations of the St. Petersburg State University has established a Central and Eastern European Association of International Studies, Prague-St. Petersburg (1996). Along with the representatives of the Central and Eastern European countries some scholars from Russian regions have joined the Association. With the further help of the IAN the Association managed to organize a series of conferences in Europe and Russia as well as to arrange fellowships in American universities for young teachers from the St. Petersburg State University.

In 1997 MGIMO established the association of the Schools of International Relations with financial support of the Choidiev International Foundation (Vlassov and Vasiliev 1997: 71). The Association of the Russian Higher Education Institutes on Teaching International Relations has been formed by the Ministry of Higher Education on the basis of MGIMO in 1994. It supervises and coordinates university curricula and grants institutes with licenses to open new IR programs (The Ministry of Higher Education 1997: 3–4). Around 50 universities and other institutes joined this association. However, it deals mainly with routine details of teaching and curriculum development rather than coordinates international studies in Russia. The Association may well be perceived as an instrument of state policy which attempts to protect and improve the quality of higher education in this particular field.

By late 1990s the Russian Political Science Association tried to take a lead in uniting Russian international studies. The First All-Russian Congress of Political Scientists has been held in Moscow in February 1998. A renewed RPSA has been established and a new leadership has been elected. A section on geopolitics (i.e. international relations) has been created within the Association. Currently, RPSA has three sections that are related to IR—world politics, foreign policy studies and war and peace studies (www.rapn.ru).

Finally, in December 1999 a first convention of a newly established Russian International Studies Association was held in Moscow. This facilitated both development of national IR schools and their integration into the global scholarship. RISA organizes a convention every two-three years and publishes a newsletter (www.rami.ru).

There have been several schools of foreign policy thought in post-Communist Russia, differing both in their conceptual foundations and in their approaches to specific international issues (see Figure 1 for a comparative analysis of different Russian IR schools). Along with purely Russian schools, almost all of the classic international relations paradigms—realism, idealism / liberalism and globalism (or state-centric, multi-centric, and global-centric approaches to international politics)—can be identified. It goes without saying that these schools have been relatively fluid coalitions, and condensing the complex debate into just a few categories obviously risks oversimplification. These schools do, however, provide a helpful framework for analyzing Russia's post-Communist IR discourse. Such an approach leads one to ask certain questions, seek certain types of answers, and use certain methods in theory-building, it also brings order to the analytical effort and makes it more manageable.

The Atlanticists ("Westerners")

The early stage of the Russian post-Communist IR discourse was manifested by the 'Atlanticism'-'Eurasianism' dichotomy. The Atlanticists were a relatively small but influential group of high-ranking government officials and academics who favored the pro-Western orientation of Moscow's international strategy. Foreign Minister Andrei Kozyrev became their recognized leader (Arbatov 1993, 9–10; Crow 1993, 12–3). From August 1991 to the end of 1992, the ideas of this group dominated policy formulation and implementation as well as the foreign policy discourse in Russia. For that reason, Yeltsin's foreign policy was clearly pro-Western.

The "Atlanticists" believed that the West (Western Europe and the United States) should be the main orientation for Russian diplomacy. They insisted that Russia historically belongs to the Western (Christian) civilization. They saw the main task of Russian international strategy as one of building a partnership with the West and joining Western economic, political and military institutions—the European Union (EU), North Atlantic Treaty Organization (NATO), International Monetary Fund (IMF),

World Bank, Organization for Economic Cooperation and Development (OECD), General Agreement on Tariffs and Trade (GATT) (succeeded by World Trade Organization in 1995), G-7, and so on. Mr. Kozyrev stressed that Moscow's main guideline is to 'join the club of recognized democratic states with market economies, on a basis of equality' (NATO Review, 1993, February, 7). He regarded such a partnership as the principal source of international support for Russian reforms.

During that period (1991–93) Moscow refrained from opposing NATO enlargement. Moreover, on a number of occasions high-ranking Russian officials (President Boris Yeltsin, Vice President Aleksandr Rutskoi, Foreign Minister Andrei Kozyrev, State Secretary Gennady Burbulis, etc.) proposed that Russia could itself one day become a full member of NATO (Pravda, 23 December 1991; Rossiyskaya gazeta, 7 March 1992). In the Atlanticists view, NATO was an important instrument for providing both European and trans-Atlantic security. The Atlanticists maintained that combined with the Conference for Security and Cooperation in Europe (CSCE) (transformed to the Organization for Security and Cooperation in Europe in 1993), NATO could become the starting point for the formation of a new type of Euro-Atlantic Community; one which could guarantee international stability from Vancouver through to Vladivostok,

The Atlanticists' insisted that Russia should reduce the global activities of the former USSR due to a lack of resources, and radical changes in the country's foreign policy doctrine should be implemented. They believed that a renunciation of the global imperial policy and the ideological messianism of the former Union could open up prospects for domestic reforms and facilitate Russia's national revival. At the same time, this was not to lead to Moscow's self-isolation from wide-ranging processes of international co-operation (Zagorski et al. 1992: I)

However, the Atlanticists split into two groups. While Kozyrev's followers became more assertive as to the West and the "near abroad", a number of liberal politicians, academics and journalists were in favor of "civilized dialogue" both with the West and the countries of the former Soviet Union. The liberals opposed Kozyrev's "linkage tactics" regarding troop withdrawals and Russian national minorities in the ex-Soviet republics. They were also against the maintenance of Russian military bases and a considerable military presence in the "near abroad" (Arbatov 1992; Goncharov 1992: 3).

Eurasianism

The Yeltsin-Kozyrev pro-Western line evoked painful reactions from many Russian politicians and intellectuals who tried to develop some alternative concepts of foreign policy. Since 1992 "Eurasianism" has been the first serious alternative to the pro-Western theories that were dominant in Russian foreign policy thinking during the late 1980s and early 1990s.

The "Eurasianist" concept *(evraziistvo* in Russian) became very popular among Russian intellectuals during the mid-1990s. The concept drew heavily on a philosophical school of 1920s Russian émigrés who had tried to find a compromise with the Stalinist version of Socialism. It stresses the uniqueness of Russia. One of its key postulates is that in civilizational terms Russia has never been part of Europe (Laruelle 2008, 16–49; Savitsky 2003; Trubetskoi 2003). Hence, it should choose a "third way" between the West and the East. Globally Russia should be a bridge between these civilizations.

Contemporary proponents of this theory have been split into two opposing groups. One of them resided in the reformist (so-called democratic) camp, while the other belonged to the Slavophiles.

The "Democratic" Version. The "Democrats" tried to adapt Eurasianism to their views for a number of reasons. They realized their own weakness in terms of neglecting the national question and Russian national values. The nationalists and the Communists were obviously stronger in this field and thus, in part, managed to capture the sympathy of the ordinary people by appealing to their humiliation over their national dignity. Obviously, the adoption of Eurasianism by the Democrats was part of a strategy aimed at conquering both Russian public opinion and the political elite. Furthermore, Eurasianism was a reaction by those Democrats disappointed by both the West's reluctance to admit Russia to its institutions, and the scale of Western assistance to Moscow. They understood that it was unwise to rely too heavily upon the West. By adhering to Eurasianism they tried to demonstrate to the West that it could well lose a potential ally.

Finally, the "democratic" Eurasianism reflected the geopolitical position of Russia, the need to maintain stable relations with both the East and South. Speaking at a meeting at the Russian Foreign Ministry in February 1992, Sergei Stankevich (1992, 100), the then Advisor to the President, said:

There is no getting away from certain facts. One of them is that we are now separated from Europe by a whole chain of independent states and find ourselves much further from it, which inevitably involves a definite and, indeed, a quite substantial redistribution of our resources, our potentialities, our links and our interests in favor of Asia and the Eastern sector.

As apparent from the term Eurasianism itself, the geographic frame of reference for the Eurasianist foreign policy concept implied first of all the Eurasian continent. Other regions were of peripheral interest for Eurasianism. Hence, in the methodological sense, the Eurasianist foreign policy concept was relatively close to the geopolitical school of thought (comparable with Mackinder's (1904 and 1919) "Heartland" theory).

The Eurasianist philosophy in the "democratic" version departed from a thesis on Russia's special mission in history. According to Stankevich (1992, 94):

Russia's role in the world is ... to initiate and maintain a multilateral dialogue between cultures, civilizations and states. It is Russia which reconciles, unites, and co-ordinates It is the good, Great Power that is patient and open within borders, which have been settled by right and with good intentions, but which is threatened beyond these borders. This land, in which East and West, North and South are united, is unique, and is perhaps the only one capable of harmoniously uniting many different voices in a historical symphony.

One other observer has put it in more pragmatic terms: '[...] the primary object of Russia's mission today is to be fundamental to Eurasian continental stability [...] Another aspect of Russia's mission is to guarantee at least minimum respect for human rights in post-Soviet space' (Pleshakov 1993, 22–3).

The basic idea of the Eurasianist security concept according to the "democratic" version was the notion of national interests. According to Stankevich, the national interests of any country are pre-determined by its geography, history, culture, ethnic composition, and political tradition. Stankevich believed that the Russian national idea should be one characterized by democracy, federalism, and patriotism rather than totalitarianism, imperialism and socialist internationalism. More precisely, he identified Russian national security interests as follows: self-preservation; the prevention of further collapse; the creation of a system of democracy and federalism that checks both imperial dictatorship and separatist tendencies; efficient guarantees for ethnic Russians who live in the "near abroad"; and the evolution of a strong and efficient state with a stable foreign policy (Stankevich 1994, 31–2).

The Eurasianists believed that the government had paid too much attention to the Western direction of its foreign policy, while Russia's most compelling needs were in the South and East. The Eurasianists argued that, first of all, Moscow should deal with "the arc of crisis" developing on Russia's southern borders, and with the problems which had arisen in relations with its own sizeable Muslim population. Russia, they argued, has to develop an active diplomacy to meet the challenges posed by Turkey, Iran, Saudi Arabia, and other Islamic countries. In addition, they contended that coping with these threats and challenges is more important than maintaining an active dialogue with the West on European and trans-Atlantic issues (Stankevich 1994, 24).

The Eurasianist approach gave priority to the consolidation of economic, political and security ties between the countries of the Former Soviet Union, preferably within the context of the Commonwealth of Independent States (CIS) (Travkin 1994, 34–5). The Eurasianists persuaded the Yeltsin government to make the CIS a priority for Moscow's international policy, and to initiate the Commonwealth's integration.

For the "democratic" version of Eurasianism, Eastern Europe was geographic priority number two after the CIS. In 1992–93, the Eurasianists viewed this sub-region through the prism of Russia's economic, rather than purely security, interests. They complained about the disruption of traditional economic ties with Eastern European countries, which had appeared to have re-oriented themselves towards the West. However, the school also predicted that very soon these countries would again be interested in cooperation with Russia as the Western markets would no longer have vacant niches (Travkin 1994, 38).

The Eurasianists from the "democratic" pole recommended co-operation with the Third World rather than with the industrial West (Lukin 1994, 110). While the former perceives Russia as an equal partner the latter treats Moscow as a "second-echelon" state. In addition, a number of prosperous and rich Asia-Pacific nations such as Japan, South Korea and some of the members of Association of Southeast Asian Nations (ASEAN) could be promising trade partners and a source of investment for Russia's troubled economy. Moreover, military co-operation with India and China could be important pillars for the new Eurasian security complex (Miasnikov 1994, 228–238; Sergunin and Subbotin 1996a, 24–27; Sergunin and Subbotin 1996b, 3–8; Sergunin and Subbotin 1999).

At the same time, the "democratic" version of Eurasianism has not denied the importance of keeping good relations with the West. They do not object to Russia entering either the international economy or the "defense structure of the advanced part of the world community" (Bogaturov et al. 1992, 31). In their view, Russia's most important interest consists of improving relations with the EU, and gradual integration into the European economic and political system. At the same time, Russia should oppose the transformation of Europe into a closed economic system and military-political union, just as it should oppose the appearance of a dominant regional power (Germany). For the Eurasianists from the "democratic" pole, it is best to preserve both the multipolar nature of European politics and the role of the United States in the region. Simultaneously, both the function and role of NATO should be reconsidered (Lukin 1994, 115).

The main point in the "democratic" Eurasianists' dispute with the Atlanticists has been the need to adjust the balance between the Western and Eastern directions of Moscow's international strategy. As one advocate of "democratic" Eurasianism explained, 'partnership with the West will undoubtedly strengthen Russia in its relations with the East and the South, while partnership with the East and the South will give Russia independence in its contacts with the West' (Malcom 1994, 167).

Initially, the "democratic" Eurasianists were much less influential than the Atlanticists within the Yeltsin government and Russian political elites. However, as Russian society's discontent with Kozyrev's pro-Western line increased, Eurasianism became stronger among both policy-makers and foreign policy experts. Starting to coalesce in 1992, by 1993 the "Eurasianist Democrats" were able to influence foreign policy and security debates in Russia. The theoretical framework of Russia's 1993 foreign policy doctrine (especially the setting of regional priorities) was obviously affected by "democratic" Eurasianist ideas (Kontseptsiya Vneshney Politiki 1993). The nationalists and the Eurasianists were together successful in forcing Kozyrev to link Russian military politics and troop withdrawals with national minorities' rights in the ex-Soviet republics (especially in the Baltic States).

The Slavophile Version. In contrast to the "democratic" version of Eurasianism, the Slavophiles downplayed the country's unique geopolitical position and instead stressed Russia's distinctiveness from both the West and the East. Elgiz Pozdnyakov (1993a, 6), a Russian authority in IR theory, noted:

> The geopolitical location of Russia is not just unique (so is that of any state), it is truly fateful for both herself and the world [...] An important aspect of this situation was that Russia, being situated between two civilizations, was a natural keeper of both a civilized equilibrium and a world balance of power.

According to the Slavophiles, this predetermined in no small measure the evolution of the Russian state as a great power and the establishment of a strong central authority. Unlike the "Democrats", the Slavophiles have not been frightened to label Russia as an empire and to support its revival (Pozdnyakov 1993b, 30).

Contrary to the "Democrats", the Slavophiles opposed Western assistance. They considered it irrelevant and burdensome, and proposed a reliance on Russia's own resources. They opposed Russia's joining of the Western economic, political and military institutions on the basis of it restricting the country's sovereignty. They also favored turning the protection of Russian minorities in the former Soviet republics into a top foreign policy priority. Contrary to the "Democrats", however, the Slavophiles did not rule out the use of force to defend these minorities.

Finally, they proposed to change the current geopolitical priorities by paying more attention to Russia's southern and eastern neighbors and to keep a relatively low profile in the West.

By the end of 1993, both versions of Eurasianism—"democratic" and Slavophile—found themselves, similar to Atlanticism, in a critical situation due to a number of intellectual and political factors. Other schools of thought, alternatives to both Atlanticism and Eurasianism, then became influential.

The rise of the *derzhavniki*

The emergence of derzhavniki was the end result of the process of consolidation of the three major political forces—the industrial lobby, the federal military and civilian bureaucracies, and the moderate "Democrats". This group was quickly labelled the derzhavniki or the gosudarstvenniki (proponents of state power). The term derzhavnik denotes the advocating of a strong and powerful state which can maintain order and serve as a guarantee against anarchy and instability; a relatively traditional Russian view of the state's role.

As for Russia's foreign policy, the *derzhavniki* proposed that it should be guided by the principle of self-limitation and self-sufficiency (Russia's National Interests 1992, 135). It was argued that Russia should not compete for influence as a global power. But this period of concentration on its internal problems should not, however, prevent Russia from pursuing an active foreign policy in various parts of the world. The *derzhavniki* opposed a choice between pro-Western or pro-Asian lines in Russia's foreign policy. They believed that Russia is both a European and an Asian country: According to the *derzhavniki,* the best way to define Russia's identity was to become Russian and to respect the nation's own history and values (Vladislavlev and Karaganov 1992, 36). Along with the "Democratic" Eurasianists they considered the CIS and the "near abroad" as a top priority for Moscow's security policy. 'Russia must bear its cross and fulfil its duty by playing an enlightened post-imperial role throughout the ex-Soviet Union', observed Vladislavlev and Karaganov (1992, 33):

> A decisive component of Russia's new mission in the world is to ensure, with help from the world community, that the ex-Soviet area does not become a geostrategic hole radiating instability and war and ultimately endangering the very existence of humanity.

A need for the gradual economic and military integration of the CIS has also been acknowledged. Belarus and Kazakhstan have been the most promising partners in the Commonwealth in this respect. The *derzhavniki* have put pressure on the government to create a proper CIS mechanism to provide such integrationist processes with the essential institutional support. However, they stated that Russia's assertive policy in the "near abroad" should not imply an imperialist policy. The *derzhavniki* assumed that any attempt to forcibly re-establish the Soviet Union or the Russian Empire would be fraught with danger; overstraining Moscow itself and also possibly leading to international isolation (Blackwill and Karaganov 1994, 19).

This group regarded the West as an important priority in Moscow's foreign policy and favored better relations with the West, but not at the cost of diminishing Russia's role as an independent great power with its own spheres of influence. They remained fairly sceptical as to the West's willingness and capability to help Russia in realising its reforms. They argued against an excessive reliance on Western economic assistance and political guidance and advocated an active arms export policy regardless of Western opposition. (Strategiya dlya Rossii 1992, 5).

It was the *derzhavniki* who first suggested that the West may well choose to implement a sort of neo-containment policy towards Russia because of its irritation with Moscow's less than compliant tone, its increasing concern about signs of Russian dominance in the post-Soviet space, as well as over Moscow's reluctance to accept NATO enlargement, to restrain its arms sales, and to stop playing the "Chinese card" (Blackwill and Karaganov 1994, 19–20).

The *derzhavniki* have been the leading critics among Russia's political elites over Western policies concerning NATO's expansion. They have warned that enlargement could lead to a resumption of the East-West confrontation, although in a milder form than before. They recommended that the West should delay its decision on expansion for a number of years. Moreover, both Russia and the West should propose some positive programme for Central and Eastern European countries to reduce their security concerns. There could be bilateral or unilateral Western guarantees for their security, and an early enlargement of the EU, Western European Union (WEU), and so on. In addition, Russia should develop its relations with the EU and WEU as a counterweight to NATO's offensive capabilities (Karaganov 1995, 63–64).

As a result of the December 1993 elections, which demonstrated the success of Vladimir Zhirinovskiy, the domestic basis for pro-Western policy shrunk. For many "Democrats", "statist" ideology became the only way to save the remnants of "Democratic" principles and confront the extremists, nationalists, and Communists. A significant group of Atlanticists (including Kozyrev) and the "Democratic wing" of the Eurasianists both joined the *derzhavniki*.

The so-called Kozyrev Doctrine, pro-claimed by the then Russian Foreign Minister in a speech to Russian diplomatic representatives in the CIS and Baltic states in January 1994, became a symbol of the *derzhavniki* concept of foreign policy. He declared that the vital strategic issue for Russian diplomacy was the defense of Russian minority rights in the "near abroad". He affirmed the need for a Russian military presence in this area and advocated the idea of dual nationality (Nezavisimaya gazeta,19 January 1994; Litera 1994 / 1995, 45–52).

The year 1996 took off with the appointment of a new Russian Foreign Minister. Andrei Kozyrev was replaced by Yevgeny Primakov, previously Director of the Foreign Intelligence Service. Primakov was a less controversial figure than Kozyrev: the Democrats and the government's opponents both acknowledged his professionalism and eagerness to protect Russia's national interests. He also followed the *derzhavniki* course. Primakov proposed a slightly different set of geographical priorities—the CIS, Eastern Europe, Asia-Pacific, Europe and the United States of America—to demonstrate to the West Russia's capability as a counterweight to NATO and EU enlargement (Stupavsky 1996, 10).

Realism: return of the repressed

The derzhavniki with their suspicions toward idealism and romanticism and their advocacy of national interests paved the way towards the rehabilitation of the realist school of thought. The balance of power, rather than the balance of interests, was again in fashion. National, not international, security became the matter of primary concern.

Politically the realists have belonged to different groups, although with a predominant orientation to the democratic parties and associations. The realist concept simply provides them with a common theoretical framework and ideas, which easily cross party lines.

According to the realists, Russia's national security concept should depart from the real potential of the state, provide for the rational use of resources, combine and interact with internal, foreign policy, socio-economic, scientific, technological, information, as well as all other aspects of life and work among the state's people. In fact, the realists were one of the first schools of thought in Russia to propose extending the concept of national security to include, not only "hard security" issues, but "soft security" topics as well. As the realists underlined, a security concept should contain a comprehensive analysis and classification of the existing and potential threats to Russia's security; as well as the starting points for the development and functioning of internal and external mechanisms for both the prevention and operational elimination of these threats.

In other words, the concept should be a complex of security goals and ways of ensuring them; of ways and means of achieving them that would correspond to Russia's historical position and future role. It should ensure a coordinated effort on the part of both the state and the people as a whole to provide security at the national, regional, and global levels, as well as the organization of internal and international interaction in solving urgent and long-term security problems (Shaposhnikov 1993, 11).

The realists distinguish four main categories in terms of Russia's national interests. First, there are functional interests—economic, political, social, military, humanitarian, and environmental. Second, there might he other groups of interests, depending on the degree of these interests' longevity—short-term, midterm, and standing interests. Third, interests could be categorized depending on their importance—vital, important, or marginal. Finally, domestic and foreign policy interests could he defined (National Interests 1996, 8).

The realists stress that in an interrelated and interdependent world national interests of different countries may overlap, cross, or even clash in various forms, ranging from "soft", diplomatic, to radical, military ones. The realists also distinguish two kinds of threats to Russia's security: external and internal.

The external sources of threat were defined as follows (Shaposhnikov 1993, 14–18):

(a) *political:* attempts to challenge the territorial integrity of the Russian Federation by exploiting inter-ethnic and inter-religious conflicts; territorial claims made by foreign powers; blocking integrationist processes in the CIS; creating obstacles to Russia's co-operation with the former Soviet republics and Eastern European countries; political instability in neighboring countries; human rights violations and the resultant uncontrollable mass migration from these countries; efforts to weaken Russia's role and positions in the international organizations, and so on;

(b) *economic:* the diminished economic independence of Russia, a decline in its economic and scientific-technical potential, fixing its fuel and raw material specialization in the world division of labor, restricting Russia's presence in some of the world's markets, blocking Russia's access to advanced technology, uncontrolled exports of capital and strategic raw materials, Russia's non-admittance to the international financial, trade and economic organizations, smuggling, and so on;

(c) *military:* existing and potential armed conflicts in the vicinity of Russia, the unsettled problem of nuclear weaponry in the former Soviet republics, nuclear weapon and technology proliferation, the lack of a proper border regime (especially in the south and west of Russia), the unclear status of Russian military presence in the ex-Soviet republics, the military build-up in neighboring countries and adjacent regions, and so on;

(d) *environmental:* ecological disasters in neighboring countries, long-term negative effects resulting from global environmental shifts; and

(e) *social:* the internationalisation of organized crime, drug trafficking, international terrorism, mass epidemics, the modern slave trade, and so on.

However, the realists were also keen to emphasize that at present the main sources of threat to Russia's security come from within the country which is in a deep system crisis.

Internal threats were described as follows (Shaposhnikov 1993, 14–8; Lukov 1995, 5–7):

(a) potential disintegration of the Russian Federation as a result of inter-ethnic and center / regions conflicts;

(b) socio-economic tensions stemming from economic decline, the rupture of economic ties, inflation, rising unemployment, deep social differentiation, the degradation of science as well as the education system and medical services, and so on;

(c) organized crime and corruption;

(d) cultural and spiritual degradation;

(e) the degradation of the environment; and

(f) the lack of information security.

To cope with these threats, Russia should first accomplish its domestic reforms. Only in this way will the country have the necessary resources to restore its internal, and to some degree its external stability. The realists believed that the cohesion of all levels of security—intra-regional, national, CIS, European, Asia-Pacific, global—should be reached. This should be aided by the rational and effective use of all forces and means currently at the disposal of the Russian state.

Moreover, the realists preferred political, diplomatic, economic and other peaceful methods to meet security challenges. However, they did not rule out the use of military force if differences between states' vital interests cannot be reconciled (National Interests 1996: 9–10).

The regional priorities of the realists were similar to those of the *derzhavniki*. Rogov (1993, 76) suggested that there were three main circles of Russian interests: (1) "near abroad" / CIS; (2) East Europe, the Middle East and Far East; and (3) the West (the United States and Western Europe). The remainder of the world meanwhile was of peripheral importance for Russia.

According to the realists, the "near abroad" was the first regional priority in Russia's international strategy. The main goals of Moscow's foreign policy in the "near abroad" were defined as to prevent the rise of unfriendly regimes and the emergence of ethnic and religious conflicts, to establish stable relations with its neighbors, to protect Russian citizens' human rights, to shape a common security space on CIS territory, and to resolve territorial disputes with the New Independent States (NIS) (Elections 1995, 18–20).

According to the realists, re-imposing Russia's military and political dominance over the post-Soviet space at any cost would cause many sacrifices and lead to countless failures. Instead, Russia's diplomatic inventory must contain a wide range of accurately weighed and measured economic, political, military and cultural methods which could assist with the protection of Russian interests and with the development of friendly relations with their neighbors. The realists have emphasized that CIS integration could only be achieved once Russia becomes attractive to its partners. Integration will be costly for Moscow; Russia could afford it only if its domestic reforms succeed (Elections 1195, 19).

The second circle of Russia's national interests included Eastern Europe, the Middle East, and the Far East. The realists were critical of Kozyrev's policies towards Central and East European countries because Moscow has been unable to prevent their drift towards the West both in economic and security terms. According to the realists, Eastern Europe must be shown, through clever initiatives in various fields, that it will be safer and more prosperous, not in the role of a *cordon sanitaire* thrown around Russia, but functioning as a connecting link between Eurasia and Western Europe (Elections 1995: 20).

In line with other schools of thought, the realists have stressed the Eurasian geopolitical location of Russia. However, Russian foreign policy on the continent should be defined by real interests rather than messianic ideas.

Russian policy towards the Middle East should be determined by its interests in the "near abroad"—the Transcaucasus and Central Asia. Potentially, Turkey, Iran, Iraq, Pakistan, and Afghanistan could be Russia's opponents. According to Lukin (1994), very likely, Russia will, in the years ahead, have to vigorously resist Islamic fundamentalism, the spread of which would threaten to destabilize the situation both near and inside the CIS. It was essential, however, not to be drawn into a confrontation with the biggest Islamic countries (including Iran), but to instead seek various avenues of agreement and develop mutually beneficial interstate relations. Russia must rebuff all attempts by Turkey, Pakistan and Afghanistan to encroach on Russian economic, political, and military interests (Elections 1995, 21). As for the Far East, the realists have noted Russia's weakness and declining role in the region. Rogov (1993, 76) admitted that some of the ex-Soviet republics could be drawn into the spheres of interest of such regional centers of power as China or Japan. Arbatov (1993, 72) even suggested that China may represent the greatest external security threat to Russia in the long run. He and other realists did not approve of too quick a military rapprochement with the PRC (People's Republic of China) and warned of the possibility of Russia's one-sided dependence on Beijing (Arbatov 1993, 72; Trush 1996, 4). For that reason, Arbatov (1993, 72) observed the interests of Russia in the region may best be served by the maintenance of the United States' political role and limited military presence. If the United States were to withdraw, the Japanese reaction could be none other than re-militarisation in view of the rapid growth of economic and military power in China. A clash between these two giants could draw Russia into the conflict as well. In addition to keeping the United States military presence, Russia's national interests would be best served by a new multilateral security system in the region.

According to Rogov, the third circle of Russian interests included Moscow's relations with the West, in particular with the United States and Western Europe. As for the United States, the realists saw a number of areas where the two states had common interests: (a) accomplishing

Russian economic and political reforms; (b) developing a bilateral arms control regime (in particular, further reductions in strategic armaments and a nuclear test ban); (c) preventing the rise of resurgent regional powers which could violate the existing power balance; (d) nuclear, chemical and biological weapons non-proliferation; and (c) peace-keeping (Rogov 1993, 76; 1995, 5).

At the same time, the realists have singled out some sources of tension between Russia and the United States—Russia's inability to move fast with its domestic reforms; the lack of a common enemy, which is indispensable for any military-political alliance; the model of mutual nuclear deterrence inherited from the Cold War; the United States' refusal to admit Russia into the Western community; the preservation of the system of military-political alliances set up by the United States during the Cold War; NATO and EU enlargement through admitting the Soviet Union's former "clients" but not Russia itself; NATO's aggressive policies in the Balkans and Russia's arms and dual-use technology transfers to Third World countries (Rogov 1995, 5–8).

Many of these differences could well remain in the foreseeable future. According to the realists, Russia should be firm as regards its most vital interests (for instance, preserving a common European security system and arms control regime, the prevention of a military build-up and alliances in the country's vicinity, and Moscow's dominant position in the post-Soviet security space). At the same time, Russia should avoid quarrelling with the United States over differences on secondary matters such as nuclear deals with Iran, missile engine technology transfers to India, advanced weaponry transfers to China, and so on (Rogov 1995, 9).

Concerning European security problems, the realists have focused first of all on NATO and EU enlargement. They did not oppose the latter, and regarded the former as detrimental to the regional security system. The realists did not favor NATO's dissolution. On the contrary, they acknowledged the Alliance's positive role in the maintenance of European security both in the Cold War era and beyond (Arbatov 1993, 71). But they also believed that NATO should not be extended and strengthened at the expense of Russian security According to the realists, to prevent a new clash between the East and the West the OSCE should become the main collective security organization on the continent (Arbatov 1995b; 1996, 248–9). The realists have also focused on the search for a compromise with the West. They have proposed both a delay in NATO's expansion by a number of years, and that its eventual enlargement be limited to the Visegrad countries only, and not be extended to the Baltic

States. They have also proposed a special Russia-NATO charter to ensure Moscow's security (no further expansion to the CIS countries, no military bases and nuclear weapons on the territory of new members, the continuation of arms control dialogue, and so on) (Arbatov 1995a, 146: Rogov 1995, 10–11; Trenin 1995, 20–26). The Russian-NATO Paris Agreement (May 1997) was concluded, in fact, on the basis of these principles (Rossiyskaya gazeta, 28 May 1997, 3; International' Herald Tribune, 28 May 1997, 1, 16).

The realists pointed to the Kosovo crisis as evidence of the threat emanating from the NATO-centric European security model. However, they recommended resuming a dialogue with NATO after the end of the war because they realized that it was impossible to ignore this influential pole of the world power (Arbatov 1999, 8; Pyadyshev 1999, 2).

As far as the post-9.11 world order was concerned the realists believed that the Afghanistan and Iraq wars have demonstrated the return of the world to the 19th century-like anarchical model which had been based on power politics, selfish national interests and hard competition between major players. They emphasized the inability of international organizations and international law to prevent new wars and the rise of hegemonic powers. Instead, they suggested several possible models for the 'neo-anarchical' world. Some of the Russian realists believed that the era of US unilateralism was looming ahead (Karaganov 2003, 9, 15) and advised the Russian leadership to choose the sides—either to join the US-led pole as a junior partner (Dmitrieva 2003a, 6) or try to counterbalance American superpower with the help of other power poles—EU (or certain European countries, such as France or / and Germany), China, CIS and so on (Grigoryev 2003, 6; Lukin 2003, 15; Suslov 2003, 9, 14).

Another group of realists visualized the future world as a chaotic combination of *ad hoc* and shifting coalitions where different states pursued their national interests. The realists warned the Russian leaders that since these coalitions will be of a temporary (short-term) rather than permanent (long-term) nature, Russia should not invest too much to them and should change allies and alliances when they stop to serve Russia's national interests (Andrusenko and Tropkina 2002, 1; Satanovsky 2003, 1). They pointed to US-Russia cooperation on Afghanistan (2001) and Russia-France-Germany strategic triangle in case of Iraq (2003) as examples of such *ad hoc* coalitions.

Finally, there were realists who believe that a multipolar model of the world was still possible and Russia could become one of the power poles (especially in the post-Soviet geostrategic space) (Nikolaev 2003, 9, 14;

Satarov 2003, 7). More specifically, this model of the 'manageable anarchy' could result in creating of a 'concert of powers' international security system where Russia could play a significant role. G-8 was seen as an embryo of such a less informal but more flexible and reliable security regime (Bausin 2003, 2). President Putin's speech at the Munich conference on international security (February 2007) went along the same lines (Putin 2007). Some realists suggested including China and India into G-8 and transforming it into G-10 to make this institution more authoritative and representative (Dmitrieva 2003b, 1, 4). UN Security Council should not be neglected as well. It could be useful when there is a consensus between five permanent members or it could be used by Russia (and its allies) to block (or make illegitimate) undesirable initiatives and strategies (Lukin 2003, 15).

The "Arab awakening", a series of "color" revolutions in the post-Soviet space and, more recently, the Ukrainian and Syrian crises forced the two latter realist groupings to merge and shift to a more pessimistic view of world politics. For the Russian present-day realists, it is absolutely clear that the West (particularly, the U.S. and EU) should be blamed for the Ukrainian crisis (Markov 2014). This (hard-line) school believes that by helping the nationalist forces in Ukraine to oust the pro-Russian regime of Viktor Yanukovych the West wanted to withdraw this country from Moscow's sphere of influence and sideline Russia in the post-Soviet space. They fully approve Vladimir Putin's policies on Crimea's integration to Russia and supporting the breakaway Donetsk and Lughansk people's republics (DPR and LPR). The radical version of this school even suggested not to limit the concept of 'Novorossiya' (New Russia) to Donbass only, but to include other eastern and southern regions of Ukraine to it (from Kharkov to Odessa) and help the local pro-Russian forces to "liberate" these territories from the Kiev-based "junta" (Krutikov 2014).

As for the future of the Ukrainian question is concerned the Russian realists believe that the 'frozen conflict' scenario is the most probable one because the warring parties have no more resources to continue the conflict in its open form (Guschin et al. 2015). This option will not bring peace and stability to the region but can stop military activities, killing civilians and create necessary conditions for rebuilding region's economy and social institutions.

This scenario is possible in an environment where neither of the parties is interested in serious concessions or compromises, but at the same time they are not in a position to implement their maximalist program. Ukraine has limited resources for defeating the separatists if it does not want to risk escalating tensions with Russia (including Moscow's direct military involvement). Meanwhile, if Russia were to increase support to the self-proclaimed republics of Donbass, it would risk entering a new Cold War. The West is interested in cooperating with Russia on the issues of Iran, Syria, Afghanistan, North Korea, as well as in the fight against the Islamic State, and fears Moscow's unilateral strengthening of its positions in the 'near abroad' as well as the transformation of Russia's foreign policy into a Eurasian version of the 'Monroe Doctrine'. In this case, concerns about heightened stakes could play the role of deterrent.

Under this scenario, Russia would become a donor to the Donbass republics while guaranteeing the survival of the population and largely assuming the responsibility of rebuilding their infrastructure. For Moscow, support for the DPR and LPR would not simply be an element of pressure on Kiev, but an attempt to build a political system modeled on Transnistria with a gradual reduction in the role of warlords.

In this case, Ukraine would not agree to official negotiations with the DPR and LPR authorities and would focus on building up its armed forces, as well as carrying out the military reform. Special attention would be paid to the country's eastern regions, including the Ukrainian parts of the Donetsk and Lughansk regions, in terms of economic aid and decentralization. In many respects, it would be a competition between Ukraine (with the West's support) and the unrecognized republics (with Moscow's support) in terms of governance effectiveness and rebuilding infrastructure. Because of the long-term nature of the 'frozen conflict' scenario, the socioeconomic standing of Russia and Ukraine would take on particular importance, both in terms of the ability to allocate sufficient resources to solve problems, as well as competition between the Ukrainian and Novorossiya concepts.

The realist legacy has had a fairly mixed record. On the one hand, realism has contributed positively to the Russian foreign policy debate. The realists have helped to overcome the crisis in Russian foreign policy thinking which had been generated by the struggle of two extremes represented by such schools of thought as Atlanticism and Eurasianism. The realists succeeded in articulating Russia's real security interests and priorities to both domestic and foreign audiences. Moreover, the spread of their ideas made Russian security thinking more predictable and understandable for the West. The Russian national security concept which was approved by the President in December 1997 (and revised in 2000, 2009 and 2015) drew heavily upon the realist ideas (Yeltsin 1997, 4–5; Putin 2000a, 6–7 and 2015b; Medvedev 2009). On the other hand, the coming of realism with its emphasis on national interests, national security and national sovereignty implied an obvious return to the old paradigms belonging to the age of classical modernity. They failed to develop any concepts addressing the challenges of post-modernity.

Geopolitics: new opportunities in Russia?

Along with realism, its close "relative"—the geopolitical school of thought—is currently in fashion in Russia. In part, it could be viewed as a counter-reaction to Russian theories concerning Marxism and Gorbachev's NPT which both denied the role of geopolitical factors in international relations.

One additional reason why many Russian theorists have been fascinated with geopolitics is that this concept assisted them in escaping from the intellectual dead-end caused by the Atlanticism-Eurasianism political controversy. At a certain stage, the two schools realized that both the pro-Western and Eurasian orientations were imposed by ideological preferences rather than dictated by Russia's real national interests. The geopolitical paradigm was seen by many thinkers as having a solid theoretical basis compared to several other concepts. In fact, all leading Eurasianist theorists eventually became followers of the geopolitical school (Pozdnyakov 1993c and 1994; Pleshakov 1995, 101–107).

The geopolitical school departs from the assumption that every state consists of three indispensable components: territory, population, and political organization. Wherever people may live, and under whatever political system, their activities are invariably conditioned by the physical environment. Every state has unique geographical features. Its territory has a location, landscape, form, size, and natural resources. These specifics account for the equally unique historical background of any country. Of the numerous factors influencing people's activities, geography changes least of all. It underlies the continuity of national policy provided that the geographical area remains unchanged (Pozdnyakov 1992, 4).

The size of territorial possessions is a tangible element of the relative strength of a country in defending its interests. Natural resources and geography are factors for either the solidity or looseness of social and economic ties. Coupled with climate, they set a limit on agricultural production and condition internal communications and foreign trade. The country's strength should therefore be assessed primarily by looking into geography.

According to proponents of the geopolitical paradigm, today's divided world is both a political and a geographic reality to be reckoned with by the political and military strategy of every state, as well as by the concept of national security and interests. Every country's vital interests include its self-preservation as a specific cultural and historical community (Pozdnyakov 1992, 5).

Many Russian adherents of geopolitics, in fact, accept Mackinder's (1904 and 1919) and Cohen's (1963) concept of two geostrategic regions: the maritime world dependent on trade (with the United States as its core) and the Eurasian continental world (where Russia is the core). According to Pozdnyakov (1992, 7), the United States, as one of the two geostrategic regions, is now the only remaining superpower. In addition, it is trying to take advantage of this situation as a means to achieve some of its goals which, until recently, have been largely unattainable.

To geopoliticians' minds, two things are of paramount importance for the maintenance of world order and stability: (a) establishing a clear boundary between Western sea power and Eurasian land power in Europe, and (b) preserving the unity of the Heartland. According to some analysts, both of these principles of global security are seriously challenged by the reunification of Germany and the collapse of the Soviet Union. The boundary between the West and Eurasia has shifted eastward. To date, this boundary has not been properly defined. Russia, which controlled most of the Heartland, has shrunk in terms of territory and is currently unable to play the role of balancer in a geopolitically unstable world. A geopolitically unbalanced Eurasia might provoke a universal re-division of the world with its resources and strategic boundaries. In turn, it could imply a protracted period of turbulence, rift and bloody conflict. The Kosovo war, Chechnya, the civil wars in Tajikistan and Afghanistan, the Ukrainian crisis have already demonstrated some implications of the lack of such a geopolitical balance. To avoid an even worse scenario, both Russia and the West should make joint efforts to stabilize the post-Soviet geopolitical space. It could restore Russia's historical mission to be the mediator and to serve as a safeguard against forces aiming at worldwide domination. Echoing Mackinder's three geopolitical theses, Pozdnyakov (1992, 12) coined his own geopolitical formula: "He who controls the Heartland can exercise effective control over world politics, above all by maintaining a global geopolitical and power balance, without which lasting peace is unthinkable."

There is a group of Russian geopoliticians who believe that presently the control over natural resources rather than over territories matters.

According to the "resource geopolitics" school, the maritime powers (led by the U.S.) aim to establishing their control over the regions which are rich in natural (first and foremost energy) resources (Dugin 2002). That's why they aspire to installing pro-Western regimes in the Middle Eastern, North African and Central Asian countries. For the same reason, they aim to preventing Russia's industrial modernization on the high tech basis and secure its status of the West's "raw materials appendage". This type of geopoliticans calls on the Kremlin to restructure the Russian economy from the resource export-based model to the innovative one and by doing this to overcome the country's "resource curse". On the other hand, the geopoliticians suggest that Russia should lead a coalition of nations rich in natural resources to protect their collective interests vis-a-vis resource consumers (Dugin 2012).

Some Russian theorists prefer to produce "soft" geopolitical concepts which do not neglect the plurality of factors influencing international politics, but regard geography or spatial dimensions as the most important ones. According to one definition, geopolitics is about 'how the states use spatial factors to identify and attain their political purposes' (Vestnik MGU 1994, 3). According to Pleshakov (1994, 32), geopolitics

> can be defined not only as objective dependency of some nation's foreign policy from its geographic location but also an objective dependency of an international actor from the totality of material factors which provide this actos with control aver the space.

Some scholars, such as Gadzhiev (1997, 4, 16–39), view geopolitics as a subfield of political science or equivalent of IR theory which emphasizes the spatial-temporal dimensions of world politics.

For other specialists, the geopolitical paradigm is a theoretical departure in order to justify their reading of Russia's foreign policy priorities. Sorokin (1995, 8) believes that geopolitics as a discipline consists of two parts: fundamental geopolitics which produces a theoretical outlook of the world, and applied geopolitics which aims at policy-relevant recommendations. For example, this group of geopoliticians use geopolitics to prove the importance of the "near abroad" and adjacent regions for Moscow's national interests (Razuvayev 1993a; 1993b, 109–116; Podberezkin 1996, 90–94).

Despite the seemingly old-fashioned argumentation, the geopolitical paradigm is likely to retain its influence in the Russian foreign policy debate in the foreseeable future. Not only the existence of a theoretical vacuum, but the current geopolitical challenges and the need to define Russia's national identity (including national interests and security politics) make this paradigm both significant and attractive to Russian policy-makers and analysts.

The idealist / liberal paradigm

Despite the dominance of the realist / geopolitical paradigm, the idealist / liberal perspective on international relations is also represented in Russia. In fact, Atlanticists drew upon some idealist principles. Idealism emphasises globalisation trends in the world economy which strengthen the trend toward global management of economic and political developments and generally increases the relevance of international legal frameworks, thus reducing global anarchy. Idealists believe that the development of multilateral institutions and regimes could guarantee stability of the international system. Although the trend toward a multipolar world is not neglected within the idealist / liberal perspective, it argues that the future development of the international system is no longer predominantly determined by the shape and outcome of rivalries among the major centers of economic and military power, but increasingly by the dynamics of their common development and interdependency (Khrustalev 1992; Zagorski et al. 1992, 5–13). The idealists / liberals argue that the geopolitical drive for control over territories does not matter anymore, and suggest that it should be replaced by geo-economic thinking (Zagorski 1995a, 5–8).

The debate between realists and idealists in Russia on more practical aspects of diplomacy has mainly concentrated on two issues: integration of the post-Soviet space and European security. For instance, Zagorski (1995b, 263–270) argued that the real dilemma of Russian politics in the CIS was not further disintegration *versus* integration, but rather reintegration *versus* eventual "natural" new integration on the basis of democratic and market reforms yet to be completed. Zagorski also argued that to pursue the latter option one needed to recognize that the major building blocks of the experience of the EU did not apply to the CIS and another North American Free Trade Area (NAFTA)-type of soft integration should be the goal.

In the 2000s, the liberals pushed forward the idea of a "multi-track" integration which included several models ranged from the Russian-Belorussian Union State (confederation), Customs Union and Eurasian Economic Union to some loose cooperative arrangements under the CIS auspices.

Priority was given to further development of the EEU which was seen as a "brain-child" of Russian liberalism. A treaty aiming for the establishment of the EEU was signed on 29 May 2014 (i.e. after the beginning of the Ukrainian crisis) by the leaders of Belarus, Kazakhstan and Russia, and came into force on 1 January 2015. Treaties aiming for Armenia's and Kyrgyzstan's accession to the Eurasian Economic Union were signed on 9 October and 23 December 2014, respectively. Armenia's accession treaty came into force on 2 January 2015 and Kyrgyzstan's one—on 8 May 2015.

Along with the basic liberal principles the EEU introduced the free movement of goods, capital, services and people and provides for common transport, agriculture and energy policies, with provisions for a single currency and greater integration in the future. The union operates through supranational and intergovernmental institutions. The supranational institutions are the Eurasian Commission (the executive body), the Court of the EEU (the judicial body) and the Eurasian Development Bank. National governments are usually represented by the Eurasian Commission's Council.

The EEU's creation was a result of a difficult compromise between Vladimir Putin and Kazakhstan President Nursultan Nazarbayev, who suggested the idea of the Eurasian economic integration in mid-1990s. Where Putin had wished for a common parliament, common passport, and common currency within the EEU, Nazarbayev remained steadfast in confining the organization to a purely economic union. Kazakhstan (as well as Belarus and Armenia) have repeatedly emphasized that the EEU is a pragmatic means to get economic benefits, not meddling into what Russia is doing politically or following its international course. According to one Kazakhstan expert, "We are quite pragmatic about membership, anticipating economic and social dividends. Astana is interested in preferences for the export of energy to Russia and its transit to other countries" (Russian International Affairs Council 2015a).

The Ukrainian crisis has put the EEU in a radically different situation. None of the EEU member-states recognized Crimea's take-over by Russia and forced them to make emphasis on their sovereignty in international politics. For example, Astana is mindful of the fact that ethnic Russians still make up nearly a quarter of Kazakhstan's population, and there is a discernible history of secessionist attempts in northern Kazakhstan. The economic crisis in Russia provoked by the downfall of oil prices and Western sanctions impedes the implementation of the EEU integration projects. For example, trade between the three EEU founding states (Belarus, Kazakhstan and Russia) had fallen nearly 13% in the first quarter of 2014 (Shapovalov 2014).

As for the future of the EEU the liberal experts ((Michel 2014; Russian International Affairs Council 2015a) suggest three scenarios:

- The first scenario is the optimistic one. According to this option, the EEU eliminates all barriers to trade and economic cooperation between the memberstates enters a phase of sustainable development based on implementation of the EEU Treaty and associate documents. Tajikistan overcomes its border disputes with Kyrgyzstan, harmonizes its legal and technical standards with the EEU ones and joins the Union in the near future. Some other countries like Uzbekistan and Turkey may express their interest in rapprochement with the Union. The EEU's relations with other countries in the near and far abroad advance constructively, including through the establishment of free trade areas. By 2025, the EEU emerges as a solid interstate bloc setting the agenda for integration processes in the post-Soviet space. Economic integration within the EEU creates favorable conditions for the start of a monetary and political union.

- The second option is a muddling-through scenario. Due to divergent goals and interests among the member-states, the EEU proceeds slowly, giving rise to diverse problems and frictions between its members, which gradually lose interest in participation. For some time, Russia artificially retains the Union and its governing structures, although with diminishing interest and energy because of the growing domestic problems. Finally, the Union tends to transforming into a loose intergovernmental association operating on an explicitly formal basis like the former Eurasian Economic Community.

- The third scenario is the pessimistic one. Since Russia is unable to become an attractive economic and political power in Eurasia and because of the external pressures / competition from China, EU, U.S. and WTO (upon Belarus' and Kazakhstan's accession) the non-Russian member-states lose their interest in the EEU and it eventually collapses. Putin's plans to make the EEU a new geoeconomic and geopolitical pole will collapse as well.

The first scenario is seen by the Russian liberals as both the mostly desirable and highly probable one while realists and geopoliticians oscillate between the second and third options.

As to European security, in the 1990s, the major controversial issue was NATO enlargement. While mainstream thinking has put forward the geopolitical argument against enlargement, the liberals have argued for a cooperative solution to the issue, which would strengthen and institutionalize interaction between Russia and the West. The basic argument of liberals has been that the predominant interest of Russia in Europe should be the strengthening of multilateralism as a guarantee that there will be no return to balance of power politics in Europe (Tyulin 1997, 187).

Pro-Western liberals viewed no serious threat stemming from NATO enlargement. They believed that NATO extension was a natural reaction of the former Soviet satellites to Russia's unpredictable behaviour. They criticized Yeltsin for his failure to persuade the Central and Eastern European countries that Russia posed no threat to their security any longer. The liberals also were discontent with Yeltsin's inability to make full use of the opportunities that were opened to Russia in the framework of different security arrangements ranging from Partnership for Peace (PfP) to OSCE programs (Kortunov 1996, 74–75).

The liberals considered NATO as the main guarantor of stability in Europe (in particular in relations between Western and Eastern Europe) (Maksimychev 1994). They believed that Russia was interested in NATO's responsibility for the stability of borders in Central and Eastern Europe, a region with a number of potential hotbeds of instability that could endanger Russia and the CIS member-states. The liberals thought that once NATO accepted the Central and Eastern European countries, which are currently anti-Russian, it will no longer have an incentive to be hostile to Moscow and that they would become more benevolent neighbors to Russia. In this view, partnership between NATO and Russia could become an instrument of conflict resolution in Russia's relations with its neighbors (Kozin 1994). The liberals also emphasized that the Western direction was the only one where Russian national security interests have not really been challenged. Moscow should have good relations with NATO to allow free hands in coping with the "arch of instability" extending from the Black Sea and North Caucasus through Central Asia further on to China (Trenin 1994).

The liberals pointed out that NATO was not an aggressive or totalitarian military organization. Rather, NATO is an alliance of democracies (Kortunov 1996, 75). It is a defensive rather than offensive security organization. The liberals maintained that Russia has to focus on its domestic problems such as economic decline, organized crime, environmental decay, nationalism and separatism which they consider much more dangerous than NATO enlargement. They proposed that Russian diplomacy should be focused not on resistance to NATO expansion, but on dialogue with NATO on disarmament and confidence-building (Churkin 1995).

More generally, NATO has been regarded as a mechanism that helped modernize societies, overcome nationalistic aberrations, and condition the thinking and behavior of new political elites (Kortunov 1996: 76). Some liberal analysts even believed that "national humiliation" experienced by Russia in the case of NATO enlargement was useful for the future democratic transformation of this country. According to some accounts, NATO's extension forced Yeltsin (a) to progress with economic reforms; (b) to pay more attention to Russia's neighbors such as Belarus, China, Iran, and Japan; and (c) to start real military reform (Makarov 1997: 9). According to the liberals, NATO overreacted to Milosevic's Kosovo politics by bombing Serbia but should remain Russia's main partner in ensuring European security (Orlov 1999, 15; Trenin 1999, 1, 4).

Realists and idealists disagree on the nature of the post-Cold War European security model. In the 1990s, realists believed that in an age of multipolarity only a flexible pan-European security system could guarantee a balance of power on the continent and the national sovereignty of particular countries. They hoped that the OSCE, the only organization where Russia acted on an equal footing with other major Western powers, could be the core of such a security system. Liberals, however, were quite pessimistic as regards the possibility of creating an effective pan-European structure where Russia could have a major say. According to Zagorski (Zagorski and Lucas 1993, 77–107; Zagorski 1996, 67), a "Big Europe" was emerging as a result of the expansion of West European and trans-Atlantic institutions rather than on the basis of the only pan-European organization such as the OSCE. Transformation of these organizations and especially of the EU into the pillars of a "Big Europe" could not but result in the marginalization of current pan-European structures, in particular of the OSCE. This reduced the available options for Russia's integration into European developments.

The main objective of Russia's foreign policy should not be joining Western European organizations, but using cooperation with them to facilitate its own integration into the world economy and the community of democratic states. This aim might be attained not only through membership, but also by creating mechanisms of "extra-institutional" cooperation between Russia and the EU, NATO and other organizations. For example, the liberals were satisfied with projects and initiatives such as EU's Northern Dimension that aimed at integrating Russia's north-western regions into the single European economic, social and cultural space or Russia-NATO 20 (19 + 1) cooperative format (Ryabov 2003, 14).

In the 2000s, however, the Russian foreign policy schools' views on the European security architecture and its institutions have significantly changed. While the realists became increasingly skeptical about the OSCE and the possibility to create a viable regional security system on its basis, the liberals, on the contrary, put this organization in the center of the European security order. For example, the draft of a European Security Treaty (EST) proposed by then President Dmitry Medvedev (November 2009) was obviously inspired by the liberal / globalist idea of a "Greater Europe" ("Europe from the Atlantic Ocean to the Urals). The EST draft outlined the contours of a new European security architecture and proposed the idea of a special security treaty of binding nature (Medvedev 2009).

The Medvedev initiative aimed to the revival of the OSCE as the only pan-European security organization where all countries of the region (including Russia) acted on the equal footing. Over the last decade (especially after the 1999 Kosovo war) the OSCE has been nearly paralyzed, and other international organizations (NATO and, to some extent, the EU) have claimed the role of leading security guarantors on the continent. Russia has expressed discontent with this situation and aspired to a more equal position in the European security system. At the same time, the EST draft envisioned a greater role for other regional organizations (EU, CIS, CSTO) in providing security on the European continent. Despite some criticism of the EST draft (Sushko 2009–2010; Trenin 2009; Tsypkin 2009), the Russian liberals have fully supported Medvedev's initiative and later expressed their disappointment with the position of the EU and NATO member states which did not endorse this idea.

Presently, liberal school's attitude to the OSCE is rather contradictory. On the one hand, the liberals are quite critical about the role of this organization in conflict prevention, management and resolution, including the Georgian (2008) and Ukrainian (2014) ones. The Russian liberal analysts believe that the OSCE was often too slow and indecisive, its capacities and mandates were too limited and implementation process was inefficient. As for the conflict in the Ukrainian south-east the liberals often accused the OSCE Special Monitoring Mission to Ukraine of being biased (in favor of Kiev).

The liberals have also dropped (at least for a while) the idea of making the OSCE a backbone of future European security architecture. Rather, the liberals have more pragmatic and shorter-term plans to use the OSCE for solving existing problems, including the conflict in and around Ukraine.

However, on the other hand, the liberal school is not interested in further marginalization of the OSCE because it remains the only pan-European institution where Russia acts on equal footing and the only authoritative conflict management mechanism available to Moscow for the time-being. Given the deep crisis in relations between Russia and two powerful security actors in Europe—the EU and NATO—because of the Ukraine crisis, it seems unlikely that a fully-fledged partnership will be formed with them in the mid-term perspective.

The Russian liberal experts suggested a number of improvements to revive the OSCE and secure its key role in the European security system (Tauscher and Ivanov 2015, 18–20; Zagorski 2014):

- To develop a code of conduct for the OSCE member-states in the areas they define as most problematic.

- To adopt an OSCE Charter (constituent document), which could help to transform the organization from a regional arrangement into a full-fledged treaty-based regional organization under Chapter VIII of the UN Charter. The Charter would reaffirm, in a legally binding form, the *modus operandi* of the OSCE, its structures and institutions, as it has been established to date by relevant decisions of the OSCE decision-making bodies.

- To approve a Convention on the International Legal Personality, Legal Capacity, and Privileges and Immunities of the OSCE that was finalized in 2007 but was not signed to date.

- To expand the OSCE Conflict Prevention Center's powers as regards conflict monitoring and early conflict prevention.

- To resume the pan-European dialogue on conventional arms control in the framework of the OSCE Forum for Security Cooperation.

- To revive discussions within the OSCE on the modernization of the Vienna Document on confidence and security-building measures.

As far as the global security regime is concerned the Russian liberals are anxious about the decreasing role of international organizations and international law and the rise of unilateralism in the aftermath of 9.11 (Volkov 2003, 7). There was a split among the liberals on the nature of the emerging world order. One part of the liberals insisted that Russia should aim at restoring of the crucial role of international organizations and law in world affairs. Particularly, they advised the Russian government to bring the Iraqi question back to UN and handle it within the world community rather than within the "coalition of winners" (Ivanov 2003, 1, 6). Other group of liberals is close to the realist camp by suggesting to switch from traditional international organizations to more flexible and informal institutions (such as G-7 / 8) and the "concert of powers" model (Bausin 2003, 2). They hope that this could help to prevent the complete collapse of the world order and keep the chaos of international politics at the manageable phase.

Although liberals are unable to dominate or even influence Russian IR discourse significantly, they play a useful role by challenging realism / geopolitics and providing these schools with an intellectual alternative.

Globalism

The Russian globalist IR paradigm consists of several schools. First of all, there are two main versions of Marxist-inspired political thought in Russia. The first is more traditional and is exemplified by the Communist Party of the Russian Federation (CPRF), led by Gennady Zyuganov. The second one is close to social democracy and has been developed by certain organizations and authors such as the Gorbachev Fund, Alexander Yakovlev, Dmitri Furman and so on. The former group can be called traditionalists, whilst the latter can be named Social Democrats.

Traditionalists. The Communists have been unable to reconcile themselves to the demise of the Soviet Union and to the country's loss of great power status. They believe that Gorbachev and Yeltsin led the USSR to defeat in the Cold War and finally to its collapse. These two leaders are regarded in fact as national traitors (Elections 1995, 7).

As some pro-Communist experts have suggested, in the search for a national security doctrine Russia should choose between two alternatives: the domination of national-state interests over cosmopolitan ones and Russia's independent position in the international relations system; or an orientation towards "Western values and the joining to a "community of civilized countries" (Podberezkin 1996, 86). The CPRF opts for the first alternative. The Communists emphasize the invariable nature of the country's national interests, which do not depend on a concrete regime or dominant ideology. They believe that the main Russian national interest inherited from its history consists of preserving the country's territorial and spiritual integrity. The idea of a powerful state based on multi-ethnicity is equivalent to the Russian national idea. Thus, the breakdown of the Soviet Union and weakening of the Russian state have undermined Russian security and worsened its geostrategic position.

As for threat perceptions, pro-Communist analysts have singled out some global developments that could challenge Russian national security (Podberezkin 1996, 88): (1) resurgent powers that aim at changing their regional and global status and which may affect the world power balance (Germany, Japan, China, India, Brazil, South Africa); (2) the rise of regionalism in the world (such as EU, NAFTA, ASEAN) which could potentially increase Russia's isolation; (3) the aggravation of global social, economic and environmental problems; and (4) a decrease in the significance of nuclear deterrent force and the rise of unstable regional alliances with high conflict potential.

The Communists have also advocated a number of measures to prevent a further weakening of Russia's international authority (Podberezkin 1996, 88): (1) the non-expansion of United Nations (UN) Security Council membership; (2) strengthening the UN Security Council's role in peace-keeping and solving of international conflicts with minimal Russian involvement in peace-keeping operations; (3) improving the nuclear non-proliferation regime; (4) observing the principle of equality and reciprocity in concluding nuclear arms control agreements with the United States; and (5) opposing the scheme "Europe without Russia" or attempts to replace the OSCE with NATO as the principal security organization on the continent.

The Communists believe that Russia is not part of the West nor of the East. It should define its own, independent way. At the same time, the Communists are not really fascinated with Eurasianism, seeing both Russian and world history as the result of objective processes rather than messianic ideas. However, they acknowledge the need for a national ideal or doctrine that could consolidate Russian society (Podberezkin 1995, 89).

Moreover, a number of regional priorities could be identified as part of the Communist foreign policy platform. Similar to the Eurasianists and the *derzhavniki,* the Communists regard the CIS and "near abroad" as the first priority for Moscow's foreign policy. As they believe that the Soviet Union has been dissolved illegally, the Communists have tried to foster the reunification of the former Soviet republics. Even so, they have ruled out the use of force to restore the USSR. According to Zyuganov, this should be done on a 'voluntary basis' (Pushkov 1995, 4; Zyuganov 1995, 86). Along with some liberals and nationalists, the Communists have put pressure on the Yeltsin government to protect Russian minorities abroad.

The Communists believe that the breakdown of the Warsaw Pact, Russian troop withdrawals from Eastern Europe and the loss of Moscow's control over this region have generated new threats to Russia's security (Elections 1995, 7). The CPRF has pointed out that NATO's eastward expansion violates the strategic balance in Europe in a number of ways. The enlargement inevitably destroys the existing "security buffer" between Russia and NATO. It also brings NATO's military presence to Russia's borders, including military bases and probably nuclear weaponry. Furthermore, it may provoke a Russian military build-up on its western and north-western borders, and accelerate the creation of a military alliance within the CIS, while resuming the confrontation between the East and the West on the military bloc basis. It may also challenge Ukraine and Moldova's status as neutral states, cause the collapse of the Conventional Forces in Europe (CFE) Treaty,[6] and undermine the OSCE's role as the backbone of the European security system (Elections 1995, 8–9). The Communists have also pointed to NATO's Kosovo intervention as a "natural" result of NATO enlargement and warned that Kosovo-like operations next time could be repeated in the CIS space, including Russia (Guseinov 1999, 4).

According to other assessments, the aim of the United States is to undermine Russia's economic, scientific-technical, and military capabilities, and also to isolate Moscow from promising trade partners and markets (in particular, in areas such as advanced technologies and arms trade). The West's motive for doing so, it has been argued, is to hopefully prevent Russia's transformation into a potential rival (Podberezkin 1996, 90).

To put pressure on both the "pro-Western" Yeltsin government and NATO, the Communists undertook some measures through their faction in the parliament. That faction has proposed to revise the CFE Treaty in accordance with the "new realities" and voiced its negative attitude to ratification of the START II Treaty[7] until the United States and NATO have changed their position on the Alliance's extension. The Communists have again threatened to restart discussion of Russia's participation in the PfP program (Zyuganov 1997, 20–23). Finally, the CPRF faction has, together with the Liberal Democrats, urged the government to oppose the NATO countries' drive in the Balkans through bilateral channels and multilateral institutions. During the Kosovo war the Communists also suggested the

---

6   Treaty on Conventional Armed Forces in Europe, signed in Paris on 19 November 1990.
7   Treaty between the United States and USSR on the Reduction and Limitation of Strategic Offensive Arms.

lifting of the arms embargo and sending of the most advanced Russian weaponry to Serbia. They strongly objected to the resumption of Russian-NATO dialogue in early 2000 saying that this might encourage NATO to make further interventions (Migranyan 1999, 1, 6; Zaitsev 1999, 3).

The *derzhavniki* and realists agreed in principle with the Communists on their assessment of the implications of NATO's enlargement and the Kosovo war. However, they pointed out that it was wrong in the first place to represent the NATO member-states as a completely united organization with regard to enlargement and the Kosovo intervention, and to ignore the difference of opinion between various political forces on the pace and scope of enlargement and the necessity of the "humanitarian intervention" in the Balkans. They also stressed that the decision on enlargement has been made in an attempt to overcome NATO's identity crisis and to cope with post-Cold War threats rather than being targeted against Russia. The same was true in case of the Kosovo war. NATO intended to demonstrate that it was the only security organization that can effectively solve security problems on the continent. Lastly, they argued that there could be a compromise between the Alliance and Russia to guarantee Moscow's security and minimize both the enlargement's or the Kosovo war's detrimental effects. Such compromises were finally achieved at the Paris summit (May 1997) and during the series of Russian-NATO meetings in early 2000 (Rogov 1997, 9; Trenin 1999, 1, 4).

The Communists, however, did not stop criticizing the Kremlin for its "appeasement policies" with regard to NATO. For example, they heavily criticized the Putin administration for "swallowing" the 2004 round of NATO's eastward expansion that included three post-Soviet republics (Communist Party of the Russian Federation 2011).

As for other regions, the Communists have proposed to restore Russia's links with its traditional friends and allies such as Iraq, Libya, North Korea, and Cuba (Communist Party of the Russian Federation 2011). This could prevent America's unchallenged world-wide leadership and provide Russia with profitable orders for its troubled arms industry. They have accepted a *detente* in Sino-Russian relations as well as active arms export policy in the region because it strengthens Russia's international authority and supports the defense industry. Many leaders of the CPRF are fascinated with the Chinese model of socialism and believe that Gorbachev should have used the PRC's experience to reform the Soviet Union. At the same time, the CPRF is concerned with the future security orientation of China and the correlation of forces in the Asia-Pacific area which is turning out to be quite unfavorable for Russia (Zyuganov 1995, 87).

The CPRF has strongly supported President Putin's 2014 decision to reintegrate Crimea to Russia and support the Donbass rebels. They also supported the Kremlin in its military intervention to the Syrian conflict (Polyakov 2016). The Communists, however, noted that these moves should be made in a more decisive way, irregardless the Western opinion.

It should be noted that, unlike in the domestic sphere, the CPRF has failed to produce any coherent and clearly pronounced foreign policy doctrine. Instead, it has operated with an amalgam of the party leadership's statements and remarks, which have made it difficult to reconstruct the CPRF's foreign policy platform. Despite its significant domestic influence, the CPRF has, in fact, been unable to influence the Russian discourse on IR theory.

The Social Democrats

After his resignation in December 1991, Mikhail Gorbachev and a number of his close friends (Aleksandr Yakovlev and Georgi Shakhnazarov being the most prominent among them) committed themselves to the creation of a social-democratic movement in Russia to confront *inter alia* the Communist-nationalist coalition. The Gorbachev Fund and the journal *Svobodnaya Mysl* (Liberal Thought) became the most important pillars for the emerging social democracy in Russia. Although the so-called Social Democrats failed to form any influential political coalition comparable with the *derzhavniki,* the Communists or Zhirinovskiy, they were able to produce some foreign policy concepts, which affected the Russian IR discourse.

Similar to the Eurasianists, Social Democratic security thinking has focused on the concept of stability. Internal stability has been defined as cohesion within the political system, adherence to normal democratic procedures concerning the rotation of ruling elites, the absence of pressing ethnic and social conflicts, and a healthy functioning economy (Bogomolov 1994, 142). International stability has been seen as the balance of interests among major international players (contrary to the balance of power in the past) (Kolikov 1994, 12).

Along with other schools of thought, the Social Democrats have contributed to the Russian discussion of national interests. Contrary to the Gorbachev doctrine of 1980s that was grounded on the unconditional priority of "all-human" interests over national interests, the Social Democrats have admitted that national interests is the subject of primary concern for any country. They define national interests as a manifestation of the nation's basic needs (survival, security, progressive development) (Brutents 2014; Krasin 1996). National interests may be subjective in terms of their form or way of expression, but they are definitely objective in terms of their nature. In a nation-state, national interests are usually synonymous with state interests. In multi-national countries (like Russia) the articulation and representation of national interests are a much more complicated process involving numerous political actors and requiring more time and effort to achieve a public consensus.

The Social Democrats, however, do not limit themselves to the acknowledgement of the significance of national interests. They believe that in an interdependent world international actors cannot afford to solely pursue their own interests. Since the international environment has become multi-dimensional, the actors should take into account both the national interests of other players and universal (all-human) interests. According to the Social Democrats, narrow-minded nationalism is absolutely outdated and detrimental not only to the world community but, in the end, also to a nation conducting a nationalist policy (Utkin 1995a; 1995b, 1–2). They realize that democracy in the international relations system is still in its infancy, and few "all-human" values have taken root in humankind's mentality The Social Democrats regard the creation of a global civil society as the only way of replacing national interests with "all-human" values. In their view, a world civil society could be based on a system of horizontal links between both inter-governmental and non-governmental organizations dealing with economic, political, environmental and cultural issues (Krasin 1996, 12). Some experts have proposed the creation of a world government to resolve global problems and to save humankind from imminent catastrophe (Shakhnazarov 1996: 79). Thus, the Kantian (1795 / 1957) project of 'perpetual peace'—the methodological basis of the NPT and its current proponents—could be put into practice.

The Social Democrats perceive the world as moving from a unipolar (United States as the only superpower) towards a multipolar structure. None of the countries or ideologies will be able to impose its model on the others. The Social Democrats disagree with Fukuyama's (1992) thesis on the world-wide domination of the liberal-democratic model. Various civilizational models will compete in the foreseeable future. A future world will be born out of the process of the interaction of two contradictory processes—integration and regionalization. The future poles of power will emerge on the basis of economic, religious, and cultural differentiation.

Some analysts distinguish Arab-Muslim, Europe-centric (including the United States), Eurasian (including Eastern Europe), South Atlantic, Indian, and Asia-Pacific centers ((Andreev and Petukhov 2015; Dakhin 1995, 85). Others point to North America, the EU, Eurasia, the Islamic world, and Asia-Pacific as the main future poles (Kolikov 1994, 13). In any case, these developments will make the world less predictable and more multidimensional than has been the case so far.

Which identity should Russia choose? The Social Democrats usually pay tribute to the Eurasian geographical position of the country, but they emphasize that, from a cultural and civilizational point of view, Russia is part of Europe and Russians are part of the European nation (Gorbachev 1992; Kolikov 1994, 5). For that reason, Russia should aim at entering pan-European economic, political, and security structures. "Europe" is also defined in a civilizational rather than geographical sense: the Gorbachevian project of a Common European House or "Europe from Vancouver to Vladivostok" is still popular among the Russian Social Democrats (Andreev and Petukhov 2015).

The Social Democrats have proposed a model of "multidimensional partnership" that is directed at co-operation with the major players of the world regardless of their geographical location. According to this model, Russia's policy should not be based on playing geopolitical "cards" (Chinese, American, European). Instead, it should be oriented to establishing long-term and stable bilateral relations as well as to promoting multilateralism (Andreev and Petukhov 2015; Brutents 2014; Voskresenskiy 1996, 99). However, it remains unclear which methods should be used to create such relations and how to convince other powers to accept this model.

To sum up, the social-democratic foreign policy doctrine has taken over many concepts and principles of Gorbachev's NPT. The latter, however, was complemented with some advocacy of Russia's national interests and balanced policies towards the East and the West.

The environmentalists. The environmentalist version of Russian globalism was one of the first to re-define the concept of security in the post-Soviet period. As Academician Alexei Yablokov, the leader of the Russian "greens" in the 1990s said at the conference on Russian foreign policy doctrine in February 1992, "National security is no longer purely military. I am sure that Russia's national security is environmental by at least one-third" (A Transformed Russia in a New World 1992, 98). Contrary to military or geopolitical threats which are mainly hypothetical, ecology directly affects the nation's economy, health and climate.

Under the pressure of environmentalism, nearly all leading schools of foreign policy thought included an ecological dimension in their concepts of security. A special section on ecological security was put into the National Security Concepts of the Russian Federation of 1997 (Yeltsin 1997, 4–5).

Environmentalists believe that traditional diplomatic methods are not sufficient for resolving ecological problems which have now tended to become global rather than national or regional. They believe that Russia, along with the entire world, should develop New Thinking based on a common interest in survival in the face of global problems (Plimak 1996, 42–52).

Environmentalists are quite radical in their recommendations regarding solutions to global problems. They recommend the dissolution of political boundaries and a de-ideologizing of international relations (of course, except for environmentalism itself). In order to cope with ecological problems, they say that humankind should be able to forecast both the near and distant future, considering all the components of these problems in their historical and physical developments. Since only scientists are able to make good forecasts, this stratum should be elevated to the very top of society and charged with political management as well. National and international economies should be based on new technologies targeted at the rational exploitation of natural resources. Contrary to public and private properties, cooperative property will be the best form of ownership to deal with environmental issues. Furthermore, trans-national rather than national bodies should be in charge of global problems as nation-states are unable to cope with them any longer (Burlak 1992, 16–24).

According to the environmentalists, managing ecological problems is merely the first step in humankind's progressive development. The main objective looming ahead is to move from a program of survival to that of sustainable development. The latter can be described as a social order based on harmonious relations with nature and the prevention of major internal and external threats to stability and social well-being (Belkin and Storozhenko 1995, 32–41).

It goes without saying that these ideas are by no means original. Russian environmentalists have borrowed many of them from their foreign 'colleagues'. The Rome Club papers, the Brundtland Commission report, and the ideas of Bertrand Russell are among the most authoritative theoretical sources for the Russian ecologists (Burlak 1992, 20–21).

However, the environmentalists have been less successful in their attempts to influence Russian discourse on future security challenges. Russian foreign policy makers and analysts regard this part of environmental-ists' problematique an exotic intellectual exercise which is hardly relevant for present-day Russia. They are concerned with Russia's compelling needs (including some ecological issues) rather than with challenges in the distant future. However, this situation may change if Russia is able to resolve its most acute social and economic problems, and hence is more able to pay attention to ecology.

Peace research school. PRS is one more globalist school in Russia. Methodologically it is based on Johan Galtung's (1964 and 1969) theory of structural violence which is very popular among the Russian peace researchers (Vorkunova 2009). This school tries to explain why the vio-lence is deeply embedded both in the society and international relations system. This group of peace researchers believes that the structural vio-lence as a socio-political phenomenon is deeply rooted in the capitalist society and economy and constantly reproduced by the capitalist mode of production. They believe that the forms of contemporary exploitation are different from those depicted by Marx, Engels and Lenin but the essence of this phenomenon is still the same and it will continue to generate vio-lence and conflicts both domestically and internationally.

It is interesting to note that along with the structural violence, its cul-tural variation is increasingly becoming a popular theme within the Rus-sian peace research. The critical peace researchers believe that in the era of global communications the cultural violence can be even more ef-fective than its direct or structural versions. They note that the so-called 'color' revolutions in the post-Soviet space and Arab countries were often generated or at least facilitated by the West with the help of public diplo-macy based on the cultivation of liberal / democratic values among the local youth and political opposition. For this school, the cultural violence can be even more dangerous than other forms of violence because it not only reinforces other 'angles' of the 'conflict triangle' (Galtung and Jacob-sen 2000) but it can also have long-term negative and unexpected effects (Kubyshkin and Tzvetkova 2013; Sergunin and Karabeshkin 2015; Ste-panov 2014; Vorkunova 2009).

The peace research school notes that in general usage 'peace' con-veys the notion of 'the absence of war' and not any particular ideal condi-tion of society. This broad consensus view of peace is, of course, unsatis-factory from the point of view of this peace research sub-school since we need to know more about the nature of a possible world without armed conflict. According to Galtung (1985 and 2006), peace seen merely as the absence of war is considered to be 'negative peace' and the concept of 'positive peace' has been used to describe a situation in which there is neither physical violence nor legalized repression. Under conditions of positive peace, war is not only absent, it is unanticipated and essentially unthinkable. A state of positive peace involves large elements of reciprocity, equality, and joint problem-solving capabilities. There have been many different proposals as to the positive definitions: integration, justice, harmony, equity, freedom, etc., all of which call for further conceptualization. Analytically, peace is conceptualized by the Russian scholars in a series of discrete categories ranging from various degrees and states of conflict to various states of co-operation and integration (Sergunin 2015).

The dominant trend in the Russian peace research is to interpret peace as synonymous to the category of sustainable development (Samarin 2008; Sergunin 2015; Stepanov 2014). Some scholars believe that 'positive' peace can be seen as a sort of a social order where not only violence, exploitation and major security threats are absent but also the favorable conditions for human creativity are provided (Sergunin 2012; Vorkunova 2009).

As far as the PRS' positions on conflict resolution and mediation (CRM) are concerned it offers a broader understanding of conflict than other IR paradigms. The PRS approach is based on the assumption that conflicts are a natural product of various contradictory processes in the society. The PRS does not reduce the causes of conflict to the legal ones (as, for example, the liberals do); among the sources of conflict peace researchers identify the economic, social, identity, political, military, environmental, cultural, ideological, religious and other factors (Bikbulatova 2009; Dmitriev 2000: 76–93; Orlyanski 2007: 19–22; Sergunin 2015).

Thereafter, the PRS does not limit the CRM methods and techniques to the legal instruments and procedures. This school believes that to resolve a conflict and preclude its reemergence, its causes should be eliminated first and foremost. For this reason, this school's CRM arsenal is much richer and more complex. In addition to the instruments that the 'legalists' suggest (e.g. negotiations, cease-fire, truce and peace agreements, peace-keeping and peaceenforcement mechanisms, etc.), peace researchers offer a broad agenda for post-conflict peace-building and development that envisage a radical transformation of the society and its institutions with the aim to eradicate the causes of the conflict (Sergunin 2015; Stepanov et al. 2007; Stepanova 2003).

To prevent new conflicts the PRS suggests creating an early warning / monitoring mechanism. The latter should be based on a system of indicators that should monitor dangerous developments and identify conflict-prone areas. Such a system could be helpful in detecting and preventing conflicts at an early phase.

In contrast with the legalist approach which relates the CRM activities basically to the state and statist instruments, the PRS believes that conflicts can be resolved and lasting peace is possible if not only governments but also societies talk to each other and develop non-hierarchical, horizontal contacts. That's why peace researchers welcome an active participation of non-state actors in the CRM activities: people-to-people, NGO-to-NGO, company-to-company contacts, the so-called 'people's' or 'civil diplomacy' (Sergunin 2015).

Despite its marginal positions in the Russian expert-analytical community, the PRS continues to provide the Russian scholarship with innovative approaches and useful insights into basic IR issues such as causes of war and conflict, nature, sources and manifestations of violence, essence and ways of achieving both 'negative' and 'positive peace', transformation of the international relations system in the post-Cold War era and so on (Sergunin 2015). In addition, this type of research continues to challenge Russia's predominant IR paradigms, thus forcing them to develop their concepts, argumentation and research techniques.

The "right radicals"

There are a number of radical and extremist organizations in Russia. They were united primarily by their rejection of Yeltsin's domestic reforms and by criticism of his pro-Western foreign policy. At the same time, there are also major disagreements about both the meaning of Russian history and the appropriate model for the future. Hence, they have been unable to go beyond negativism and to develop a coherent, forward-looking agenda of their own.

The Liberal Democratic Party of Russia (LDPR) led by Vladimir Zhirinovskiy is the most important of the right radical organizations. The LDPR faction was the largest one in the Russian Duma in 1993–95. The party also had influential positions within the Russian parliament in 1995–99.

It is difficult to reconstruct Zhirinovskiy's foreign policy concept due to the lack of its elementary logic and the extravagant form of expression of his ideas. One should take into account his many statements that often contradict each other. It seems that Zhirinovskiy prefers geopolitics as his theoretical basis, but at the same time he may borrow some ideas belonging to other schools of thought. All these circumstances should be taken into account in the process of analysing Zhirinovskiy's foreign policy views.

According to Alexei Mitrofanov, the former LDPR representative in the Committee for International Affairs of the State Duma, Russia's national interests included (Elections 1995, 11):

- creating more favorable international conditions for the country's economic and political development;

- securing the country's national security and international stability;

- restoring Russia's strategic boundaries and its historical geopolitical space;

- restoring the Russian state within its natural frontiers, primarily bringing Ukraine and Belarus back to Russia;

- regaining Russia's rights to the ports in the Black and Baltic seas as well as passages to Western Europe;

- restoring Russia's role as a world superpower, which is consonant with its geopolitical predestination; and

- preventing any outside interference in Russia's internal affairs.

The "near abroad" was priority no. 1 for the LDPR. On the one hand, the LDPR's leaders have called for the end of Russian assistance to other former republics of the Soviet Union and have declared that they did not want them as part of Russia, at least in the near future. On the other hand, however, he has also envisaged a Russia that includes all the territory of the former Soviet Union, suggesting that the former republics will experience further trouble and seek to subordinate themselves to Russia for economic and security reasons. As for Russia itself, he has suggested a new, expanded Russia which would have no separate republics based on nationality, and Russians would be essentially *primus inter pares,* with other nationalities allowed to maintain their cultural but not political identities (Komsomolskaya Pravda, 22 January 1994).

As for Russia's relations with Ukraine, at the film premiere of the film *Taras Bulba* in 2009 Zhirinovsky stated: "Everyone who sees the film will understand that Russians and Ukrainians are one people—and that the enemy is from the West" (Barry 2012). In February 2010 he claimed that Eastern Ukraine would become part of Russia "in five years" claiming that "the population is largely Russian" and called President-elect of Ukraine Viktor Yanukovych "basically Russian". With the start of the 2014 Ukrainian crisis Zhirinovsky supported reintegration of Crimea to the Russian Federation and the Donbas rebels. He has also strongly endorsed the concept of Novorossiya, that aimed at secession of eastern and southern regions from Ukraine, and even suggested himself as a potential president of a new state (http://www.ntv.ru/novosti/1207197/).

The Baltic States, according to Zhirinovskiy, would be part of Russia, except for Tallinn, which would be a separate city-state, and three cities in Lithuania which would form a small Lithuanian state. Koenigsberg might some day be returned to Germany. On 10 August 2014, Zhirinovsky threatened Poland and Baltic states with carpet bombing, doom and wiping out (http://www.interpretermag.com/russia-this-week-roots-of-pro-rus sian-separatists-in-russian-ultranationalist-groups/).

With respect to Finland, Zhirinovskiy has emphasized that there would be 'no problem' (Elections 1995, 11). But if Finland were to seek the return of Karelia, then all of Finland would have to be ceded to Russia (Morrison 1994, 109). In Zhirinovskiy's vision, Russians living outside Russia would be given dual citizenship and Russia would defend them, primarily with economic instruments of power.

In Eastern Europe, according to Zhirinovskiy, three cities in north-western Poland would become part of Germany, and Lvov in Ukraine might be given to Poland as compensation. He did not oppose Poland's joining NATO. On the other hand, he warned that the Eastern European countries could become Western servants and advised them to remain neutral. He also insisted on dissolving NATO because the Warsaw Pact had already been dissolved (Morrison 1994, 122).

In Zhirinovskiy's view, Slovakia might want to become part of Russia. The Czech Republic would go to Germany. Austria and Slovenia should unite, perhaps along with Germany. Bulgaria would get the Dobrudja portion of Romania. Greece should return Thrace to Bulgaria. In the former Yugoslavia, the Serbs, Croats, and Bosnians would all keep their existing borders. He proposed that all foreign or UN forces withdraw from the former Yugoslavia so that the warring parties could settle the conflict by themselves, but he also said that Russia and the Balkan states would together solve all the Balkans' problems (Morrison 1994, 100).

The LDPR considered the United States to be the principal anti-Russian power, intending to break Russia up into a multitude of states dependent on the West. However, due to American strength Russia is bound to co-operate with Washington in various fields, especially in the maintenance of international security (Elections 1995, 12; Ennis 2014).

Such cooperation, however, has its limits when Russia's vital interests are at stake like, for instance, in the case of the Ukrainian crisis which, Zhirinovsky maintains, was provoked by the U.S. He still believes that Russia is the target of a global plot orchestrated by the United States and involving fighters from the self-styled Islamic State and nationalist Ukrainian troops. "America is everywhere, the West is everywhere, NATO is everywhere. Everything is organized against Russia," Zhirinovsky said during a talk show on Channel One, Russia's most popular TV station (Ennis 2014).

In his early book, Zhirinovskiy (1993) proclaimed as a geopolitical concept the necessity for Russia to gain access to the Mediterranean Sea and Indian Ocean by military conquest. Viewing this 'last dash' as the "task of saving the Russian nation", he argued that Russia needed to secure access to these warm water routes in order to thrive, and that it needed to subjugate its southern neighbors in the Caucasus, Central Asia, Turkey, Iran, and Afghanistan to eliminate threats posed by pan-Turkism and pan-Islamism. He claimed that Ankara was planning to establish a greater Turkey reaching from the Adriatic to Tajikistan. This would allow Turkey to dominate Slavic populations in the former Yugoslavia and Bulgaria, while placing extreme pressure on Russia *via* the Caucasus and Central Asia. He argued that Moscow must fight back by leading a pan-Slavic and an anti-Turkish alliance, perhaps in partnership with a resurgent Germany. He suggested that a military conquest to the south would be the basis for a renaissance of a Russian military that has fallen on hard times in the 1990s (Izvestiya, 21 January 1994).

In November 2015, after the incident of a Russian jet plane shot-down by a Turkish F-16 after an alleged air-space violation, Zhirinovsky said that Russia must detonate a nuclear bomb on the Bosphoros, to create a 10 meters high tsunami wave that would wipe out at least 9 Million Istanboulites in a speech he gave to Duma (http://argumenti.ru/society/2015/11/425179).

With regard to the Russian-Japanese relations Zhirinovsky proposed at some point to sell the disputed Kurile Islands to Japan for 50 billion USD (http://news.bbc.co.uk/2/hi/europe/667745.stm).

According to Zhirinovskiy, a religious war between Islam and Christianity can take place in the foreseeable future. Only Russia could prevent such a war. He commented that "Russia could be a factor for stability It could stop the process of disintegration in Europe, the Balkans, and Central Asia [...]" (Morrison 1994, 125).

In an interview, Zhirinovskiy projected a trilateral German-Russian-Indian axis, linking together an expanded Germany, a new Russia that would include most of the former Soviet Union and some additional territory; and India. With some two billion people linked together, Zhirinovskiy imagined that the world would take whatever form this axis imposed upon it. India and Russia together could neutralize China, and Germany and Russia could either neutralize or control Europe (Morrison 1994, 110–111). Namely, the LDPR fears Chinese "ethnic aggression" against the Russian Far East and favored using tough economic, administrative, and military methods to stop Beijing (Elections 1995, 13). However, after his 2005 visit to China Zhrinovsky said that the "Chinese threat" to Russia is exaggerated (http://viperson.ru/articles/zhirinovskiy-likvidiroval-kitaysku yu-ugrozu).

Despite the influence of the Liberal Democrats in domestic affairs, their impact on foreign policy issues has been moderate. The "Zhirinovskiy phenomenon" has shifted Russian security debates slightly to the right, but has had no direct effect on official foreign policy and military doctrines as well as on theoretical discourse.

Postpositivism in Russia?

Until recently, Russian scholarship has been quite indifferent to postmodernism as a school of Western political thought. The Russian academic community has mainly ignored both the postmodern problematique and the discussions around it. Indeed, prior to the 2000s many Russian theorists were not even aware of this particular school. In the 1990, when postmodernism has gained its momentum in the Western social sciences, few Russian philosophers and historians have tried to implement postmodernist approaches to their research (Kharitonovich 1995, 248–50; Vizgin 1995, 116–126). In the meantime, some political scientists have studied postmodernism as one of the Western schools of political thought (Konyshev and Sergunin 2013; Makarychev and Sergunin 1996; Sergunin and Makarychev 1999).

Predominantly postmodernism was regarded as being irrelevant for Russian political discourse. Russian foreign policy experts were especially unfriendly to postmodernism because, they thought, it neither provided them with a theoretical framework for producing national interests or geopolitical concepts nor with practical advice on concrete issues. However, some have suggested that a certain postmodern insight could be evolving in Russia due to some peculiarities in the national mentality. Russians have never been happy with the project of modernity grounded on rationalism, a belief in linear progress and the decisive role of science and knowledge. Even Marxism, a typical product of modernity has been adapted to Russian conditions. Russians have never perceived other civilizations as hostile; on the contrary, they have been quite open to dialogue with other civilizations and cultures.

However, even in the 1990s, there was growing feeling among Russian scholars that the country has already entered the postmodern epoch. There are completely new temporal and spatial dimensions in which individuals and society live in the period of transition. Moral values and individual perceptions of the surrounding world have significantly changed as well. At the same time, Russia's economic and technological potential, social structure, and political system still remain in the age of modernity. This typically postmodern discrepancy between an individual's material conditions and his / her psychological and spiritual orientations was gradually emerging as a fashionable theme in Russian social science literature in the 1990s. In her essay published by the main Russian political science journal *Polis,* Busygina (1995) depicted a mysterious urban world of *post-perestroika* Moscow representing a mixture of Soviet and capitalist, Russian and Western, values and modes of living.

Another adept in postmodernism believed that in the postmodern epoch politics has been freed from economics, ideology and intellectuality; it needs no longer any legitimacy, and power appears in its "pure sense"—as power for power itself (Kachanov 1995, 38). Other academics did not share the anti-rationalist and anti-foundationalist views of postmodernists but acknowledged the existence of the postmodern era with an absolutely new political system, actors and rules of the game which should be examined with new research methods (Panarin 1997, 93–123, 172–80).

It should be noted, however, that, in the 1990s, for many Russian academics postmodernism was simply a sort of "intellectual game" or "entertainment"'. When dealing with security issues, experts still turned to more traditional theories. At the same time, postmodernist thought has already begun to influence Russian foreign policy discourse in the 1990s—at least in areas such as modelling the new world order, Russia's place in world civilization, defining national interests, and so on. For example, Ilyin (1995, 48–9) rejected the very idea of postmodernity because he did not believe in the end of history or man. However, he offered a relatively postmodern world-view by describing the evolution of the international relations system from the Westphalian, Vienna, Versailles and Yalta models to the present one which emerged as a combination of nation-states with "post-urbanist mutations of civilizations" and "global villages / *choritikas"* (from Greek *choritika*—rural, country, territorial). The latter he interprets as transterritorial, transnational and global political systems based on telecommunications and political rhetoric.

Some Russian postmodernists applied the so-called grammatological civilizational model borrowed from the Western poststructuralists to explain the causes of conflict between different nations and civilizations. This model had pretensions of being more accurate than Huntington's notorious "clash of civilizations" theory. According to this model (Kuznetsov 1995, 98–99), a system of writing is a more important civilizational connecting link between members of a nation than, say, religion or culture. Present-day Russia, for instance, is a rather loose formation from a religious point of view but, in terms of writing (Cyrillic alphabet), it is far more homogeneous. Chinese dialects differ so greatly that language functions as a common vehicle only in writing.

There is a "war of alphabets" in the world: most of the peoples and groups now at war use different systems of writing, that is, they belong to different civilizations. Some groups either waging war or involved in some other conflict include: Serbs (Cyrillic alphabet; Orthodoxy)—Croats (Latin alphabet; Catholicism), common language, Serbo-Croatian; Nagorny Karabakh (Armenian alphabet, Armenian Church)—Azerbaijan (switching from the Cyrillic to the Latin alphabet; Islam); Greek Cypriots (Greek alphabet; Orthodoxy)—Turkish Cypriots (Latin alphabet; Islam); Russians (Cyrillic alphabet; Orthodoxy)—Chechens (who in 1992 tried to switch from the Cyrillic to the Latin alphabet) (Kuznetsov 1991, 96). In addition, there are parties to conflicts professing a common religion but using different alphabets: (1) Orthodoxes: Moldavians (Latin alphabet)—Transdniestr Republic composed of Russians and Ukrainians (Cyrillic alphabet); Abkhazians (Cyrillic alphabet)—Georgians (Georgian alphabet); Georgians (Georgian alphabet)—South Ossetes (Cyrillic alphabet); Greeks (Greek alphabet)—Macedonians (Cyrillic alphabet); (2) Muslims: central Tajik government (Cyrillic alphabet)—guerrillas (Arabic alphabet), *etc.* (Kuznetsov 1995, 97).

"Small" civilizations used to be a source of tensions in international relations because they struggle for their survival. They wage wars against more powerful civilizations, thereby making history. Postmodernists are very sceptical with regard to the capabilities of international organizations to cope with the destabilizing potential of "small" civilizations.

Adherents to the grammatological model, however, have found it difficult to convince many Russian scholars that a system of writing is the main source of intra- and international conflicts. This model (Kuznetsov 1995), they argue, describes the symptoms of conflict rather than its causes. Indeed, contrary to the grammatological explanation, one can find numerous examples of conflicts both between and inside nations using the same alphabet: intra-Arab conflicts, Latin America, China-Taiwan, wars between the European nations, civil wars (from American to Russian), and so on. At the same time, the grammatological model can be heuristically valuable for understanding the history of, and current borderlines between, various civilizations (Kuznetsov 1995).

As to security issues, Russian postmodernists argued that Russia should not base its policy on the concept of national interests. The latter, they believed, was "heuristically non-productive", "theoretically weak", and "politically harmful" (Kapustin 1996, 13).

The postmodernists have "deconstructed" the national interest concept in order to demonstrate its lack of meaning. For them, this concept is a mere camouflage for parochial interests. In reality, so-called national interests reflect neither a state's nor a nation's interests. Those, in fact, are interests of the elite, which runs the government. By imposing its perception of national interests on society the ruling elite tries to legitimize its dominance and control over both state and society. Each *stratum* or group has its own version of national interests, but only the most powerful group's version becomes officially recognized doctrine. This, however, does not mean that the success of any particular concept necessarily corresponds to the real interests of the majority of the country's population. For that reason, foreign policy based on *quasi*-national interests can be detrimental to a significant part of society (Kapustin 1996, 16–19).

While the national interest concept was useful and productive during the early modernity, today it represents merely a "conservative Utopia". The postmodernists have categorized this concept and the revival of realism in Russia and other countries as a "primitive communitarian response" to the dominance of universalism in the age of modernity. According to a postmodernist reading, the national interest concept tends to protect "speciality" (or even "exceptionalism") against "universality" which was imposed on humankind by the Enlightenment. But this extreme leads followers of the national interest concept to an intellectual and political dead-end. Theoretically, to prove your uniqueness or special rights over something you should—one way or another—use some universal matrix. Otherwise you have no criterion with which to compare different objects. Politically, by defending only its national interests a country could provoke an endless confrontation with other international actors (Kapustin 1996, 28).

The postmodernists have argued that the concept of national interest has become obsolete in the age of the global or world economy, information and communications. It does not fit into a new world order which presupposes that states give up a substantial part of their national sovereignty in favor of supranational organizations (including security matters).

The postmodernists warned that the search for Russian national interests may divert the country away from its path towards democracy. In a global sense, this can lead to confrontation with other powers, which deny universal values and pursue only national interests of their own. For them, liberal democracy *versus* Islamic fundamentalism, one ethnic nationalism against another, exemplifies such a confrontation. The only way out is to get rid of both extremes—universalism and communitarianism. The old universalities which proved either wrong or anti-democratic should be abandoned. Instead, new universal norms should be discovered based on multiculturalism, tolerance, self-criticism, and a dialogue culture (Kapustin 1996, 28). At the same time, however, the postmodernists have avoided building concrete models of security either for Russia or the world.

Since late 1990s the most recent version of postpositivism—social constructivism—has become popular in some Russian academic groupings. In contrast with postmodernism, social constructivists not only criticize / deconstruct traditional IR theories but also try to produce theoretical approaches of their own.

Russian social constructivists prefer to view international problems through the prism of the notion of 'identity'. If identities were formed in a confrontation way ('we' and 'others' approach) it may lead to a conflict between states, ethnic and religious groups, etc. If identities are built on the basis of a dialogue / tolerance principle it is conducive to international cooperation (Morozov 2006 and 2009).

Following the Barry Buzan and Ole Wæver's securitization theory, the Russian postpositivists believe that most of security threats are artificially construed by nations themselves (or—more exactly—by elites) (Morozov 2006). To adequately design its foreign policy Moscow should desecuritize its mentality and fundamentally revise its international priorities and relations with other countries and multilateral institutions.

Russian social constructivists mainly focus on regional / subregional issues or country-to-country relations. There are quite interesting constructivist studies on international security (Makarychev 2002, 88–94 and 2007; Medvedev 1998; Morozov 2006), trans-border cooperation (Makarychev 2005; Morozov 2005; Reut 2000), regionalism / globalism dichotomy (Makarychev 2002 and 2003), geographic / spacial dimensions of world politics (Zamyatin 2004) and EU-Russia relations (Makarychev 2006; Medvedev 1998 and 2006; Morozov 2009).

It is hard to believe that postpositivism could become an influential school in Russian foreign policy thinking in the foreseeable future. There are at least three main obstacles to the growth of their influence. *First,* Russia is still at the stage of trying to define its own national identity and, therefore, realist concepts such as national interests, national security, power balance and so forth will remain attractive both for academics and policy planners for many years. *Second,* those versions of postpositivism that limit themselves only to "deconstruction" are unable to produce any new theory (because they are opposing the very idea of theorizing). *Finally,* Western science has already passed the peak of postpositivist discourse (late 1980s-early 1990s) while Russia was still relatively isolated from these discussions. Thus, Western postpositivists probably missed their best opportunity to gain a following in Russia. Nevertheless, as Russia continues to progress with its reforms and opens up to greater international co-operation, it will inevitably face the postmodern *problematique.* Responses to postmodern challenges will not necessarily be given by the Western-like postmodernists; although perhaps they could be found by some other schools of thought.

A foreign policy consensus?

Along with the polarization of Russian foreign policy elites and public opinion, there was a clear tendency towards consensus on foreign policy since late 1990s. The NATO intervention in the Balkans in 1999 and post-9.11 events served as an additional spur to the emergence of such a consensus. The discussions of 1990s resulted in defining some common principles on which the major schools have agreed (see Figure 1). The contours of an emerging consensus could be described as follows:

1. Realism and geopolitics have become widely recognized theoretical concepts regardless of the schools' political and ideological orientations.

2. The priority is given to Russia's national interests; the secondary role is awarded to "all-human" or cosmopolitan values.

3. Russia should remain a great power with a major voice in the international community.

4. Other goals should not be given priority in Russia's foreign policy over the country's domestic needs. Foreign policy should serve

these needs rather than be a goal in itself (as it was often in the Soviet time).

5. Russia's main national interest consists of ensuring the country's security and territorial integrity.

6. Today, world security includes not only military and geopolitical but also societal, environmental, cultural and other dimensions vital to the individual and society.

7. Russia should not be biased in favor of either the West or the East. Instead, its policy should he even-handed and oriented to cooperation with all countries. In fact, a moderate version of Eurasianism was tacitly accepted by the Russian foreign policy elites.

8. Among Moscow's regional priorities, the "near abroad" is the most important one. Russia has special geopolitical, strategic, economic and humanitarian interests in the post-Soviet geopolitical space and should be recognized as an unchallenged leader in this area.

9. Russia should resist to the rise of American unilateralism but, at the same time, maintain a cooperative US-Russia agenda on issues such as fighting international terrorism, non-proliferation of weapons of mass destruction, arms control and disarmament.

10. Russia should be more assertive in voicing its specific interests in relations with the West. It should not hesitate to differ with Western views if Russia's vital interests are at stake.

11. Moscow should be more realistic in assessing the West's attitudes to Russia, in particular its position on Russia's admission to the Western economic, political and military institutions.

This consensus has made it possible to produce a number of governmental concepts and doctrines such as the foreign policy concepts (1993, 2000, 2008 and 2013), military doctrines (1993, 2000, 2010 and 2014) and national security concepts / strategies (1997, 2000, 2009 and 2015). It should be noted, however, that a consensus has been reached mainly on those issues dealing with Russia's immediate security needs. While many schools are able to identify threats to the country's security, they are still not ready to go beyond negativism and construct a positive security concept for the future.

Russian IR schools continue to differ on many important theoretical and practical issues: the meaning of Russia's national interests and security; the correlation between "hard" and "soft" security; the future of national sovereignty; the role of international organizations in ensuring national and international security; civilizational orientations; the use of military force in international relations; functional and regional priorities; particular ethnic, religious and territorial conflicts, and so on.

The Russian IR discourse still aims at responding to the fundamental question: what is Russia about? This discourse is a way to nation-building rather than to defining the country's future foreign policy and security agenda. This is hardly surprising, given Russia's newly born polity, culture and even boundaries, as well as its unfinished reforms. It is understandable why fairly old-fashioned approaches such as Eurasianism, realism, and geopolitics could come to dominate Russian security debates. As these concepts refer to national interest, national security, national sovereignty and territory they seem a reliable theoretical basis for searching for a national identity. Russian and other countries' experience shows that these concepts may provide both society and the political elites with some intellectual support for building a foreign policy consensus. However, as the country departs modernity and faces the challenges of postmodernity many quasi-reliable paradigms (including realism / geopolitics) do not work.

What can easily be predicted, however, is that Russian security debates will not stop with the reaching of a consensus on a realist / geopolitical basis. That is the starting point rather than the end of these debates. With the achievement of a certain level of socio-economic and political stability, new concepts with an emphasis on individual and societal security will likely challenge collectivist and state- or nation-oriented theories. The entire landscape of the Russian discourse on security will be even more diverse in the years to come. Plurality rather than unification and consensus-building will probably become the main characteristic of this discourse. A completely different set of priorities could be the focus of future security debates: ensuring domestic stability and territorial integrity, preventing the rise of hostile powers and alliances may be replaced by concerns such as the environment, mass disease, international terrorism and narco-business, migration, the increasing vulnerability of economic and information networks, and so on.

Figure 1.   Major principles of the Russian foreign policy schools: comparative analysis

Schools \ Principles	NPT	Atlanti-cism	Eurasia-nism	Derzhav-niki	Realists	Libe-rals	Neo-Commu-nists	Social Demo-crats	Peace researc-h	Right Radicals	Post-positivis-m
Country's geopoliti-cal status	'civilized' 'super-' power	'normal' great power	great power	great power	great power	'civilized' great power	great power	great power	'civilized' great power	great power	Not interested
Country's civilizatio-nal status	Part of the global civiliza-tion	Part of the Western civilization	Eurasian civilization	Western / Eurasian civilization	Eurasian civilization	Part of the Western civiliza-tion	Eurasian / Western civilizatio-n	Part of the Western civilization	Part of the global civiliza-tion	Eurasian civilization	Part of the global civilization
Geopoliti-cal orienta-tion	The West	The West	Eurasia	Eurasia	Eurasia	The West	Eurasia	The West	Multi-vectored strategy	North / South relations	Multi-vectored strategy
Security interests	Preva-lence of univer-sal over national interest-s	Balance of universal and national interests	Preva-lence of national over universal interests	Prevalenc-e of national over universal interests	Preva-lence of national over universal interests	Balance of universa-l and national interests	Preva-lence of national over universal interests	Balance of national and universal interests	Balance of universal and national interests	Preva-lence of national over universal interests	Desecuriti-zation

Chapter 3.
Threat Perceptions, Foreign Policy, Military and National Security Doctrines

To understand the nature and orientation of Russia's foreign policy it is very important to examine how the country identifies challenges to its security. This is also helpful for explaining how the national security discourse and ideas, developed by various foreign policy schools, are translated into concrete political initiatives and implemented by practitioners. In defining its national security doctrine (including threat perceptions) in the 1990s, Russian policy makers and analysts faced numerous problems. One of them was lack of a point of departure, because there hadn't been a pre-existing doctrine (at least, not in the formal sense). What had been called the Soviet national security doctrine, in reality, was a mixture of ideological dogma and real political considerations, typically camouflaged by peaceful rhetoric (Kremenyuk 1994: 88). The very concepts of "national interests" and "national security" were rejected because of the dominance of cosmopolitan ideas. At the same time, the concept of security was interpreted in purely military terms. Other (the so-called "soft") aspects of security (such as economic, societal, environmental, information, and other dimensions) were nearly completely ignored. For all these reasons, the Russian post-Communist theorists and practitioners had to start from scratch.

Drafting of the security concept began in the late Soviet period, but was never completed due to, firstly, rapid changes in the international environment and political upheavals, and, secondly, the related political infighting between competing interest groups, both factors remaining a regular feature of the Russian political scene. The persistent failure of the country's political elite to reach a consensus on the security concept further complicated attempts at drafting a series of other documents, including Russia's military and foreign policy doctrines, which, logically, had to be built on the security concept. This chapter examines the evolution of Russian military threat perceptions over the last two decades as well as various factors contributing to this process. Since some issues of the "soft" security problematique are discussed in other parts of this volume, this chapter will examine primarily traditional "hard" or military aspects of Russian threat perceptions that still play a significant role in Russian strategic thinking. The analysis below focuses primarily on the official Russian documents, but informal discussions among Russian strategic experts and academics are also taken into consideration. The evolution of the Russian post-Soviet national security, military and foreign policy doctrines and strategies evolved in several phases.

- The *first*, formative, period took place in 1991–1993, when the new Russian politico-military elites tried to apprehend new domestic and international realities and formulate the country's national interests and relevant strategies. First national security-related documents were adopted.

- The *second period* (1994–1999) was characterized by attempts to define more precisely Russia's threat perceptions and national security interests (on the one hand) and develop a more coherent and integrative national security strategy (on the other). Particularly, a national security doctrine, that integrated previous similar documents, was adopted in 1997.

- The *third period* (2000–2006) was related to Russia's efforts to re-assess its national security strategy because of the second Chechen war, NATO military intervention in Kosovo, NATO's eastward enlargement, and wars in Afghanistan and Iraq. A new set of military and national security doctrines was adopted in 2000, and the military reform that aimed at radical restructuring of the Russian armed forces was speeded up.

- The *fourth period* (2007–2014) was marked by Russia's more assertive foreign and security policies both in the "near" and "far" abroad, Moscow's growing anti-NATO, and, especially, anti-American sentiments, and attempts to restore its former military strength (albeit for different purposes and on a different basis). There was some rapprochement between Moscow and Washington, when the Obama administration launched its "restart" policy on Russia (early 2009). However, as basic Russian national security documents demonstrate, Moscow's threat perceptions still have a strong anti-NATO / U.S. flavor.

- The *fifth period,* that started in the aftermath of the Ukrainian crisis in early 2014 and continues to the present day, entailed a serious revision of Russia's doctrinal basis. Threat perceptions and regional priorities were reconsidered to cope with new security challenges.

Early concepts

Immediately after the collapse of the Soviet Union, the Yeltsin government, surprisingly, found itself as the only relevant military successor of the USSR. For the period of several months the Russian leadership simply did not have a coherent and clear vision of its future security strategy. The new Russian government was hesitating between the desire to keep a unified control over the military structures of the CIS,—especially of its nuclear forces that were based not only in Russia but also in Belarus, Ukraine and Kazakhstan,—and the plans to create national armed forces.

Initially, the new Russian leadership pushed the idea of creating collective armed forces of the CIS with a command center in Moscow (without national armies). However, this idea very soon failed because, for various reasons (civil or inter-state wars, nationalistic / anti-Russian sentiments among the local elites, etc), CIS member states started to form their national armies. By spring 1992 President Yeltsin had to abandon the idea of keeping a unified CIS military structure and decided to create independent Russian armed forces and develop Russia's national security strategy.

Russia's Law on Security of 1992

On 5 March 1992 President Boris Yeltsin signed "The Law on Security of the Russian Federation" which the Supreme Soviet (the then Russian Parliament) had initiated. The Law established some legal and institutional frameworks for Russia's security policy. It was a rather interesting document from both the theoretical and the practical points of view. First of all, it defined the very notion of security: "Security is freedom from internal and external threats to vital interests of the individual, society and state" (Yeltsin 1992, 5). In line with the foreign political thought, the authors of the document singled out not only state and military security but also economic, social, information, and ecological aspects of security. Contrary to the Soviet legislation, which had focused on state or party interests, this document declared priority of interests of the individual and society. It also established a national security system of the newly born Russian Federation. Along with already existing bodies such as the Ministry of Foreign Affairs, Ministry of the Interior, Ministry of Security, Foreign Intelligence Service, Ministry of Environment, the Law recommended setting up the Security Council, the Ministry of Defense, and several committees including the Border Guards Committee and so on.

However, this document was too abstract and vague to design a coherent national security strategy. It mainly focused on domestic issues and lacked proper legal and conceptual grounds for a number of important areas such as foreign policy and military reform. A special section on threat perceptions was lacking as well. Moreover, in adopting this legislation the leadership of the Supreme Soviet was eager to use it as a tool in the power struggle with the President. With the adoption of the new Russian Constitution in December 1993, which established a new system of government, some provisions of the Law became outdated.

Russia's foreign policy concept of 1993

In early 1993, the Foreign Ministry presented a foreign policy concept of the Russian Federation that was consequently approved by the Supreme Soviet (the then Russian Parliament) and President Boris Yeltsin (Ministry of Foreign Affairs of the Russian Federation 1993, 3–23). It was the first time that post-Soviet Russia adopted a comprehensive foreign policy doctrine. Despite numerous inconsistencies and shortcomings, this document clearly described Russian national interests and foreign policy priorities. Its basic premise was that Russia's foreign policy must meet fundamental national interests, primarily the need to preserve the sovereignty, independence and territorial integrity of the country, strengthen its security in every respect, revive Russia as a free and democratic country, and provide favourable conditions for the formation of an efficient market economy, in keeping with the status of a great power, and for the entry of the Russian Federation into the world community. The document suggested a greater emphasis on the economic aspect of foreign policy in order to mobilize international support for Russian economic reforms, integrate the national economy into world economic relations in competitive forms, ease the burden of military spending, solve the problem of foreign debt, support Russian business, and carry out conversion projects. It called for giving priority to the interests of the individual, and to human and minority rights.

According to this concept, Russia was to exercise its responsibility as a great power to maintain global and regional stability, contribute to conflict prevention, and promote democratic principles such as rule of law and human and minority rights protection. The document emphasized Russia's commitment to political and diplomatic methods and negotiation rather than to the use of military force, the admissibility of the limited use of force in strict accordance with international law to ensure national and international security and stability. The aims of the military strategy were outlined as follows: a) transformation of the international relations system from a bipolar, bloc-based model into one of co-operation; facilitating the arms control and disarmament process; b) bringing the military potential in line with a new pattern of challenges and threats and in accordance with the principle of reasonable defense sufficiency; c) a military reform should be conducted on the basis of a national security concept, and it should take into consideration the economic and social potential of the country.

The concept did not see any serious threats to Russia's security. Even the Baltic States, that discriminated against Russian-speaking minorities and pushed the Russian Federation to withdraw its armed forces from their territory, were seen as promising international partners. The only exception was the Third World that had initially been characterized as the main source of threats to regional and global security. However, in the document's sections dealing with regional issues developing countries were depicted as an important resource for Russia's successful global strategy. In general, the document can be characterized as liberal and pro-Western in its spirit. This did not come as a surprise because the concept was mainly prepared by the team of the Atlanticists although some regional priorities were affected by the Eurasianist school.

The Russian military doctrine of 1993

The new military doctrine was approved by the Russian Security Council on 2 November 1993 and made public. According to the document,

> "The Basic Provisions of the Military Doctrine of the Russian Federation are part and parcel of the security concept of the Russian Federation and represent a document covering Russia's transitional period—the period of the establishment of statehood, implementation of democratic reform, and formation of a new system of international relations. They represent a system of views, officially accepted by the state, on the prevention of wars and armed conflicts, on the development of the armed forces, on the country's preparations to defend itself, on the organization of actions to ward off threats to the military security of the state, and on the use of the armed forces and other troops of the Russian Federation to defend the vital interests of Russia" (Yeltsin 1994, 6).

In contrast with the earlier versions of the military doctrine and the foreign policy concept of 1993, this document clearly defined both external and internal sources of military threats. The doctrine singled out ten major external challenges to Russia's military security:

1. territorial claims of other states on the Russian Federation and its allies;

2. existing and potential seats of local wars and armed conflicts, above all in the direct proximity of the Russian borders (there was a special section on the attitude of Russia to armed conflicts);

3. the potential use (including the unsanctioned use) of nuclear and other mass destruction weapons owned by some states;

4. the proliferation of nuclear and other mass destruction weapons, their delivery vehicles and latest military technologies, coupled with the attempts of certain states, organizations and terrorist groups to achieve their military and political ambitions;

5. the potential undermining of strategic stability by violations of international agreements in the sphere of arms control and reductions and the qualitative and quantitative arms build-up by other countries;

6. attempts to interfere in the internal affairs of and destabilize the internal political situation in Russia;

7. the suppression of the rights, freedoms and legitimate interests of citizens of the Russian Federation in foreign states;

8. attacks on military facilities of the Russian armed forces situated on the territory of foreign states;

9. expansion of military blocs and alliances to the detriment of the interests of Russia's military security; and

10. international terrorism.

In a separate section, the document highlighted five crucial factors facilitating the escalation of a military danger into a direct military threat to the Russian Federation:

1. the build-up of forces on the Russian borders to limits which upset the existing balance of forces;

2. attacks on the facilities and structures on the Russian border and the borders of its allies, border conflicts and armed provocations;

3. the training of armed formations and groups on the territory of other states for dispatch to the territory of the Russian Federation and its allies;

4. the actions of other countries which hinder the operation of the logistics system of the Russian strategic nuclear forces and of state and military control of, above all, their space components; and

5. the deployment of foreign troops on the territory of states adjacent to the Russian Federation unless this is done to restore or maintain peace, in accordance with the decision of the UN Security Council or a regional agency of collective security, by agreement with Russia.

Along with the external threats the new doctrine identified seven major internal threats against which the armed forces and other services may be used:

1. illegal activity of nationalist, secessionist and other organizations, designed to destabilize the internal situation in Russia and violate its territorial integrity and carried out with the use of armed force;

2. attempts to overthrow the constitutional regime and disorganize the operation of bodies of state power and administration;

3. attacks on the facilities of nuclear engineering, chemical and biological industries, and other potentially dangerous facilities;

4. the creation of illegal armed formations;

5. the growth of organized crime and smuggling on a scale where they threaten the security of citizens and society;

6. attacks on arsenals, arms depots, enterprises producing weapons, military and specialized equipment, and organizations, establishments and structures which have weapons, with the aim of capturing them; and

7. illegal proliferation of weapons, munitions, explosives and other means used for subversion and terrorist acts on the territory of the Russian Federation, as well as illegal drug trafficking.

The section on threat perceptions had many important implications. Along with the systematic description of these threats, it demonstrated rather substantial changes in Russia's strategic thinking. In contrast with the Soviet strategic thinking, the new doctrine did not identify the USA and NATO as a primary source of military danger. Rather, they were warned not to provoke a new confrontation by violating the strategic balance, military build-up in the regions adjacent to Russia, NATO expansion, and so on. This implied that Russia also would refrain from any destabilizing actions.

Instead of the traditional threat from the West, other challenges such as armed conflicts, subversive activities and territorial disputes in the post-Soviet space were seen to be a major danger. This was understandable because, by the the document was adopted, all but two FSU (former Soviet Union) inter-state borders were disputed, and 164 different territorial-ethnic disputes were identified in this region (Dick 1994, 3).

The doctrine, however, did not specify what kinds of territorial claims and local conflicts really threatened Russia's security, and which ones might be potentially dangerous. For example, the Russian-Japanese dispute on the Kuriles went back to WWII, and Russian-Norwegian disputes on exclusive economic zones (EEZs) and maritime borders in the Barents Sea dated back to the 1920s (until it was resolved in 2010).

However, these conflicts did not create an immediate military threat to the Russian Federation. Moreover, most of the countries in dispute with Russia were simply unable to pose a military threat for lack of sufficient capacity. Conversely, these countries feared the potential use of military force by Russia in pursuit of her interests.

The proliferation of weapons of mass destruction and international terrorism, which have been on the periphery of the Russian strategic priorities in the previous doctrines and drafts, were given a rather important status in the 1993 doctrine. Above all, this brought Russia closer to leading Western countries, which also consider these phenomena to be the most dangerous international developments.

Identifying violations of own citizens' rights in foreign states and attacks on own military facilities in foreign countries as potential sources of military threat is a rather common stance for security doctrines not only in Russia but also in other world powers. However, from a legal point of view, it was not clear who could be considered Russian citizens in the FSU countries, and what was, at the time, the status of the Russian military bases in these republics. The Russian foreign policy concept of 1993 acknowledged, that Russia was only beginning the process of negotiating and concluding relevant agreements with the former Soviet republics. In fact, the lack of a legal framework for the relations with the FSU countries gave Russia a certain number of excuses for interventions in the "near abroad" (Ra'anan 1995, 21–22).

The most significant change in the Russian threat perceptions occurred with regard to internal threats. The Law on Security of 1992 only mentioned that some of these might exist. The General Staff draft of the military doctrine (1992) simply ignored the very possibility of internal threats to Russia's security and therefore did not foresee any internal mission for the armed forces. This view was a result of the military elite's belief, that the armed forces should protect the country only from external enemies, not internal ones. The latter should be the business of the Ministry of the Interior and security services.

However, accepting reality, the military doctrine of 1993 acknowledged that there were many dangers stemming from domestic developments. This inevitably led to a commitment of the military to an internal role. As the failed coup of August 1991 and the attack on the Russian parliament in October 1993 demonstrated, the armed forces had already been involved in domestic power struggles.

The new reading of military threats has led to new approaches to military strategy, as well as to an appropriate organization and training of the armed forces.

Since the main threat to stability and peace in the post-Cold War period comes from local wars and armed conflicts, the document called for a re-targeting of the Russian armed forces from large-scale war to low intensity conflicts. The main aim of the use of the armed forces and other services in armed conflicts and local wars, the doctrine said, was "to localize the seat of tensions and stop hostilities at the earliest possible stage, in the interests of creating conditions for a peaceful settlement of the conflict on conditions suiting the interests of the Russian Federation" (Yeltsin 1994, 9). Military operation in armed conflicts and local wars should be carried out by peacetime groups of forces (those which organized for peace-time conditions, i.e. have incomplete personnel and arsenals; in the war-time period they are reorganized to be full-fledged military units), deployed in the conflict area. In case of need, they might be strengthened by a partial deployment and re-deployment of forces from other regions.

According to the document, the priority was to develop the armed forces and other services designed to deter aggression, as well as mobile elements, which can be quickly delivered and deployed in the required area and can carry out mobile operations in any region where the security of Russia might be threatened. When faced with conventional war, the armed forces must act decisively, using both defensive and offensive methods to destroy the enemy. The armed forces should

1. repel enemy attacks in the air, on land and at sea;

2. defeat the enemy and create conditions for ending hostilities at the earliest possible stage, and for signing a peace treaty on conditions suiting Russia; and

3. carry out military operations together with the armed forces of allied states, in accordance with international obligations of the Russian Federation.

A number of tasks have been set up by the doctrine for other services:

1. to ensure a stable operation of intelligence, control and communication systems, and to seize and keep the initiative in different spheres;

2. to isolate the intruding groups of forces of the aggressor;

3. to flexibly combine firepower and manoeuvre;

4. to ensure close co-operation of the arms and services, including special services of the armed forces and to co-ordinate the plans of using the armed forces and other services in armed conflicts and wars, and in performing joint tasks;

5. to hit the facilities of the enemy's troop and weapon control systems.

This combination of defensive and offensive methods was an important distinction from Gorbachev's military concept that had been oriented only to defensive operations.

Some military experts were concerned with the fact that the doctrine said nothing about the country's role in regional security systems; this omission could be interpreted as an intention to ensure Russia's security by unilateral, purely national efforts (Davydov 1996, 267).

Despite the focus on local conflicts, the military doctrine of 1993, however, said nothing about the need for a different force structuring, equipping and training for low intensity operations. Besides, as some military experts noted, the emphasis on mobile forces could be seen as a preparation for an intervention in the "near abroad" (Dick 1994, 4; Grigoriev 1995, 6).

In the document, the requirement to deploy troops outside the Russian territory is specifically stated. This resulted both from threat perceptions and Russia's international obligations (peacekeeping operations, military bases, joint groups of forces, etc.). It was underlined that, irrespective of the terms of deployment, Russian military formations, deployed on the territory of other states, remain a part of the armed forces and should act in accordance with the procedure, established for the Russian armed forces on the basis of bilateral and multilateral treaties and agreements. However, some specialists believed that, despite the reference to international agreements and commitments, the document left open the possibility that such agreements could be imposed by Russia on weaker states (Davydov 1996, 267).

The doctrine did not exclude the possibility of large-scale war. It mentioned that, under certain conditions, armed conflicts and local wars can develop into an all-out war. Factors, which increase the danger of a conventional war escalating into a nuclear war, can be deliberate actions of an aggressor, designed to destroy or undermine the operation of strategic nuclear forces, early warning systems, and nuclear and chemical facilities. The document also included a provision according to which any, including limited, use of nuclear weapons even by one of the sides can provoke a mass use of nuclear weapons, with catastrophic consequences.

The doctrine clarified Russia's nuclear policy, which had not been updated since the Gorbachev period. It was declared that the goal of the Russian Federation's nuclear policy is to avert the threat of a nuclear war by deterring aggression against Russia and its allies. Therefore, nuclear weapons were no longer regarded by the Russian strategic planners primarily as war fighting means. Instead, their main use was seen as a political deterrent to nuclear or conventional aggression. This marked the shift in Russian strategic thinking to a Western-like concept of deterrence, compensating for conventional weakness. The most distinct departure of the new Russian nuclear doctrine from the Soviet one was Russia's abandonment of the principle of no-first-use (introduced by Leoinid Brezhnev in 1982). At the same time, the document promised that Russia would never use its nuclear weapons against any state party to the Non-Proliferation Treaty (1968), which does not possess nuclear weapons, unless:

> "(a) such a state, which is connected by an alliance agreement with a nuclear state attacks the Russian Federation, its territory, Armed Forces and other services or its allies; (b) such a state collaborates with a nuclear power in carrying out, or supporting, an invasion or an armed aggression against the Russian Federation, its territory, armed forces and other services or its allies" (Yeltsin 1994: 6).

In one way or another, all NATO members, China and Japan as nuclear states or the allies of nuclear powers, the Baltic States, and Central and Eastern European countries, should they join NATO or WEU (Western European Union), fell under these categories.

The reaction of Russia's international partners to the repeal of the no-first-use principle was rather contradictory (Davydov 1996, 267). On the one hand, they considered this shift to a Western concept of deterrence as evidence of a greater inclination towards openness and frankness in military matters on Russia's part: few people in the West took the old Soviet doctrine of "no-first-use" seriously. They understood that Russia's new nuclear doctrine reflected Moscow's intention to rely mainly upon nuclear deterrence in order to compensate for its conventional weakness and keep its status of a world power. On the other hand, they perceived this change as a clear message to them, especially to the Baltic states and the Visegrad countries (Czech Republic, Hungary, Poland and Slovakia) that they would become exceptions if they joined NATO, or the WEU, or supported any Western intervention in Russia or the "near abroad"—for instance, by giving rights of passage or providing bases. This also put pressure on Ukraine, which was delaying the transfer to Russia of the nuclear weapons, deployed on its territory during Soviet times (Dick 1994, 2; Lockwood 1994, 648).

Along with these innovations, the document confirmed Russia's long-standing interest in (a) a comprehensive nuclear weapon test ban; (b) reduction of nuclear forces to a minimum, which would guarantee against a large-scale war and maintain strategic stability, and eventual elimination of nuclear weapons; and (c) strengthening of the non-proliferation regime and making it universal.

Since internal armed conflicts were now also regarded as a considerable threat to the vital interests of the country, the objectives of using armed forces and troops for domestic purposes were described as follows: to localize and blockade the conflict zone; to suppress armed clashes and disengage the warring sides; to take measures to disarm and eliminate illegal armed forces and confiscate weapons from the population in the conflict zone; to carry out operational and investigative operations in order to remove the threat to internal security; to normalize the situation as soon as possible; to restore law and order; to ensure social security; to render the requisite assistance to the population; and to create conditions for a political settlement of conflicts. These functions had to be fulfilled mainly by the Interior Troops. However, as the document prescribed, separate elements of the armed forces and other services (the border guards and counter-intelligence) might be used to help law-enforcement bodies and Interior Ministry troops to localize and blockade the conflict zone, preclude armed clashes and disengage the warring sides, and protect strategic facilities.

Remembering the general military dislike of internal missions, General Manilov of the Security Council explained, that the armed forces could only be used "when nationalist or separatist groups are active, using armed violence and posing a threat to Russia and its integrity, or when attempts are made to use force to overthrow the constitutional system, or when nuclear facilities are attacked, and also when illegal armed formations are being created" (Dick 1994: 4). Thus, the new doctrine laid a legal foundation for the use of the armed forces in internal conflicts such as Chechnya (Davydov 1996, 267). And since the interior troops were insufficiently manned and equipped, the use of the armed forces in internal operations was inevitable,—which has been amply confirmed by the two subsequent Chechen wars.

The National Security Concept of the Russian Federation (1997)

On 17 December 1997 President Yeltsin signed Decree No. 1300, approving a new Russian national security concept. It outlined Russian national interests and the major threats to the country's security, and established a set of domestic and foreign policy goals, aimed at strengthening Russia's statehood and geopolitical position. As the document emphasized, the concept was "a political document, reflecting the officially accepted views of the goals and state strategy in ensuring the security of the individual, society and the state against external and internal threats of a political, economic, social, military, technogenic, ecological, information and other character with account of available resources and opportunities" (Yeltsin 1997, 4).

Similar to the Law on Security (1992) and the Duma draft of the Law on National Security (1995), the new doctrine departed from the broad understanding of security and focused not only on the interests of the state but also on the interests of the individual and the society. According to one of the authors of the concept, Deputy Secretary of the Security Council Leonid Mayorov, this document, which had been in the works for several years, comprehensively reflected, for the first time in Russian history, the system of views on the security of the individual, the society and the state (Chugayev 1997).

In fact, the concept was more like guidelines, or a theoretical foundation, on which one could build such essential programme documents as the military doctrine and the economic security doctrine. This was also the basis for military reform. At least, now it was much clearer what sort of armed forces Russia must have, and which conflicts these forces should prepare for. It was specified in the preamble, that "The Concept is the basis for the development of concrete programs and organizational documents, related to the national security of the Russian Federation" (Yeltsin 1997, 4).

The paper described the global situation and Russia's place in the world. Similar to the foreign policy concept of 1993, the paper saw the rise of a multipolar world as the most important characteristic of contemporary world dynamics. According to the doctrine, Russia should find its own "niche" in this complex world structure and even become one of its "poles". Even though the document still mentioned, *en passant*, the need for Russia to retain its status of a world power, it did not insist on Russia's global responsibilities and interests (as some previous doctrines had done). On the contrary, the paper acknowledged that Russia's capacity to influence the solution of cardinal issues of international life was greatly diminished.

The document singled out both positive and negative factors affecting the country's position in the world system. Interestingly, the paper pointed to the changing nature of world power in the post-Cold War period. "While military force remains a significant factor in international relations, economic, political, scientific-technical, ecological and information factors play a growing role" (Yeltsin, 1997, 4).

The document noted that some prerequisites had been created for the demilitarization of international relations, strengthening the role of law in conflict resolution, and that the danger of a direct aggression against Russia had diminished. There were some prospects for Russia's greater integration into the world economy, including some Western economic and financial institutions. Russia shared common security interests with many states in areas such as nuclear non-proliferation, conflict resolution, combating international terrorism, environmental problems, and so on. At that point, the paper arrived at an important conclusion that Russia's national security may be ensured by non-military means.

At the same time, a number of international and, especially, domestic processes undermined Russia's international positions. The shift of world power from military-strategic parameters to economic, technological and information dimensions intensified international competition for natural, financial, technological, and information resources as well as for markets. Some states did not accept a multipolar world model. In some regions, traditions of the "bloc politics" were still strong, and attempts to isolate Russia could be identified (the document referred to NATO's enlargement and to the Asia Pacific). The document stated that the Russian domestic environment was not very conducive to developing an active foreign policy. Russia had yet to develop a unifying national idea, which would not only determine its view of the world but also transform the society. The country's economic, scientific and demographic potentials were shrinking. The former defense system had been disrupted and the new one was yet to be created.

However, the concept was quite optimistic with regard to the country's prospects. It stated that Russia had all the prerequisites for maintaining and strengthening its position in the world. Russia possessed a sizeable economic, scientific and technical potential as well as natural resources. It occupied a unique strategic position in Eurasia. The country had created a democratic system of government and a mixed economy. The paper also mentioned Russia's century-old history, culture and traditions which could be an important spiritual resource for rebuilding the country.

The new national security concept asserted that Russia faced no immediate danger of large-scale aggression, and that, because the country was beset with a myriad of debilitating domestic problems, the greatest threat to Russia's security was now an internal one. The document said: "An analysis of the threats to the national security of the Russian Federation shows that the main threats at present and in the foreseeable future will not be military, but predominantly internal in character and will focus on the internal political, economic, social, ecological, information, and spiritual spheres" (Yeltsin 1997, 4). This was a distinct departure from previous doctrines. Even the military doctrine of 1993 was based on the assumption that the main threat to Russia's security was posed by external factors such as local conflicts or territorial claims.

As some analysts emphasized, no less important was the fact that for the first time it was substantiated at such a high official level (the President, Security Council, and Parliament) that there was no external military threat to Russia (The Jamestown Foundation Prism, 9 January 1998). The concept clearly suggested that the current relatively benign international climate afforded Russia the opportunity to direct resources away from the defense sector and toward the rebuilding of the Russian economy (Yeltsin 1997, 4).

In general, it placed this rebuilding effort in the context of continued democratization and marketization. In particular, the document focused on the dangers posed by Russia's *economic* woes, which were described frankly and at length. The concept highlighted a number of major threats to economic security such as a substantial drop of production and investments; destruction of the scientific and technical potential; disarray in the financial and monetary systems; shrinkage of the federal revenues; growing national debt; Russia's overdependence on export of raw materials and import of equipment, consumer goods and foodstuff; "brain drain", and uncontrolled flight of capital.

The document also pointed to internal *social, political, ethnic* and *cultural* tensions that threatened to undermine both the viability and the territorial integrity of the Russian state. Among these it singled out social polarization, demographic problems (in particular, decline in birth rates, average life expectancy, and population), corruption, organized crime, drug trade, terrorism, virulent nationalism, separatism, deterioration of the health system, ecological catastrophes, and disintegration of the "common spiritual space."

Along with the major internal threats to Russia's security, the document identified a number of dangers stemming from *international* dynamics. The doctrine highlighted the following sources of external threat: territorial claims; attempts of foreign countries to use Russia's domestic problems for weakening its international positions or challenging its territorial integrity; local conflicts and military build-up in the country's vicinity; mass migration from the troubled CIS countries; proliferation of weapons of mass destruction; international terrorism and drug-trafficking, and growing activity of foreign intelligence services. These, however, were of less significance than internal threats.

In general, this shift in Russia's threat perceptions can be evaluated as a positive move with three main advantages. Firstly, this was a step to a more realistic estimation of Russia's domestic and international problems. Secondly, given Russia's limited resources, the doctrine helped to establish a proper system of political priorities. Finally, it almost eliminated xenophobia in Russia's relations with the West and, thus, laid foundations for a more intense international co-operation.

As for the document's drawbacks, two minor comments can be made. Firstly, some threats (environmental, information, spiritual, etc.) were merely mentioned but not substantiated. Some of them, however, were described implicitly in the section on the national security strategy. Secondly, there were some grounds for concern that "securitization" of Russian domestic politics, i.e., identification of main security threats inside rather than outside the country, under certain circumstances might result in a sort of a "witch hunt". To prevent this, some analysts believed, individuals and the civil society should serve as a check on the state and should not allow the state to be the sole agency in national security matters (Chugayev 1997; Sergunin 1998).

Along with explaining Russia's national interests and threat perceptions, the doctrine determined ways and means of the country's security policy. According to the document, —the *chief purpose* of ensuring national security of the Russian Federation is to create and maintain such an economic, political, international and military-strategic position of the country, which would provide favourable conditions for the development of the individual, the society and the state, and preclude a danger of weakening the role and significance of the Russian Federation as a subject of international law, and of undermining the capability of the state to meet its national interests on the international scenell (Yeltsin 1997, 4).

The document set up a number of *particular objectives* in the task of ensuring the national security of the Russian Federation: a) to develop the country's economy and pursue an independent and socially oriented economic course; b) to further improve the legislation and strengthen law and order as well as the social and political stability of Russia's society, statehood, federalism, and local self-government; c) to shape harmonious inter-ethnic relations; d) to ensure Russia's international security by establishing equal partnerships with leading countries of the world; e) to strengthen state security in the defense and information spheres; f) to ensure the vital activity of the population in a technogenically safe and environmentally clean world.

With regard to Russia's military policy, the national security concept served as a post-facto justification for the downsizing of Russia's armed forces that had occurred since the Soviet Union's dissolution, and for the continued restructuring, envisioned in the Kremlin's still evolving military reform programme. By emphasizing domestic rather than foreign threats to Russia's security, it seemed also to justify the rapid strengthening of the country's internal security forces, relative to the regular army during the past ten years, even if defense reform plans aimed to moderate that policy somewhat. In a related fashion, the document described an alleged threat to Russian economic interests posed by foreign competitors, and underscored the importance of the role played by Russia's intelligence services in countering it.

The document also emphasized the overriding importance of Russia's strategic forces to the country's security and again disavowed the no-first-use principle. With regard to conventional weapons, the concept proclaimed a policy of "realistic deterrence" in discarding officially any effort to maintain parity with the armed forces of the world's leading states. The concept highlighted the importance of Russian participation in international peacekeeping missions as a means of maintaining Russia's influence abroad.

The document declared that, in preventing war and armed conflicts, Russia preferred political, economic and other non-military means. However, as the "non-use of force" (Art. 2,7 of the UN Charter) had not yet been fully implemented as a norm of international relations, the national interests of the Russian Federation required sufficient military might for its defense. The document said that Russia might use military force for ensuring its national security, proceeding from the following principles:

- Russia reserved the right to use all the forces and systems at its disposal, including nuclear weapons, if the unleashing of armed aggression results in a threat to the actual existence of the Russian Federation as an independent sovereign state.

- The armed forces of the Russian Federation should be used resolutely, consistently up to the point when conditions for making peace which are favourable to the Russian Federation have been created.

- The armed forces should be used on a legal basis and only when all other non-military possibilities of settling a crisis situation have been exhausted or proved to be ineffective.

- The use of the armed forces against peaceful civilians or for attaining domestic political aims shall not be permitted. However, it was permitted to use individual units of the armed forces for joint operation with other services against illegal armed formations that present a threat to the national interests of Russia.

- The participation of the Russian armed forces in wars and armed conflicts of different intensity and scope shall be aimed at accomplishing the priority military-political and military-strategic tasks meeting Russia's national interests and its allied obligations.

The doctrine underlined that Russia had no intention of entering into confrontation with any state or alliance of states, nor did it pursue hegemonic or expansionist objectives; it would maintain relations of partnership with all interested countries of the world community.

The concept reiterated Russia's opposition to NATO enlargement and called for multilateral collective security organizations such as the UN and the OSCE to play a greater role in ensuring international security. The paper called on the international community to create a new Euro-

Atlantic security system on the basis of the OSCE as well as to strengthen (with Russian participation) multilateralism in the Asia Pacific. The national security concept formally stated what had long been a cornerstone of Russian declared foreign policy: i.e., that the rebuilding of Russia is best served not by a passive diplomatic posture, but rather by an aggressive and multi-faceted diplomacy, aimed at winning membership, or increasing Russia's influence, in various international organizations, while simultaneously striving to make Russia an important global player.

The Putin-1 era

Late in Yeltsin's last and early in Putin's first term, three major factors changed Russia's threat perceptions: the financial collapse of 1998, NATO military intervention in Kosovo (1999), and the second Chechen war (started in 1999 as well).

The August 1998 crisis, to an extent, undermined the popularity of liberal concepts (including a positive attitude to globalization) in the country by exposing Russia's vulnerability to the international economy and financial markets. Some specialists believe that the fundamental sources of the crisis were internal policy failures and economic weakness, but it was precipitated by the vulnerability of the rouble to speculative international financial markets (Wallander, 2000, 2). Moreover, because Russia's economy began to recover in the aftermath of the decision to devalue the rouble and implement limited debt defaults, the crisis reinforced statist arguments, that a less Western-dependent, more state-directed policy of economic reform could be Russia's path to stability and eventual prosperity. One of the lessons of the 1998 financial meltdown was that globalization may be a source of threat to Russia's economic security.

As a result of the Kosovo war in 1999, Russia again became suspicious of NATO's real character and its future plans. In the Russian view, in the case of Kosovo NATO—contrary to previous declarations of its in-. tentions to be transformed from a military-political to a political-military organization—demonstrated, that the Alliance still chose to remain a "hard" security organization and continued to reproduce a Cold War-type logic and policies. Moreover, NATO demonstrated its ambitions to be a major (if not the sole) security provider in Europe, trying to sideline other regional organizations, such as OSCE, the EU, the Council of Europe, the Council of the Baltic Sea States, etc. In addition, the Kosovo war coincided with adoption of a new NATO strategic doctrine that turned out much more expansionist than the previous ones (Wallander, 1999, 4). In particular, the new doctrine envisaged NATO's further eastward enlargement, redeployment of its military infrastructure closer to the Russian borders, and even military operations beyond its traditional "zone of responsibility" (in fact, globally). Finally, the Kosovo crisis gave the Russian military the much needed argumentation to force through its view, that a large-scale conventional war was not nearly so remote a possibility as stated in the national security concept-1997 (Ball 1999, 2).

The second Chechen war affected Russian threat perceptions as well. First of all, it demonstrated that in the modern era international and domestic terrorisms are intertwined, and it is impossible to fight them separately. In addition, it turned out that the financial, military and technical base of terrorism on the North Caucasus was so strong that it was unrealistic to wage the war only by special forces and internal troops (without the help of regular armed forces). As mentioned, Russia's previous military and security doctrines allowed only limited and short-term involvement of the regular army. It should be also noted that Moscow was both disappointed and irritated by what it called a Western "policy of double standards" with regard to Chechnya.

On the one hand, Western countries called on Russia to join a "global war on terror" after 9 / 11, and Moscow responded in a positive way. But, on the other hand, the West treated Chechen rebels as "freedom-fighters" rather than terrorists, providing Chechen leaders with political asylum, allowing Chechen representative missions to wage anti-Russian propaganda in Europe and the US, and heavily criticizing Russia for human rights violations in the region. Such a policy contributed to the rise of new mutual suspicions and mistrust in Russia's relations with its Western partners.

In 2000, under the new President Vladimir Putin, a series of new security-related documents was adopted: the national security concept, the military doctrine, the foreign policy concept, and a brand new information security concept.

The national security concept-2000 was the most significant document for understanding Russia's new approaches to its security policies. There was a difference between the concepts of 1997 and 2000. The most important aspect of the 2000 concept was that it elevated the importance and expanded the types of external threats to Russian security. The concept no longer stated that there were no external threats arising from deliberate actions or aggression. It provided a substantial list of external threats, including: the weakening of the OSCE and the UN; weakening Russian political, economic, and military influence in the world; the consolidation of military-political blocs and alliances (particularly further eastward expansion of NATO), including the possibility of foreign military bases or deployment of forces on Russian borders; proliferation of weapons of mass destruction and the means of their delivery; weakening of the CIS, and escalation of conflicts on CIS members' borders; and territorial claims against Russia (Putin 2000a, 4).

In several places the 2000 concept emphasized, that the natural tendency of international relations after the Cold-War confrontation was toward the development of a multi-polar world, in which relations should be based upon international law, with a proper role for Russia. It argued that, contrary to this tendency, the United States and its allies under the guise of multilateralism had sought to establish a uni-polar world outside of international law. The document warned that NATO's policy transition to the use of military force outside its alliance territory without UN Security Council approval was a major threat to world stability, and that these trends could create the potential for a new era of arms races among the world's great powers. The concept-2000 links the internal threat of terrorism and separatism (clearly with Chechnya in mind) to external threats: it argues that international terrorism involves efforts to undermine the sovereignty and territorial integrity of Russia, with a possibility of direct military aggression. However, in dealing with these threats the document calls for international cooperation (Putin 2000a, 4).

Threats to Russia's security, listed in the military doctrine of 2000, were virtually the same (Putin 2000b). Perhaps there was only one exception: in addition to the threats, mentioned in the national security concept of 2000 and in the military doctrine of 1993, the new document points to a new threat of an information war against Russia as an important factor of the contemporary security environment in the world.

The military doctrine of 2000 describes in detail the nature of contemporary and future wars, distinguishing the following trends:

- The use of high-precision and non-contact weapons (with a minimal involvement of ground forces);

- An emphasis on the predominant use of air / space and mobile forces;

- An aspiration to destroy an enemy's military and administrative command structures; making strikes on military, administrative, economic and infrastructure objects throughout the whole enemy's territory;

- Widespread use of methods of information war—both world-wide and inside the enemy's country;

- Potential technical catastrophes as a result of strikes on nuclear, chemical and industrial installations and communications;

- Involvement of irregular / paramilitary formations in waging war (along with regular armed forces);

- The high risk of escalation of an armed conflict to a large-scale war in terms of a number of participants and the use of weapons of mass destruction (WMD).

Depending on the level of confrontation, the doctrine singles out the following types of armed conflicts:

- Armed conflict—intra-state (Chechnya, Transnistria, Georgia-Abkhazia, Georgia-South Ossetia, the civil war in Tajikistan) or inter-state (Russia-Georgia);

- Local war (Iran-Iraq in the 1980s, Armenia-Azerbaijan: Nagorny Karabakh);

- Regional war with the participation of a group of states (Afghanistan, both Iraq wars);

- Large-scale war (both world wars). Russian strategists see the possibility of a large-scale war as purely theoretical.

With political and economic stabilization and subsequent economic growth in Russia under President Putin, Russia's foreign and security policies became more assertive. President Putin's "Munich speech" of 10 February 2007 exemplified a new Russian stance (Putin 2007). Although there were no radical changes in Russia's basic threat perceptions, President Putin emphasized some interesting nuances in Russia's approaches to international security. Moscow's security concerns were related to the following recent developments:

- The unilateral use of military force by the U.S. and its allies (in Kosovo, Afghanistan and Iraq). The Russian Federation was also discontent with regular U.S. military threats to Iran, Syria and North Korea.

- The weakening of traditional international security institutions such as the UN (Security Council) and the OSCE where Russia is represented on an equal footing with other countries. President Putin said that the crisis of these organizations was a result of a deliberate strategy, conducted by a small group of states, interested in creation of a uni- rather than a multi-polar world.

- NATO's eastward extension and the growth of its military infrastructure on the Russian borders.

- The U.S. plans to deploy elements of the BMD defense system in East and Central Europe (in Poland and in the Czech Republic).

- Lack of progress in arms control and disarmament. In particular, Putin criticized other nuclear powers for their reluctance to join existing arms control regimes and to reduce their nuclear arsenals. The Russian President also criticized NATO for its unwillingness to ratify the 1999 Adaptation Treaty on Conventional Forces in Europe that aimed at significant force reductions and development of confidence-building and security measures in Europe. In protest against NATO's position, Putin suspended Russia's participation in the CFE Treaty in 2007.

- Lack of efficient cooperation between Russia and its Western partners in fighting international terrorism. Putin reiterated Russia's famous stance on the Western "policy of double standards" and proposed that the international community pursue a more intense cooperation in this sphere.

Russian security thinking under Putin was also deeply affected by a series of the so-called "color" revolutions (Ukraine, Georgia, and Kyrgyzstan). It has resulted in a certain re-assessment of Russian security perception regarding the "near abroad", particularly in implementing "tightening of the screw" policies. The Russian leadership now believes, that Russia cannot be a great power in the region (and a pole of the world multi-polar system) if it cannot keep its central position in the former Soviet space. Along the same lines, Putin has tried to re-animate the CIS collective security structures such as the protection of the common CIS borders, a single air defense system, and the creation of the collective rapid reaction forces.

The Medvedev era

Dmitry Medvedev, elected as a President in 2008, has repeatedly stated that his foreign and security policy course will continue the strategy of his predecessor, and that there should be no expectations of major changes in Russia's threat perceptions and security policies.

However, the beginning of his presidency was marked by two security challenges that had previously been seen as highly hypothetical: the inter-state military conflict with Russia's participation (South Ossetia) and "energy wars" (the Russian-Ukrainian gas conflict).

When in August 2008 Georgia attacked South Ossetia and the Russian peacekeepers located there, the Russian government, for the first time in its post-Soviet history, had to execute a full-fledged peace-enforcement operation, forcing Georgia to return to a *status-quo* situation. It was made clear that the Russian armed forces were ill-prepared for such an operation (although the Russian military doctrine had foreseen the possibility of a limited armed conflict). It took a long time to re-deploy forces from North to South Ossetia. The mobile forces were almost not engaged in the operation. The air and electronic intelligence were inadequate, and this inevitably led to failures in the chain of command and losses in manpower and military equipment. It has been reported that the Russian General Staff has initiated a special investigation to draw lessons from the South Ossetian conflict.

The "gas war" with Ukraine, with its rather serious repercussions for Europe, has demonstrated Russia's vulnerability in the energy sector, and its dependence on the transition countries, and challenged its credibility as a reliable energy supplier.

In both cases (South Ossetia and Ukraine) Russia called for multilateral decisions. To avoid conflicts similar to that between Russia and Georgia, President Medvedev proposed a new Trans-Atlantic Security Charter (June 2008), that was later transformed into the draft of the European Security treaty (29 November 2009).

The proposed document purported to lay the foundation for a new international security architecture in this huge region. A multilateral mechanism to prevent and solve local conflicts was proposed (Medvedev 2009). Although the US and EU reaction to Medvedev's proposal was cautious, the proposal itself was not completely rejected, and further discussions were suggested (Cartwright 2009; Champion 2009; Emerson 2009a). In addition, at the EU-Russia summit in November 2008 the EU and Russia decided to intensify their cooperation on external security, including conflict management and joint peacekeeping operations throughout the world (http://www.infox.ru/authority/foreign/2008/10/28/document2001.phtml).

As mentioned, in 2010 Russia and Germany launched the initiative to establish an EU-Russia Committee on Foreign and Security Policy to discuss the most important issues pertaining to European security. The EU-Russian discussions on the local conflicts such as Transdnistria and Nagorny Karabakh resumed in 2010 (http://news.kremlin.ru/transcripts/9730).

As far as the problem of reliable energy supply to Europe was concerned, President Medvedev has also proposed to create an international control mechanism that could monitor the supply process. It was presumed that the issue of energy security would become an important part of a new EU-Russian cooperation agreement that is now under negotiation. In addition, President Medvedev invited European energy companies to actively invest in the construction of alternative gas pipelines that could be independent of transit countries (the so-called "Nord Stream" and "South Stream" projects).

Medvedev has continued Putin's course on strengthening the CIS collective security system (i.e. the Tashkent Treaty of 1992). In 2009 he signed an agreement with President Alexander Lukashenko on the creation of a single Russian-Belarussian air defense system, and completed the creation of collective rapid reaction forces of the CIS (mainly consisting of the Russian airborne troops) (Rossiyskaya gazeta, 5 February 2009, 1–2).

The new version of the Russian foreign policy concept was adopted by President Medvedev a month before the military clash with Georgia, in July 2008 (Medvedev 2008). In line with the liberal IR paradigm, the new concept ascertained that there was no clear border between internal and external means to ensure national security. For this reason, Russia's international course should be subordinated to more general—primarily domestic—needs, such as help in completing socio-economic reforms and making Russia a competitive actor in the globalizing world.

According to the 2008 foreign policy doctrine, Russia's *global priorities* included:

- *New world order* that should be based on principles of equality, mutual respect, mutually beneficial cooperation, and international law. Again, in line with liberal thought, the primacy of multilateral diplomacy was underlined. The UN should be a centerpiece of the new world order but other multilateral arrangements, such as G-8, "big troika" (or RIC) and BRIC, could be helpful as well.

- *The supremacy of international law,* which should be, on the one hand, protected from any efforts to undermine its principles and, on the other hand, further developed within the framework of the UN, the CIS and the Council of Europe.

- *Ensuring international security,* which was interpreted in a broader sense, including not only "hard" (arms control, non-proliferation of WMD, conflict resolution, peace-keeping, etc.) but also "soft" security problematique (fighting international terrorism and trans-national organized crime, solving environmental problems, mass diseases, information security, natural and technogenic catastrophes, etc.).

- *International economic and ecological cooperation,* that should be oriented to the protection of Russian national interests (particularly, in the energy sector) and based on the principle of sustainable development.

- *International humanitarian cooperation and human rights protection.* Along with the development of people-to-people contacts, the document called for popularization of the Russian culture and language as well as a more active participation of civil society institutions in international activities.

- *Public diplomacy,* that should aim at explaining Russia's national interests and foreign policy objectives as well as at creating a positive image of Russia on the international arena.

Among the regional priorities the following areas were identified as the most important:

- The *CIS* geopolitical space. The document put forward the task of reviving the CIS and further developing the related organizations (such as the Eurasian Economic Cooperation, Customs Union, CSTO and the Shanghai Organization of Cooperation).

- *Europe.* The new concept aimed at creating a new—safer and more stable—European security architecture by concluding a European Security Treaty and reviving Russia's cooperation with regional and sub-regional organizations, such as the Council of Europe, the OSCE, NATO, CBSS, BEAC, the Arctic Council, etc.

- *North America,* including the US and Canada.

- *Asia-Pacific,* including ASEAN, China, Japan, both Koreas, India and the Middle Eastern countries.

- *Africa.*

- *Latin America.*

The document also contained a special section, describing the Russian foreign policy-making mechanism and procedures. Similar to the foreign policy concept of 2000, the new doctrine was a rather short and general document. The paper did not contain any particular details; rather, its basic goal was to define the principal / conceptual foundations of Russia's international strategy.

The new Russian National Security Strategy (NSS), adopted by Presidential Decree No. 537 on 12 May 2009, incorporated the recent developments into the Russian strategic thinking (Medvedev 2009). In comparison with preceding documents, the NSS was more strategic and forward-looking. In particular, the NSS was oriented to mid- and long- rather than short-term security needs. It was also harmonized with other Russian strategic documents such as, for instance, the Concept of the Long-Term Socio-Economic Development of the Russian Federation for the Period up to 2020.

The NSS paid much more attention to human (individual) security than previous national security doctrines. The document interpreted human security in terms of "soft" rather than "hard" security problematique. This type of security was treated as the need to improve the quality of life of Russian citizens, economic growth, development of science, high tech, education, health care system, culture, and environmental improvement.

The list of military threats remained almost unchanged (compared to the 2000 documents), but they were presented in a slightly different way. For example, the doctrine distinguished between threats to the state and society, on the one hand, and to the individual, on the other. It was a bit more detailed than preceding documents in the description of the sources of military threats to Russia. According to the NSS, the Russian nuclear doctrine remained intact, although the paper emphasized (at least at the level of a political declaration) Moscow's loyalty to its strategic aim of comprehensive nuclear disarmament.

The novelty of the NSS was its introduction of the system of indicators to characterize the state of affairs in the field of national security. This system of indicators included the following parameters:

- The level of unemployment.
- The decile coefficient.[8]
- Consumer price increase rates.
- External and national debt as a percentage in the GDP (%).

---

8   The decile coefficient (DC) is a correlation between the incomes of 10% of the wealthiest and 10% of the poorest population (Coefficient Decilny 2011). This coefficient reflects the level of income disparity and social differentiation. The DC varies from 5 to 15. Experts believe that if the country's DC is more than 10, there are grounds for social instability and even an uprising. According to the Russian Committee on Statistics, the Russian DC for 2010 was 14 (http://www.gks.ru/free_doc/new_site/population/urov/urov_32kv.htm).

- Governmental spending on health care, culture, education and research as a percentage in the GDP.

- Rates of annual modernisation of weapons as well as military and special equipment.

- Supply rates for the country's demand for military and engineering personnel.

Although these indicators were incomplete, the very idea of using them to monitor the national security system was innovative and relevant. The NSS foresaw the possibility of regular renovation of the indicator system.

The new Russian military doctrine was adopted by President Medvedev on 5 February 2010 (Medvedev 2010). Similar to the NSS, it was designed, in a way, to take into account the latest developments in the world strategic situation, including the post-Russia-Georgia military conflict realities. As compared with the military doctrine of 2000, the new document paid more attention to the socio-economic aspects of the Russian military strategy as well as to the defense diplomacy (with special emphasis on security cooperation with Belarus, CSTO and SCO).

In the immediate aftermath of President Dmitry Medvedev signing the new Russian military doctrine most foreign analysts' attention focused on the fact that a first preemptive nuclear strike was not mentioned in the document and on the attention given to NATO as the chief source of "danger" to the security of the Russian Federation (Russian Military Doctrine 2014). Comments by NATO's leadership that the doctrine was not a realistic portrayal of NATO were reported by the press, but there was no strong criticism of that aspect of the doctrine. Instead, Russian authors drew attention to the gap between Russia's conventional military capabilities *vis-a-vis* NATO and its reliance on nuclear weapons in a conventional conflict.

Russian Foreign Minister Sergey Lavrov drew the attention of then NATO Secretary General Rasmussen to the wording of Russia's military doctrine which says that the security risks are caused not by NATO itself but by the "desire to give the military potential of the North Atlantic Treaty Organization global functions carried out in violation of the standards of international law, to move the military infrastructure of NATO member states to Russia's borders including by expanding the bloc". The doctrine also speaks about the risks due to "developing and deploying strategic missile defense systems which undermine global stability and violate the present balance of forces in the nuclear missile sphere, and also the militarization of outer space, the deployment of strategic nonnuclear systems of high precision weapons" (Medvedev 2010).

The Putin-2 era

In February 2013 Putin, elected for his third term in 2012, released a new Russian foreign policy doctrine (Putin 2013a). It differed from the 2008 version in its conceptual assumptions. As far as the existing world order was concerned the document stated that the international environment was still seen to be "decentralizing" as Western influence declined and to be in transition to a "polycentric world" that was both "turbulent" and increasingly competitive. But while the 2008 doctrine noted the steady overcoming of the legacy of the Cold War and "the end of the ideological era," the 2013 doctrine made no reference at all to the Cold War. Instead it placed greater emphasis on the world's "civilizational diversity," competition over values and the negative impact of a "re-ideologization" of international affairs.

Some Western experts argued that the new Russian doctrine, although acknowledging some of the international problems such as the continuing "crisis" in Afghanistan, did not provide an adequate framework for dealing with them. Others questioned the feasibility of some of Russia's aims, not least the attempts to build up its role in BRICS and to develop the EEU into a sustainable entity (Hansen 2013; Monaghan 2013; Simons 2013).

The 2013 doctrine was quite optimistic about a future world order. The document acknowledged threats and challenges to Russia's security, but it also emphasized opportunities and the need for the country to be active. As the doctrine noted, Russia "will work to anticipate and lead events" (Putin 2013a) As part of this, it emphasized the importance of soft power, famously defined as the ability "to shape the preferences of others" (Nye 2004).

Following the foreign policy concept a new international information security doctrine has been adopted on July 24, 2013. The document had a detailed description of security threats in the field of information and communication technologies (ICTs). It identified cyber crime and terrorism as well as information warfare as new security threats both to Russia's national security and global security. The doctrine called on the CIS, CSTO, SCO and BRICS countries, G8, G20 as well as the international community at large to cooperate on combating transnational cyber crime and terrorism. Particularly, the document endorsed the Russian initiative to conclude an international, UN-based, agreement on fighting transnational cyber crime (Putin 2013b). The document also suggested ways and means how to promote Russia's positive international image with the help of ICTs.

The Ukrainian crisis that started in 2014 entailed an essential revision of the Russian foreign and national security policies' conceptual / doctrinal basis.

Such a revision has started from Russia's military strategy. On 26 December 2014, an updated version of the military doctrine was signed by President Vladimir Putin (2014). The amendments were approved by the Security Council on December 19, 2014. The new doctrine highlighted "NATO's military buildup" and the bloc's expansion toward the Russian borders as being the main external dangers to Russia's security. Other threats mentioned in the document include the development and deployment of the U.S. BMD systems, the implementation of the "global strike" doctrine, plans to place weapons in space, deployment of high-precision conventional weapons systems as well as evolving forms of warfare such as, for example, information warfare. For the first time, the protection of Russia's national interests in the Arctic in peacetime was assigned to the Russian armed forces.

The doctrine showed increased Russian interest in improving its own ability to use precision conventional weapons. For the first time, the concept of non-nuclear deterrence was introduced in the document. This became a reflection of the fact that most of the military threats that Russia faces now are of non-nuclear character and can be successfully met with conventional means. But the central question of when Moscow might feel compelled to use nuclear weapons seems unchanged from the position laid out in the previous (2010) doctrine (Russian Military Doctrine 2014). In general, the new version of the military doctrine retained its defensive nature.

Among the domestic sources of danger, the doctrine identified internal threats as being activities aimed at destabilizing the situation in the country, terrorist activities to harm the sovereignty and territorial integrity of Russia, fuelling inter-ethnic and religious conflicts as well as actions involving anti-Russian and antipatriotic propaganda (especially among the young people).

The new doctrine differed from the previous one in treating internal threats to the country as the military ones. The 2010 strategy merely referred to "attempts at violent change of the Russian Federation's constitutional order," "undermining sovereignty, violation of unity and territorial integrity" (Medvedev 2010) while the new document added "the destabili-zation of the domestic political and social situation in the nation" and even "information-related activity aimed at influencing the population, primarily the country's young citizens, with the goal of undermining the historical, spiritual and patriotic traditions in the area of defending the Fatherland" (Putin 2014). Such a broad interpretation of internal threats may lead to perceptions of any political opposition as an activity requiring a military response.

In late July 2015 President Putin approved a new version of Russia' maritime doctrine that included both naval and civilian components (Putin 2015a). As the Russian vice-premier Dmitry Rogozin has explained, the novelty of the document was that it emphasized the priority of two re-gions—North Atlantic and Arctic where NATO activities and international competition for natural resources and sea routes continued to grow and required Russia's "adequate response" (Russia revises navy Doctrine 2015). Along with the naval forces the nuclear icebreaker fleet will be modernized by 2020.

In parallel, Russia's Security Council worked on updating Russian na-tional security and information security doctrines through 2020, a move that should bring the two into line with Russia's 2014 military doctrine. The updates were partly in response to "the developments of the Arab Spring, in Syria and Iraq, [and] the situation in and around Ukraine," Security Council Secretary Nikolay Patrushev said. He specifically mentioned NATO's build up in Eastern Europe as a catalyst for the decision to amend its doctrines. "The United States and NATO are growing more and more aggressive [with] respect [to] Russia. They are building up their of-fensive potential in the direct proximity [of] our borders and are actively deploying a global missile defense system," said Patrushev (2015).

As far as the information security doctrine is concerned the Security Council said the new document will prioritize "strengthening state guaran-tees of privacy, improving the competitiveness of Russian products," and improving hardware and software to beef up national information security infrastructure (TASS 2015).

On December 31, 2015, Russian President Vladimir Putin approved a new NSS. The doctrine paid a great attention to the internal aspects of Russia's security. Particularly, security threats such as terrorism, radical nationalism and religious fanatism, separatism, organized crime and cor-ruption were identified.

To mitigate the above risks Russia will seek economic growth, devel-opment of the country's scientific-technical potential, "the preservation and augmentation of traditional Russia spiritual and moral values as the foundation of Russian society, and its education of children and young people in a civil spirit" (Putin 2015b). This includes "the creating of a system of spiritual-moral and patriotic education of citizens."

As for the external threats, the NSS-2015 accused the West of causing the Ukrainian crisis, fomenting "color revolutions," destroying "traditional Russian religious and moral values," "creating seas of tension in the Eurasian region," and pursuing "multifarious and interconnected" threats to Russian national security (Putin 2015b). The document noted a threat emanating from the biological weapons. "The network of U.S. biological military labs is expanding on the territories of countries neighboring Russia," it said.

The NSS-2015 underlined that "Russia's independent foreign and domestic policy" has been met with counteraction by the US and its allies, "seeking to maintain its dominance in world affairs." The new NSS also declared that Russia has demonstrated the ability, "to protect the rights of compatriots abroad" (Putin 2015b).

The doctrine has got a hostile reaction from the Western expert community. According to one account,

> "The 2015 NSS is a blueprint for Moscow's reestablishment of a militaristic, authoritarian state that gains it legitimacy through the blatant promotion internally of nationalism and fear of an imminent Western military threat. Confrontation with the West is now the order of the day as Russia seeks to reassert its "great power" dominion over the former states of the Soviet Union and divert domestic attention away from a declining economy" (Payne and Schneider 2016).

The Western analysts also fear that protecting the rights of Russian ethnic minorities abroad can include military invasion and territorial annexation, as, they believe, Moscow has demonstrated in Georgia and Ukraine.

To conclude, the NSS-2015 marks the culmination of a rather long process in deteriorating relations between Moscow and the West and in how the Russian security elite perceives security threats and challenges. On the other hand, Russia's new national security doctrine signals that Moscow is still open to cooperation with its Western and other foreign partners.

Chapter 4.
Foreign Policy Decision-Making System

The collapse of the Soviet polity and the re-emergence of the independent Russian state had many serious implications for the country's foreign policy decision-making system. Decision-makers had to operate within a completely new political environment—domestic and international. The Communist Party monopoly was abolished, the role of ideology in foreign policy making was downplayed and some democratic rules of the game established. In contrast with the Soviet period when foreign policy making was handled by a narrow circle of top party and executive officials, the Russian decision-making system became more diverse, transparent and receptive to external impulses. With the help of lobbies, political parties, parliamentary factions, independent 'brain trusts' and the mass media, Russia's post-Communist society was able to influence governmental and non-governmental actors, elites and non-elites. Sometimes it is difficult to distinguish between domestic and foreign policies—they are closely intertwined—and the boundary between them became more transparent and permeable with the construction of a new political system.

The new Russian decision-making mechanism did not have a blank slate with which to work. The Russian leadership had to deal with the remnants of the formidable Soviet foreign policy apparatus and its personnel. It took quite a while to reorganize the old structures, adapt them to the new reality, select proper personnel and provide the new machinery with guidance. This process is still far from complete: Both institutes and decision-making procedures are still evolving.

The new constitutional system included new institutions, political actors (such as the presidency), interest groups, a multi-party system, and think tanks. The roles and functions of old players—foreign, defense and security agencies, legislature, mass media and public opinion—were all reconsidered. The purposes and motivation of the foreign policy mechanism have radically changed as well. The country's international strategy is no longer oriented to the struggle with capitalism or competing for global hegemony with the U.S. Instead, Russia has re-defined its international status and resources to cope with the absolutely new set of security challenges and a new system of national interests. It is also important to underline that Russia had to create a new decision-making mechanism simultaneously with and in the course of nation-building. This multiple transition was extremely difficult and the cause of numerous mistakes and shortcomings.

It should be noted that a country's decision-making system not only reflects foreign policy debate in the society but it also is, to some extent, a product of this debate and an instrument which helps to put ideas and doctrines into practice. Decision-makers are the part of this debate, consumers of the products of discourse, instruments of implementation and a feed-back loop at the same time.

This chapter focuses on how Russia's foreign and security policies have been made in the post-Communist era. In particular, it pays attention to the powers, roles and functions of actors and institutions participating in the decision-making process. Both governmental and non-governmental actors are examined. It further assesses the efficiency of the foreign policy and national security mechanism and identifies major problems in its organization and functioning.

The decision-making process involves two types of actors—governmental (the presidency, numerous executive agencies, the Russian parliament, regional and local governments, etc.) and non-governmental (interest groups / lobbies, political parties and associations, religious organizations, think tanks and—to a certain extent—the mass media[9]). Let's start our analysis of the Russian decision making process from the role of governmental actors.

Governmental actors

The government foreign policy decision making mechanism took its current shape by the mid-1990s. A proper legal and doctrinal basis (the Russian Constitution of 1993, presidential decrees of 1992–93) was later followed by a series of decisions establishing the status of different agencies in foreign policy (federal laws on security (1992), international treaties and foreign trade (both—1995), delimitation of powers between the federal center and regions in the sphere of international politics (1999), the concept of foreign policy (1993), military doctrine (1993), the national security concept (1997), etc.). A more-or-less clear division of labor between vari-

---

9   The vast majority of the Russian academic community does not view the Russian mass media as an independent actor neither in domestic nor foreign politics. Rather, Russian experts believe that mass media is used by other (more power actors) such as oligarchs, political parties, government, etc., as an instrument in their power struggle.

ous executive agencies as well as between the executive branch and the legislature has been established (although some squabbling between them occasionally occurs even now). Foreign policy and national security agencies have finalized internal structural and procedural reforms.

There are three levels of foreign policy decision-making in Russia among state actors—federal, regional and local. The first (federal) level is represented (as elsewhere) by the executive and legislative branches.

Among the **federal executive bodies** two main types can be distinguished—President-related (the President and his administration) and the Cabinet of Ministers-related (ministries, committees, services, etc.) although some agencies of the government have a double subordination (to the President and Prime Minister). Among executive agencies involved in Russia's shaping of foreign policy, four categories can be singled out: diplomacy / policy (Ministry of Foreign Affairs); national security (Ministry of Defense, intelligence community, etc.); economy (Ministry for Economic Development & Trade, Ministry of Finance, Customs Committee, etc.); and society / culture-oriented (*Rossotrudnichestvo,* Ministry of Social Development & Health Care, Ministry of Culture, Ministry of Education & Science, etc.) bodies (see Figure 2).

According to current legal regulations, the *Ministry of Foreign Affairs* (MFA) is a key executive agency in the Russian foreign policy decision-making mechanism. On February 25, 1992 President Boris Yeltsin signed a decree putting himself in direct control of the MFA as well as the Ministries of Security, Justice, and the Interior. The decree stipulated that presidential decisions should appoint and remove these ministers and their deputies (Rossiyskaya Gazeta, 1992, 27 February; Diplomatichesky Vestnik, 1992, no. 6).

On November 3, 1992 Yeltsin issued an edict that increased the Foreign Ministry's authority. To coordinate the foreign policy activities of different executive bodies, the document stressed that the MFA was entrusted with the function of coordinating and monitoring work by other ministries to ensure a unified political line by the Russian Federation in relations with foreign states and in participation in international organizations and forums (most importantly, presidential activities). Executive agencies should coordinate with the MFA draft treaties and agreements as well as publication of the dates of forthcoming visits abroad by Russia's state leaders and foreign leaders' visits to Russia and reports of their progress (Rossiyskaya Gazeta, 1992, 18 November, 7).

The leading role of the MFA in coordination of Russia's foreign policies has been confirmed by the MFA's Charter (approved by the presidential decree of March 14, 1995) (Code of the Russian Federation, 1995, no. 12, Art. 1033) and especially by another decree of March 12, 1996 "On the Co-ordinating Role of the Ministry of Foreign Affairs of the Russian Federation in Conducting of a Unified Foreign Policy of the Russian Federation" (Code of the Russian Federation, 1996, no. 12, Art. 1061).

According to the then Foreign Minister Andrei Kozyrev, "Russia has a presidential foreign policy. The Ministry of Foreign Affairs acts as the steersman and main coordinator of all branches of foreign policy under parliamentary monitoring" (Crow 1993, 4).

His successor Yevgeny Primakov has also emphasized that all the key ministries accept the fact that the MFA is the country's main foreign policy organ (Izvestiya, 1996, 9 August).

Presidents Vladimir Putin and Dmitry Medvedev have confirmed the leading role of the MFA in coordinating Russian foreign policy decision making. However, the presidents and top officials from the Presidential Administration have also emphasized on several occasions that final foreign policy decisions rest with the President.

In practical terms, however, the role of the MFA in the decision-making process varied because its ground rules were rather unstable (especially in the 1990s). From the very beginning the MFA has never been the only or ultimate decision-maker of Russia's foreign policy. Despite the fact that the Ministry was the only agency with formal responsibility for overseeing international policy, other ministries (such as the Ministry of Defense, the intelligence community, the Customs Committee, etc.) and especially the President and its Administration interfered with policy making. As far as some specific regions (CIS, Europe, Asia Pacific) are concerned the Ministry of Economic Development (MED) is often the main rival of the MFA because the lion's share of Russia's relations with these regions concerns the economy, trade, WTO-related issues, Kaliningrad problem, etc., where MED has priority.

Figure 2.   Governmental actors

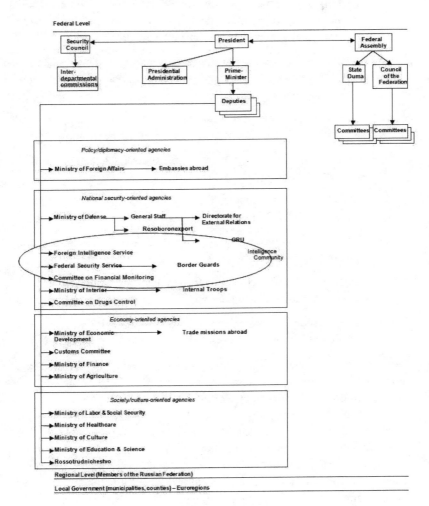

The MFA has the following responsibilities in the policy-making process:

- Gathering and processing data on Russia's foreign relations and providing the President, prime minister and other relevant executive agencies and the Parliament with such information

- Writing policy papers with the aim of attracting the attention of key players to particular problems and suggesting recommendations for solution.

- Making prognoses on regional and global developments as well as on Russia's bilateral relations with particular countries.

- Negotiating with foreign countries on specific issues and drafting treaties and agreements.

- Diplomatic correspondence with foreign countries and multilateral organizations.

- The organization of official Russian delegations' trips abroad and reception of foreign visitors in Russia.

- Maintaining routine connections with Russian embassies, consulates and trade missions abroad.

- Coordination of foreign policy activities of Russian executive agencies at all levels (federal, regional and local).

The MFA has two types of structural units (departments)—regional and functional. Regional departments are in charge of African, Asian, Asia-Pacific, European, Middle Eastern, Latin American and North American affairs. MFA's functional units (e.g., the Foreign Policy Planning Department; Department for International Organizations; Department for Non-proliferation & Arms Control; Department for Humanitarian Cooperation & Human Rights; Department for Liaison with Members of the Russian Federation, Parliament & Public Associations; Legal Department; Protocol Department; Consular Service Department, etc.) are involved in making of Moscow's foreign policy on over-arching and issue-based priorities (see Figure 3).

Along with these departments, the MFA administrative structure includes a Collegiate body, a consultative group which comprises deputy ministers, department heads, the Minister's Executive Secretary, and his Adviser. The Collegiate body discusses mainly internal administrative matters such as the improvement of structure of the Ministry and the Russian missions abroad and the reorganization of the consular service. The Executive Secretariat assists the Minister in managing the work of the MFA. There is also a Group of Advisers, staffed by senior diplomats, and Ambassadors at Large assigned special responsibilities such as conflict resolution or arms control negotiations. Deputy Ministers' responsibilities relate to particular functional or regional areas of Russian international policy and include overseeing the work of other departments.

National security-oriented agencies are represented first of all by the *Ministry of Defence* (MoD). The Ministry of Defence of the Russian Federation was formally established on the 16th March 1992, with President Yeltsin fulfilling the role of minister. On the 18th May he was replaced by General Pavel Grachev, a former Commander of the Soviet Airborne Forces, who played a critical role in obstructing the August 1991 plotters.

A radical change has taken place in civil-military relations in post-Communist Russia. Soviet-era controls and supervisory agencies have been eroded, but no authoritative civilian institutions and conventions about the limits on military involvement in political matters have emerged to take their place. There were some hopes that a sort of civilian control over the military would be established. Some experts suggested the appointment of a civilian Defence Minister who should be a President's representative among the military establishment rather than a representative of the military elite in the entourage of the President. According to this view, the Defence Minister should deal with issues such as military R&D, the defence budget, while strategic planning and operational control over the armed forces and military training should be the General Staff's responsibilities (RIA-Novosti: Russian Executive & Legislative Newsletter, 1996, June, nos. 22–28, 1). There were also some more radical proposals such as the withdrawal of the General Staff from the MoD, its re-subordination to the Defence or Security Council, and the assumption by this body of the role of chief co-ordinator of all 'power' agencies' activities (RIA-Novosti, 1997, 20 January 1997, 1–2).

Figure 3. Organizational charter of the Russian Foreign Ministry

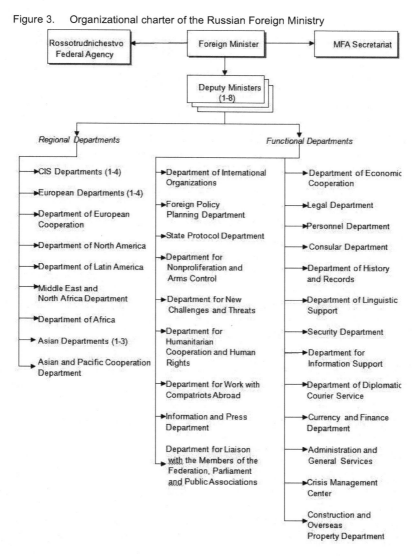

However, Yeltsin's decisions were half-hearted and cosmetic rather than substantial in nature. He limited MoD "reforms" to appointing some civilians to the minor positions and prohibiting political activity in the armed forces while the whole ministry's structure remained intact.

From the moment of its creation, the MoD appeared to be engaged in a determined struggle to recapture the influential position in foreign policy matters occupied by its Soviet predecessor. According to the Russian Constitution, the Laws on Security of 1992 and 2010 and the Law on Defense (October 1992), the President is the Commander-in-Chief of the armed forces, operating through the General Staff. The Security Council is the political body that controls Russia's military establishment. Between 1996–98, the Defence Council played an important role in military reform planning. The MoD is responsible for the development and implementation of military, technical and personnel policy. The functions of the General Staff include developing proposals relating to Russian military doctrine, and to the structure, composition, deployment, and tasks of Russian armed forces.

While the MoD was assigned political and administrative functions, the General Staff directed operational and strategic planning and the management of troops (Yeltsin 1992b). Although in the new regime the MoD's approval was formally required for any decisions affecting its sphere of competence (and its representatives were routinely included in delegations dealing with arms control and defense matters), there was a strong sense (at least in the early 1990s) that its views were being ignored and that options for the future were being foreclosed. Remarkably, Grachev became a full member of the Security Council only after he proved his loyalty to the President, once again by supporting Yeltsin in his confrontation with the Supreme Soviet in September-October 1993.

At the same time, the weakness of central authority and the lack of a sound decision-making system in the first half of the 1990s meant that the Russian military establishment enjoyed considerable autonomy and was able to gradually increase its influence on security policy. Its links with civilian politicians and expatriate communities provided the defence establishment with additional channels of influence on Russian decision-making.

It was President Putin who was able to establish an effective civilian control over the armed forces. Under Anatoly Serdyukov (2007–2012), the first really civilian Defense Minister, the Russian armed forces had undergone the most serious structural changes in the post-Soviet era. In contrast to the Yeltsin (and partially Putin-1 and 2) administrations who tried simply to downsize the huge Soviet-born military monster, the Medvedev and Putin-3 teams intended to create a principally new army. The Kremlin aimed at making the armed forces adequate to, on the one hand, the nature of domestic and external threats to Russia's military security and, on the other, Russia's economic, technical, demographic, and intellectual capabilities. The priority was to develop the armed forces and other services designed to deter aggression, as well as mobile elements, which can be quickly delivered and deployed in the required area(s) and carry out mobile operations in any region where the security of Russia might be threatened. The core idea of the Russian military reform was the transformation of the armed forces from a conventional mobilization army to a permanently combat-ready force (Makarychev and Sergunin 2013b).

Under three Putin and Medvedev administrations the MoD has continued to lose its influence on foreign policy decision-making. Prior to the Ukrainian and Syrian crises the presidents have assigned the MoD predominantly internal missions such as military reform, the war in Chechnya, etc. Even the CIS collective security system, including peace-keeping operations in the post-Soviet space and in the Balkans or arms control were no longer the MoD's preferential areas. The ministry looked often more like an instrument of implementing policies rather than a decision-maker.

To summarize, there were ups and downs in the defense agency's influence on the decision-making process. Being created and properly institutionalized later than many other Russian governmental bodies, the MoD and General Staff have had to wage permanent bureaucratic warfare to secure their interests and authority. This often resulted in open confrontation with the MFA and presidential structures as well as inconsistencies in Russia's policies in Europe. In the 1990s, the military establishment managed to retain its positions in areas such as CIS military integration, peace-keeping in the post-Soviet space and Balkans, arms control, military-technical cooperation with European countries and military-to-military contacts. The military lobby's influence increased in the periods when the President badly needed the army's support in domestic political struggles (i.e. the confrontations with Parliament in 1993 and 1998, wars in Chechnya) and decreased when the Kremlin's positions were more-or-less stable. The general tendency, however, has been that with a strong President and Foreign Minister, and the pressing goal of military reform, the defense agency's attention has eventually turned from international to domestic issues.

The intelligence community includes four major services: the Foreign Intelligence Service (FIS); military intelligence—the GRU (Glavnoe Razvedavatel'noe Upravlenie—the Main Intelligence Directorate of the General Staff); the FSS (Federal Security Service); and the Committee on Financial Monitoring (CFM).

The FIS is the most important agency in terms of decision-making. Through its stations in foreign countries and analytical services in Russia, the FIS gathers a huge amount of information that often serves as a crucial factor for decisions taken by key Russian actors (including the president). The GRU is focused on military espionage and its possibilities to influence the decision-making process are quite limited. In addition, the GRU is subordinated to the General Staff and the Defense Minister and so is unable to be an independent actor compared to other members of the intelligence community.

The FSS is mostly pre-occupied with counter-intelligence and rarely involved in purely intelligence operations. However, after the series of the 'color' revolutions in the post-Soviet space in 2004–2005 (Georgia, Ukraine, Kyrgzstan) Putin assigned the FSS the task to monitor the whole situation in the 'near abroad' (with the emphasis on potential uprisings and terrorist activities). It remains unclear whether the FSS has such capabilities because traditionally this function belonged to the FIS which incidentally was quite sceptical (and to some extent jealous) with regard to the presidential decision.

The CFM is a key agency to control financial flows to and from Russia. This body is considered as a crucial for economic / financial security of the country. Since the EU is Russia's main trade partner and source of foreign investment and technologies the CFM pays special attention to all transactions between them to prevent illegal activities.

The power / national security-oriented sector is also represented by the Ministry of the Interior and the Committee on Drugs Control. Together with the Border Guard Service (a part of the FSS) and the Customs Committee their contribution is crucial to Russia's cooperation with international partners on fighting organized crime. Cross-border crime constitutes an important area, and a common concern for both Russia and its neighbors, particularly as to the trafficking of drugs, money, goods, stolen vehicles, and even people. These types of activities have a significant impact on people's lives, the pace of economic and political reforms and undercut government revenues. At the operational level, the police, customs and special services, and border guards need to be trained to understand the implications of international laws and conventions signed by their governments. Continued training for officials from these agencies will also increase their ability to counteract illegal activities.

Among the *economy / trade-oriented agencies*, the MED is a leading actor. The MED is predominantly occupied with domestic issues, such as planning and monitoring the macro-economic strategy of Russia. However, it has a number of international policy-related functions:

- Running Russia's foreign trade.

- Daily control over the Russian foreign trade missions abroad.

- Trade-related negotiations with individual foreign countries and international economic organizations, including the EU and W.T.O.

This has inevitably led to the numerous (however, not publicized—at least when compared to tensions with the MoD) conflicts with the MFA. The latter blamed the MED for its non-professionalism and intrusion into the MFA's field of jurisdiction. The MFA insisted that the MED's activities should be coordinated with the diplomatic agency and all the Ministry's officials should clear their statements with Smolenskaya Square[10]. The MFA has also demanded that the heads of Russian trade missions in foreign countries should regularly report to ambassadors who were seen as Russia's supreme representatives abroad. Under Putin and Medvedev, the problem was also in the inter-personal relationships between the liberal-minded heads of the MED and the rather traditionalist / conservative ministers of foreign affairs.

The Customs Committee does not play any independent role in Russia's foreign policy decision-making. Rather, it is a typical body of policy-takers, overseeing implementation. However, since its huge bureaucracy deals in practical terms with the movement of people, goods and services through Russia borders, it is important that customs officers and rules correspond to international standards. For example, in the 1990s the CBSS adopted an ambitious program aimed at sub-regional co-operation, including the need to train Russian border guards and customs officers (Diplomaticheskiy Vestnik 1996: 8, 9–11). The BEAC has developed a methodology for direct and very successful cooperation between Nordic and Russian customs authorities that could be applied also elsewhere (Eliasson 2000, 70; Council of the European Union 2001, 16). At the same time (as seen from the case on Kaliningrad), the Customs Committee can also be a source of rather destructive initiatives that hamper Russia cooperation with foreign countries.[11]

---

10 The location of the MFA in Moscow.
11 For example, in January 2001 the State Customs Committee of the Russian Federation introduced the so-called Part II of the new Russian Tax Code that in fact deprived the Kaliningrad Region from the Special Economic Zone privileges. In turn, this resulted in a social-economic crisis in the *Oblast:* the prices were up by 20–30 percent and a series of

The Ministry of Finance is also of secondary importance for decision-making on international affairs (although it is crucial in domestic politics). It is responsible for allocating funds for Russia's foreign policy apparatus and Russia's joint programs with international partners. It also oversees whether there are any violations in the use of budgetary money or not. The Ministry has its own contacts with the similar agencies of foreign countries and discusses on the occasional basis partners' financial policies.

Since Russia has a quite considerable trade in agricultural goods with foreign countries and runs a number of international agricultural projects in Russia with the aim to improving technology, management and labour productivity, the Russian Ministry of Agriculture is involved from time to time in the formulation of Moscow's international policies. Similar to many other governmental agencies, its role is of a more technical, rather than political character.

The cultural / societal bloc in the Russian government is represented by the Ministry of Labour and Social Security Development, Ministry of Healthcare, Ministry of Culture and the Ministry of Education & Science. Being not independent actors (all of them coordinate their activities with the Foreign Ministry) they developed rather intense and fruitful cooperative links with foreign countries.

For example, the Ministry of Education & Science was a subject to a number of EU cooperative programs, such as TEMPUS-TACIS (inter-university co-operation), INTAS (research co-operation), SIRIUS (lecturing program), ERASMUS-MUNDUS (academic exchanges), etc. The Ministry is crucial in terms of Russia's joining the so-called Bologna Process that aims at the harmonization and integration of the European higher education system. In 2003 the Russian Federation has pledged to complete the reform of its university system (in order to comply with Bologna requirements) by 2010 although there is a great deal of scepticism about whether it will actually be achieved among experts. The Ministry has selected several institutions to serve 'pilot universities' where things like a two-level system (bachelors and masters) instead of the specialist scheme, European Credit Transfer System (ECTS), diploma supplement and mutual recognition of European and Russian diplomas are introduced.

---

protests took place (Parlamentskaya Gazeta 2001, 14 February, 1). Under pressure of the regional authorities the office of the Procurator General (with the obvious support of the President Putin) abolished the customs' decision but the status of Kaliningrad remained unclear for several years.

Given the impressive number of the Russian governmental foreign policy actors the problem of coordination of their activities is obvious. Initially, this function should rest with the *Security Council* created by Yeltsin in 1992 (in accordance with the Law on Security). The Council consists of the President (Chair), Secretary, Prime Minister and the heads of the key national security-related agencies. The Council has a Secretariat with numerous subdivisions, expert groups, etc. The Council also serves as an umbrella for various inter-agency groups (task forces) that were created to solve or monitor specific problems (most of them are of a temporary character) (see Figure 4).

According to the Law on Security, the Council:

- Determines the foundations of Russia's domestic and foreign policies

- Identifies the country's vital interests, as well as internal and external threats to its security

- Supervises the country's military, economic, social and information security

- Makes recommendations to the President on the issues of external and internal policies

- Drafts presidential decrees on national security matters, such as foreign policy, defence, military-technical co-operation with foreign countries, organised crime, etc. (Yeltsin 1992a).

In reality, however, the Council has been unable to fulfil its coordinating role for a number of reasons.

First, being a collective body the Council consists of the representatives of different agencies which often have conflicting interests (the same is true for the Council's Secretariat). They often use sabotage tactics to torpedo their rivals' initiatives without a direct confrontation with the President or the Council's Secretary. Moreover, foreign policy issues are not a very important priority for the Council and discussed on the occasional rather than regular basis. Due to its institutional organization the Council is unable to maintain daily control over the activities of the foreign policy agencies and has to limit itself only to strategic / conceptual issues. The Council has a powerful competitor, namely, the Presidential Administration that does not want to lose its control over the Russian foreign policy apparatus. For these reasons, the Council now has a figure-head role, a body that simply stamps decisions taken by others.

It seems that the *Presidential Administration* is the real coordinator of Russian foreign policies. By the presidential decree no. 1039 (19 September 1997) a special Directorate on Foreign Policy was established within the Administration (Rossiyskaya Gazeta, 1997, 26 September). According to the presidential edict, the Directorate should draft executive initiatives and assist in drafting international treaties, plan foreign trips (in collaboration with the MFA, nominate foreign policy-making candidates and collect foreign policy information for the President.

Unsurprisingly, many of these functions overlap with those of the Security Council and make the latter a marginal or nominal player.

Moreover, the Russian presidents practicized appointing special envoys to deal with most important / complicated international issues. These Kremlin's representatives were subordinated directly to the President, i.e. his administration. For example, with the start of his second presidency Putin appointed Sergey Yastrzhembsky as a Special Assistant on EU Affairs and charged him with coordination of all Russian foreign policy agencies with European agendas (plus the Kaliningrad problem). This appointment, however, has provoked some disgruntlement on the part of the MFA and MED who perceived this position as one more redundant bureaucratic structure.

To sum up, the problem of coordination of executive agencies' foreign policies is not solved so far. Even under Putin (famous for his centralist spirit), there is a lot of unhealthy competition and tension between various governmental institutions. Russia still lacks a single (governmental) voice in international affairs and Moscow's European partners are often unsure of whom to listen and contact.

The Russian Parliament is another player on the federal political arena. In the well-developed democracies the legislature is a crucial and integral part of the foreign policy decision-making process. However, in the case of Russia the situation is different. It should be noted that with adoption of the Russian Constitution in December 1993, the President became a key figure in foreign policy making. The President "directs the foreign policy of the Russian Federation", within the framework set by the Constitution and laws of the country (Articles 80 and 86). He no longer needs Parliament's approval of ministerial appointments, or of the composition of the Security Council (Article 83).

The bicameral legislature (the Federal Assembly) has quite limited powers in the field of foreign policy. On the other hand, it is able to influence the executive in some ways. The President needs the legislature's approval of his ambassadorial appointees (Art. 83 (m)). The lower house, the State Duma and the Council of the Federation ('Senate') ratify and denounce international treaties (Art. 106 (g)). Parliament also drafts legislation related to foreign and national security policies (foreign trade, defense, conversion of the defense industry, national security, etc.). However, its power over legislation is less effective because of the extensive use of executive decrees, and the President's rights of veto.

The legislature can also adopt non-binding resolutions which have limited impact on the executive but cannot be fully ignored by the President and the government. It has some voice in the budgeting process and may cut or increase appropriations for particular foreign policy agencies. The legislature may undertake investigations. The Council of the Federation exercises the sole parliamentary say on the sending of armed forces abroad. Legislators can also appeal to public opinion to block some executive's initiatives.

Finally, the Federal Assembly develops cooperation with foreign parliaments and parliamentary assemblies of international organizations (CIS, Council of Europe, European Parliament, NATO, OSCE, etc.). However, neither of these prerogatives affords Parliament much leverage over policy and even the legislators themselves acknowledge this (Rybkin 1995, 28). The Russian Parliament's powers and impact on foreign policy cannot be compared to those of, say, the U.S. Congress.

The Parliament has an institutional framework for making and even conducting foreign policy. The State Duma has three committees which deal with international affairs: the Committee for International Affairs, the Committee for Defense, and the Committee on Economics (foreign trade, negotiations with the EU and WTO, etc.). The Council of the Federation has similar three specialized bodies. These committees comprise rather competent specialists. For example, Dmitry Kosachev, who was a Chairman of both the Duma's and Council of the Federation's committees for international affairs, is a graduate of MGIMO (Moscow State Institute of International Relations) and has a solid foreign service record.

It should be noted that, in contrast with domestic policies, the Russian legislature rarely clashes with the executive branch in the domain of international politics (with the possible exception of Moscow's policies in the "near abroad"). Rather, it usually backs the President in case of international crises or his talks with the EU, Kaliningrad, the Russian minorities in the Baltic States, Yugoslavia, Ukraine and Syria.

For example, the Parliament supported Yeltsin during the Kosovo crisis in 1999. There were a number of radicals (mainly from the Liberal Democratic Party and the Communist Party factions) who called for immediate military-technical assistance to Serbia and creation of a trilateral union between Russia-Belarus-Serbia (Rossiyskaya Gazeta, 1999, 30 March, 1; Nezavisinaya Gazeta, 1999, 1 April, 3). However, the vast majority of both the State Duma and the Council of the Federation was against Russia's direct involvement into the Balkan war. Moreover, although the Council of the Federation approved funds for sending Russian peace-keepers to Kosovo, many senators expressed their concerns about the financial and security implications of peace-keeping operation for Russia.

In the case of the Yugoslav conflict the government and Parliament have often played the famous game of "good and bad cops" where the executive has "had to" use a tougher tone with the West because of the legislative pressure.

Another example is Parliament's nearly unanimous support of the Kremlin's policies on Crimea and Ukraine in 2014 (Sergunin 2014a). With very few exceptions, both chambers ratified the treaty of reunification with Crimea. In several weeks after this, the Council of the Federation has provided President Putin with authority to use military force against Ukraine (if needed). The upper chamber has also approved Putin's military intervention in Syria in autumn 2015.

Although the legislature does not play any significant role in Russia's foreign policy decision-making, even Yeltsin has realized the need to establish a liaison / consultative mechanism to avoid or prevent unnecessary conflicts with the Federal Assembly. The positions of presidential representatives in the State Duma and the Council of Federation have been created. These officials not only monitor the situation in both houses and take an active part in committee hearings and plenary sessions. They also draft legislation, consult deputies, present president-sponsored legislation, invite experts, make a legal assessment of bills pending in Parliament, introduce presidential nominees and deliver presidential messages to Parliament (Sergunin 1999a). The presidential representatives got secretarial support from the special unit of the Presidential Administration which has around 25 employees (Rossiyskaya Gazeta, 1998, 14 February, 2).

The post of representative of the Prime-Minister in the Federal Assembly and Constitutional Court has also been established (Rossiyskaya Gazeta, 1999, 11 June, 26; Sergunin 1999a).

The legal directorates of both the presidential and Cabinet administrations are responsible for cooperation with Parliament in areas such as drafting legislation and the legislative agenda as well as legal assessment of legislation adopted by the State Duma. By a special presidential decree (7th March 1996) the Main Directorate on Domestic and Foreign Policies of the Administration has been charged with gathering information on deputies' attitude to president-sponsored legislation (Rossiskaya Gazeta, 1996, 16 March).

Interestingly, liaison offices not only participated in the legislative process but also organized training programs for government officials. For example, in March 1998 the Department on Relations with the State Duma of the Cabinet sponsored four workshops on drafting laws (Rossiyskaya Gazeta, 1998, 7 April, 2).

Some informal liaison structure has emerged as well. The Foreign and Defense ministries often sponsor conferences, seminars and round-tables where experts from Parliament are invited. Different Russian think tanks (CFDP, International Discussion Club "Valdai", Russian Council on International Affairs, etc.) are also used for informal cooperation between agencies and parliamentary committees. These informal channels of communication have been rather helpful in reaching an executive-legislative consensus on issues such as NATO and EU enlargement, a CFE Treaty, Northern Dimension Initiative (NDI), Kaliningrad problem, Russia's policies in the Baltic Sea region and on Ukraine, etc.

However, the existing executive-legislative liaison mechanism is far from perfect. It is reactive rather than proactive. It often simply follows international events and developments rather than foresees or shapes them. The presidential and Cabinet's liaison structures often duplicate each other. There is a lack of coordination between different executive agencies: This frequently thwarts the government's schemes and under-mines presidential leadership in Parliament. There is also the impression that the liaison mechanism sometimes looks like an individual (executive) business rather than a joint executive-legislative venture: While presiden-tial officials are rather persistent in pursuing their interests, the legislature remains passive and indifferent.

On a more general note, the legislature could play a more significant role in Russian foreign policy making both through its own parliamentary diplomacy and providing scrutiny and accountability of the executive (per-haps the main function of the legislature in a democratic society).

The second (lower) level of government actors is represented by the **members of the Russian Federation**. Prior to the early 1990s (when the Soviet model of federalism was camouflage for unitarianism) the Russian regions had no any say in foreign policy making. However, with the rebirth of the Russian federative system many regions saw the development of their international contacts as an important resource both for solving their internal problems and putting pressure on the federal center (to negotiate more concessions for their loyalty to Moscow).

Specialists distinguish two main forms of the regions' international activities–direct (developing external relations of their own) and indirect (influencing federal foreign policies).

Direct methods include:

- *Creating a regional legislative base.* In the 1990s, many regional governments adopted normative acts aimed at legitimizing the foreign policy of the members of the Federation. By doing this, regional elites tried to carve out their own policies and thus become more independent from Moscow. In fact, a number of these acts either contradicted the Russian Constitution or went beyond what was envisioned in it. Spheres that in the Constitution were ascribed to Moscow exclusively appeared as areas of joint jurisdiction in many documents. For example, Moscow's treaties with Bashkortostan, Kabardino-Balkariya, North Ossetia and Tatarstan granted these republics the right to defend their state and territorial integrity. Yekaterinburg, Tatarstan and Udmurtiya gained authority over the functioning of defense industries and arms export. In some documents, regions (Bashkortostan, Tatarstan) had authority to establish relations and conduct agreements with foreign states. Tuva granted the local parliament the right to declare war and peace. The Tuvinian constitution even envisaged the right of secession. Areas identified in the Federal Constitution as spheres of joint authority appeared in later treaties as the exclusive jurisdiction of regions, including cooperation with foreign governments and international organizations (Bashkortostan, Tatarstan). However, sometimes local legislation has forestalled its Federal counterpart: For example, encouraging foreign investment and land ownership (Novgorod the Great) (Joenniemi and Sergunin 2014).

In the early Putin period, however, regional and local laws were streamlined and brought into line with federal legislation (Mikhailova 2013; Reddaway and Orttung 2005).

- *Treaty-making.* Despite the heated debate on the treaty-making powers of the center and members of the Federation, the regions were quite active in this area. For example, in the 1990s, Tatarstan signed more than 50 agreements on trade, scientific and cultural cooperation with foreign countries and their administrative units. Tatarstan was the first member of the Russian Federation that signed—with Moscow's consent—a direct treaty with a foreign state (Turkey) in 1995. In the 1990s, the Russian regions concluded more than 300 international agreements, which used to be prepared solely with the assistance of the foreign ministry.

However, some agreements were signed that have bypassed Moscow. One example comes from the time when the Foreign Ministry expressed its concerns about the agreement between the Russian region of Kabardino-Balkariya and Abkhazia that formally was a part of Georgia. Another example is that of 1995 when Moscow annulled the trade treaty between Kaliningrad and Lithuania because it came into collision with Federal legislation. Despite these collisions, the treaty-making activities of the regions were one of the most effective instruments for strengthening their international prestige.

- *Establishing representative offices*. To facilitate direct cooperation with foreign countries the regions used to set up trade and cultural missions abroad. For instance, the Republic of Tatarstan established offices in 16 countries. In 1994, upon Tatarstan's request, President Boris Yeltsin sanctioned the establishment of a Turkish General Consulate in Kazan (the capital of Tatarstan). Presently, St. Petersburg has thirteen information business centers throughout the world (including one in Melbourne), eight of which are located in the Baltic and Nordic countries that St. Petersburg sees as its most valuable partners (St. Petersburg Committee on External Relations 2014).

Since federal law stipulated that representative offices should be at the expense of the regions, few subjects can afford having missions abroad. For example, Nizhny Novgorod had the only one—in the twinning region of North Rhine Westphalia (Germany) and had to close it because of the lack of finance. The city of Kaliningrad had an office in Brussels in the late 1990s but closed it because of insufficient funds. The Kaliningrad regional government had an office in Vilnius in the 2000s but had to close it after the London Arbitration Tribunal issued a distraint order on Kaliningrad's property abroad because the region had failed to pay its debt to the Dresdner Bank (Predstavitelstvo 2009).

For these (financial) reasons, the vast majority of subnational actors prefer to rely on federal structures—embassies, consulates, and trade missions—to pursue their international policies.

- *Attracting foreign investment*. Some regions succeeded in getting foreign investment (Moscow, St. Petersburg, Kaliningrad, Novgorod, Yamal-Nenets Autonomous Area, etc.). Lured by low taxes and enthusiastic local officials, a growing number of foreign investors were flocking to the Novgorod region in the 1990s. For example, in 1994–99 total foreign direct investment in the region has increased from $153 to $600 million. According to some accounts, 29 investment projects worth $1.5 billion were under consideration. At that time, 49% of the oblast's GDP was derived from foreign investment. In investment dollars per capita, Novgorod was second only to Moscow, and was rated third for its economic development in the 1990s and early 2000s (as noted by Johnson's Russia List, no. 2183, on May 18, 1998). There were about 200 foreign or joint-venture enterprises in Novgorod which played a major economic role, providing 20,000 jobs and 62 per cent of regional industrial output. Firms with foreign capital provided half the taxes paid to the region. The situation changed in the mid-2000s, when President Putin's recentralization led to a decline in foreign investment. By 2010, Novgorod oblast was only ninth in terms of foreign investment per capita (Reiting Regionov Rossii 2011).

In contrast, Kaliningrad and St. Petersburg have managed to attract foreign investment despite the Putin regime's poor image abroad and two economic crises in 1998–1999 and 2008–2010. For example, Kaliningrad oblast has exploited its marginal / exclave location to secure from Moscow special status as a free economic zone (FEZ) (1991), then a special economic zone (SEZ) (1996, 2006) (Joenniemi and Sergunin 2013). With foreign investment from Germany, South Korea, the United States, and elsewhere, Kaliningrad has built a large cluster of car factories that accounts for 15 percent of car production in Russia (Avtotor 2014). St. Petersburg has one of the best investment ratings among Russian regions and earned the highest rank (1A) in 2013. In that year, St. Petersburg attracted $8.9 billion in foreign investment, 50 percent more than in 2012 (St. Petersburg Committee on Investment 2014).

- *Creating a region's positive image*. To attract foreign investors, many regions launched dynamic PR campaigns. They arrange exhibitions and take part in international fairs. A good example is the so-called Cooperation Days aimed at developing the region's international contacts, which became a tradition in Novgorod the Great. Normally, 60 foreign firms take part in this event. Moreover, regional leaders undertake foreign trips with PR purposes. The regions publish English-language periodicals oriented to foreign audiences. In the 1990–2000s, the following regional leaders were among the most successful 'PR specialists': Dmitri Ayatskov (Saratov), Dmitry Kobylkin (Yamal-Nenets Autonomous

Area), Yuri Luzhkov (Moscow), Boris Nemtsov (Nizhny Novgorod), Mikhail Prusak (Novgorod), Mintimir Shaimiev (Tatarstan), Anatoly Sobchak (St Petersburg), and Konstantin Titov (Samara).

- *Cooperation with international organizations.* To confirm their status of global actors, many regions try to develop relations with international organizations. For example, Tatarstan cooperates with UNESCO, UNIDO, the European Congress of Municipal and Regional Governments, and the Council of Europe. Furthermore, Tatarstan is a member of the European Regions Assembly. The north-west regions of Russia cooperate with the CBSS, Hanseatic League and the BEAC. These multilateral institutions have enthusiastically supported Russian subnational actors, demonstrating that sometimes even their marginal geographic location does not preclude them from being attractive international partners. It should be noted that cooperation with international organizations is important for regions not only in terms of getting additional leverage in the power-struggle with Moscow but also in terms of opening up them for the world-wide processes of globalization and regionalization.

Indirect methods are:

- *Influencing federal legislation.* Local legislation not only legitimises the external relations of the regions but also affects federal legislation. For example, the Nizhny Novgorod law on international agreements (1995) has been used by the federal parliament to draft a law on coordinating the external relations of the members of the Federation (1999). The comments made by the Nizhny Novgorod regional legislature on the drafts of the federal laws on international treaties of the Russian Federation (1995), state regulation of foreign trade (1995), visas (1997), foreign policy powers of the Federation and its members (1999) have all been taken into account by the State Duma.

- *Taking part in federal diplomacy.* Since the federal law envisages Russian regional and local governments' participation in international activities that affect them, subnational actors have tried to influence national diplomacy. For example, the representatives of Karelia and Krasnodar assisted the Foreign Ministry in preparing treaties with Finland and Cyprus, respectively. The Murmansk authorities assisted the Russian MFA in negotiating the Russian–Norwegian Agreement on the Delimitation of Maritime Territories in the Barents Sea (2010). The Murmansk and Kaliningrad regional governments helped Russian diplomats and border guards prepare the Russian–Norwegian (2010) and Russian–Polish (2011) agreements establishing visa-free regimes for borderland residents. This was quite helpful for harmonizing Federal and regional interests.

It should be noted that subnational units' international cooperation projects do not exist in isolation but instead form part and parcel of a broader Russian strategy of cooperation with Europe. In sum, national diplomacy and paradiplomacy reinforce and complement rather than contradict each other.

- *Conflict prevention and resolution.* Over time, the federal authorities have realized that regionalization and its concomitant familiarization can serve as ways for Russia to solve problems with neighboring countries. Kaliningrad's close cooperation with Lithuania, Poland, and Germany has impeded the rise of territorial claims by these countries and has dampened their concerns over excessive militarization in the region. Moscow and Kaliningrad worked hand in glove in negotiating the 2011 Russian–Polish agreement governing local traffic along the border. Cooperation between Finland and Karelia was also conducive to the eventual solution of the Karelia issue.

- *'Verbal diplomacy'.* To influence federal foreign policies, regional leaders often make statements on particular international issues. For example, in the 1990s, Yuri Luzhkov, former Moscow mayor, protested against the division of the Black Sea Fleet between Russia and Ukraine and insisted on the Russian jurisdiction over Sevastopol and Crimea where the fleet is based. Former Nizhny Novgorod governor Boris Nemtsov made a number of negative statements on the prospects of the Russian-Byelorussia Union thus generating a grumbling reaction from Minsk (and the Russian MFA). The implications of this 'verbal diplomacy' were that it demonstrated the growing influence of the regions over Russia's international strategy and—at the same time—the absence of political culture among regional elites. In other words, 'verbal diplomacy' was rather detrimental to the Russian national interests.

- *Exploiting the Parliament.* The regions use the legislature to lobby their foreign policy interests at the federal level. The Council of the Federation, the upper chamber of the parliament, which under the Yeltsin regime was made up of the regional leaders (governors and speakers of local legislative assemblies) was the most popular vehicle for regional lobbying. For example, senators from the border regions tried to persuade the federal government that, being marginal territories and facing numerous problems, these subnational units needed special status and privileges to ensure their sustainable development. The senators often use their official foreign trips to find new partners for their home regions and promote them in the international arena. For instance, Prusak, being a chairman of the Foreign Affairs Committee of the Council of the Federation and the Vice President of the Parliamentary Assembly of the Council of Europe, often used his official position to promote Novgorod's interests. Under Putin, this practice has been continued although the composition of the upper chamber has been changed: Now it is formed by regional representatives elected by local legislatures.

- *Capitalizing upon federal infrastructure.* To influence federal foreign policy the regions use the institutional structure created by Moscow in the periphery. For example, the Foreign Ministry has established a special unit on inter-regional affairs. The Foreign Ministry, MED, Customs Committee and Federal Border Service have offices in those regions engaged in intensive international cooperation. Theoretically, these agencies should coordinate and control the regions' international contacts. However, they often serve as a region's instrument of pressure upon Moscow rather than the centre's leverage. The problem is that these agencies are dependent on local authorities in terms of housing, basic provisions and professional careers. They are usually staffed by the locals with close connections to regional elites.

Another alarming implication of regionalization is the dependence of the so-called 'power structures' (armed forces, police, special services) on local authorities. Given their lack of funds and shortage of food, energy and accommodation (especially in the 1990s), many military commanders had to apply for assistance from local governments. This casts doubts on the loyalty of the 'power structures' to Moscow.

- *Exploiting international organizations.* To put pressure on Moscow the regions managed to use not only federal institutions but also international organizations. For instance, to get a more privileged status (SEZ, visa-free or visa-facilitated regime with Lithuania and Poland) Kaliningrad quite skilfully exploited venues such as the CBSS and the EU Northern Dimension. Russia's northern regions are represented at the Regional Council of the BEAC and develop direct ties with the neighbouring regions of Finland, Norway and Sweden. With the help of the OSCE, Council of Europe and the Red Cross, Ingushetiya managed to increase the flow of humanitarian assistance to refugees from Chechnya after the first Chechen war (1994–96).

It should finally be noted that in real life the regions combine both direct and indirect methods because they are complimentary rather than mutually exclusive.

Operationally, there are three main levels of regions' international activities: Bilateral cooperation with respective subnational units of foreign countries; cooperation between the inter-regional associations and foreign partners; and cross-border and trans-regional cooperation.

Bilateral cooperation between members of the Russian Federation and foreign countries (or their subnational units) ranges from economic, social, environmental and cultural matters to security issues. For example, Nizhny Novgorod oblast has rather close relations with the North Rhine-Westphalia region, Italian Lombardy, and the French Buche-du-Rhone, as they have much in common with the Nizhny Novgorod economy.

The second level of international cooperation is through the external relations of the Russian inter-regional associations. There are a number of inter-regional associations or blocs such as the Northwest Association, Greater Volga Association, Chernozem Association, Ural Association, and the Siberian Accords Association which mainly deal with economic and social issues. The members of these associations meet several times each year to discuss issues of common interest which need coordination, (e.g. transport, communication, food and fuel supplies, and joint projects). However, along with domestic affairs, these blocs are increasingly engaging in international relations. For example, the Northwest Association led by St. Petersburg coordinates foreign economic relations of its members with the Baltic / Nordic countries. The Siberian Accords Association (19 members) is a driving force for Russian-Byelorussian integration. Its members accounted for 20% of Russian trade with Minsk in the late 1990s and early 2000s (Nechipurenko 1999, 4). Moreover, the association initiated a Siberian youth movement, 'Russian-Byelorussian Union'.

The third level of international cooperation, is cross-border (cooperative projects between regions in neighbouring countries) and trans-regional (collaboration with and within multilateral organizations). For example, Russia's north-west regions cooperate closely with Nordic countries: Finland and Karelia traditionally cooperate in areas such as the economy, transport, communication, tourism, ecology and culture. Kaliningrad has the same experience of cooperation with Lithuania and Poland. It should finally be noted that cooperation with foreign countries was crucial for many Russian regions in terms of survival. For example, after the 1998 financial meltdown Poland and Lithuania provided Kaliningrad with humanitarian assistance.

Along with bilateral channels, there are multilateral institutions such as the CBSS, BEAC, Nordic Council, Arctic Council, and Black Sea Co-operation forum. For example, at the May 1996 Visby summit the CBSS adopted an ambitious program for regional cooperation in economics, trade, finance, transportation, communications, conversion, ecology, bor-der and customs control, and fighting organized crime. Within the BEAC, two working groups—the Environment Task Force of the Barents Council and the Environment Committee of the Barents Regional Council—proved to be successful in identifying ecological problems in the region and seek-ing funds for the implementation of joint projects. Both organizations have been very helpful in implementing the so-called Northern Dimension Envi-ronmental Partnership (NDEP).

The EU is also an important player in trans-regional cooperation. The EU members Finland and Sweden are especially important as they neighbor Russia. Finland was particularly enthusiastic about the so-called "Northern Dimension" of EU policy, and hoped to serve as a bridge be-tween the EU and Russia. To promote economic co-operation between the EU and non-EU countries, Brussels has allocated resources for in-vestment and other projects in a program named "INTERREG". Under the program, Finland could enlist the economic support of the Russian re-gions if the partners are able to provide 50% in matching funds. Two of four INTERREG programs covered the northern parts of Russia: INTER-REG Barents (with a budget of ECU 36 million) and INTERREG Karelen (with a budget of ECU 32 million). After the May 2004 EU enlargement, the Union has new members that border Russia—Poland, Lithuania, Lat-via and Estonia. Currently, these countries are not very keen on intensive cooperation with Russia (for various reasons) but some sustainable trans-border links have already been formed between them and the Russian north-western regions (Kaliningrad, Pskov, Novgorod and Leningrad / St. Petersburg).

The third (and the last) level of governmental actors in Europe-Russia relations is **local government**. To date, both Russia and the EU have preferred to focus on intergovernmental or supranational levels (and from time to time on the members of the Russian Federation), virtually ignoring the role of local government. Cooperation at this level is under-developed. Meanwhile, it has become commonplace to ascertain that micro-level negotiations may be crucial for establishing horizontal networks which could serve as a solid basis for mechanisms of interdependency. In the 1990s, a number of the most dynamic Russian cities, such as Moscow, St. Petersburg, Samara, Nizhny Novgorod, Novgorod the Great, Kazan, Kaliningrad, Petrozavodsk, Yekaterinburg, etc., tried to develop their own relations with Europe although each of them had different experiences (both positive and negative).

For the Russian north-western / border municipalities, the Euroregions project (based on engagement of local governments from neighbouring countries) became an important instrument for cooperation with their European counterparts. As the European experience demonstrates, the Euroregions project is an efficient tool for solving trans-border problems and overcoming socio-economic and cultural disparities between neighbouring regions. It could be a promising venue for subregional cooperation.

Currently, local governments from three Russian border regions are the part of the Euroregions initiative—Kaliningrad, Karelia and Pskov. Kaliningard is the most dynamic Russian region in terms of Euroregions' participation. Currently, the Kaliningrad Region includes five Euroregions (Baltic, Saule, Neman, Sesupe and Lyna-Lava). Municipalities from Poland, Lithuania, Latvia, Belarus, Denmark and Sweden cooperate with Kaliningrad towns and counties in the framework of these Euroregions. They deal with issues, such as the development of regional and municipal transport infrastructure, energy sector, agricultural technologies, treatment of waste and sewage, environment, culture, etc. (Sergunin, 2006). The same problems are on the agenda of the Karelian and Pskov Euroregions.

Despite some successful projects that were implemented within the framework of trans-border cooperation (especially the Baltic and Karelia Euroregions exemplify success stories) the overall results of local government's international activities remain rather modest. The Euroregions are basically reduced to what common Russians call 'bureaucratic tourism'- i.e. exchanges between municipalities. With rare exceptions, they do not promote economic cooperation and horizontal links at the people-to-people or NGO levels. There is no clear division of labor between Euroregions (especially in case of the five Kaliningrad Euroregions). In some cases, there is an unhealthy competition for funds (EU and Russian) between different Euroregions. In other words, the Euroregions concept—being a potentially important tool for subregional cooperation—does not work properly.

Many Russian and European experts believe that the existing and future Euroregions (with Russia's participation) should become one of the locomotives of EU-Russia cooperation. For example, further harmonization of European and Russian regulatory regimes and technical standards could be a starting point for such cooperation. While general rules are established at the national / supranational level the implementation of concrete projects should be done by local companies and governments. For instance, given its unique geographical location Kaliningrad could be a pilot region in implementing such ambitious projects.

The Euroregions also can facilitate the movement of people and goods by building new and developing the existing border crossings and the transport infrastructure in the area. Currently, local governments prefer to shoulder this responsibility on the federal budget. However, by providing local government with more powers in taxation local authorities will feel themselves more responsible for this business and get more funds for implementing projects.

A better division of labor should be established between the Euroregions. For example, while the Baltic and Karelia Euroregions could keep its current specialization on subregional economic planning, the support of private entrepreneurship, environment protection and home and justice affairs (particularly, fighting organized crime), the Saule Euroregion could focus on cross-border trade and developing the transportation infrastructure. The Neman, Lyna-Lava and Sesupe Euroregions could pay more attention to development of people-to-people contacts, education, culture and cooperation between NGOs. In addition, the Neman Euroregion could focus on engaging Belarus (which is becoming an important priority for the European Neighborhood Policy—ENP) in subregional cooperation. Border crossings development could be a joint sphere of responsibility for all Euroregions.

To support Euroregion activities, the interoperability of various EU cooperative programs and instruments should be improved in the new institutional framework of EU-Russia common spaces. In short, it is essential that flexibility remains a central tenet of the EU approach. Some steps have already been taken by the European Commission over the last ten years to ensure better coordination between the different programs and some new EU financial instruments have been specially designed for the ENP. This work should be completed in the process of implementation of the roadmaps to the EU-Russia four common spaces (when the current EU-Russian tensions will be overcome).

The very nature of the existing (semi-dormant) Euroregions should be changed. Not only municipal officials should be participants of exchange programs, but also other actors such as local businessmen, NGOs, journalists, students and teachers should be involved. To strengthen cooperation within the Euroregions and its institutional basis joint structures—ventures, chambers of commerce, professional associations, etc.– should be developed. Local actors should not wait for Moscow's permission but be more proactive and initiative-minded. Especially as current Russian legislation allows local actors to establish links to similar actors in foreign countries (the Russian Foreign Ministry only asks for information about these contacts, visits and joint projects). The main problems to cooperation, however, are a lack of finance and psychological inertia, inherited from Soviet times. However, with the development of a more sustainable economy and an increase in living standards as well as overcoming the Soviet-type mentality (through civic activism and growing international contacts) these problems could be successfully solved.

The establishment of a proper legal basis for the Euroregions should also be an important priority for Russia. Moscow ratified the European convention on border cooperation as late as in 2003. There is a clear need for passing a federal law on the Euroregions because several Russian regions experience difficulties in this area.

On the theme of organization and administration, both Russian and EU representative bodies in the Russian north-western regions should initiate a series of meetings, expert seminars and workshops (with the participation of the concerned local governments from countries and regions) to discuss the future of the existing Euroregions and the prospects for the creation of other Euroregions.

Non-governmental actors

Civil society in Russia is still in embryonic form and for this reason its impact on foreign policy making is either relatively insignificant or sporadic / chaotic. At the same time, in a democratic society non-governmental actors (civil society institutions, NGOs, interest groups, etc.) play quite an important role in the shaping of a country's international course. They have several helpful functions:

- Articulation of foreign policy interests of various interest groups.

- Formulation of foreign policy objectives and platforms of various social groups.

- Mobilization of public support through political campaigns and mass media.

- Ensuring that all actors involved with useful information on the subject of public discussion.

- Lobbying governmental actors to take a relevant foreign policy decision.

- Providing a public control over the governmental international activities.

- Providing a feed-back (both positive and critical) on the effects of governmental policies.

As far as the Russian non-government actors are concerned, the following players that try to affect Moscow's foreign policy can be mentioned: business community; human rights activists; environmentalists; public policy centers / think tanks[12] and religious communities (see figure 4).

The business community. There are several Russian business groups interested in Russia's foreign economic policy: the energy sector; forestry; fisheries; transport companies; trade firms that specialize in the export and import of consumer goods; and tourist companies. Their roles and influence in Russian decision-making on international strategies are different and vary from time to time.

It is obvious that energy lobbies—oil and gas industries, Russian electricity company RAO EES and Rosatom (nuclear power agency)—is the most powerful player among the various interest groups engaged in the policy making process. These companies / agencies are key suppliers of energy to European and some Asian countries. Regardless the current EU-Russia tensions Europe's future energy management will be greatly dependent on Russian gas. According to some sources, Russian gas made up around 40 per cent of total EU gas consumption prior to the Ukrainian crisis (Eurostat 2015; Leshukov 2000, 31; Piskulov 1999, 27) and will remain at the level of no less than 30 per cent by 2025 (Kulagin and Mitrova 2015, 72). On the other hand, Europe will constitute the largest natural export market for Russia's gas, so there is a clear meeting of interests. Europe will need Russia and vice versa.

For this reason, energy companies are interested in stable and reliable economic and political relations between Moscow and Europe. Interestingly, in the 1990s (when Russia's relations with the Baltic States were quite tense for various reasons), the energy companies were opposed to

---

12 On think tanks' role in Russian foreign policy making see Chapter 2.

economic sanctions against the Baltic States and pressed the Russian government to normalize its political and economic relations with these countries. Testimony to the strength of this lobby was that under the influence of the gas-oil lobby, Moscow insisted on including a special provision on purchases of energy in a larger package settling Russian-Lithuanian relations. At that time the gas-oil lobby had a powerful agent in the Russian government: Prime Minister Chernomyrdin, a founding father of Gazprom, and a leader of the Russian gas industry.

Over the last two decades the Russian and European energy sectors have had ambitious plans to develop regional and subregional energy infrastructure. They heavily lobbied the EU and the Russian government to create an institutional framework for these projects.

As one of the results of these joint business-government initiatives, the Baltic Sea Region Energy Cooperation (BASREC) has been launched. Four ad-hoc groups have been created within the areas of electricity, gas, climate issues and energy efficiency. The dialogue between actors in the energy sector of the Baltic Sea region was an important part of the process. In the Barents Euro-Arctic Council, a wide network of actors working with energy efficiency, energy savings, and renewable energy resources has been established as well. Since its first Action Plan (2000–2003) the Northern Dimension program has energy cooperation as one of its most important priorities.

Reflecting the pressure of Russian and European energy companies the 1999 Helsinki Conference of Foreign Ministers on the Northern Dimension stressed the need for close cooperation between producing and consuming countries to establish favourable commercial conditions in the gas sector. There was a proposal to connect all the continental countries in the region, and thereby to create a joint space with common rules, to European networks and to ensure the security of supply and sufficient storage capacities for gas (Nissinen 2000, 122). The countries of the region also considered the integration of their electricity markets and the establishment of commonly accepted rules, market mechanisms and environmental framework conditions.

Figure 4.   The Russian Foreign Policy Decision Making System: Non-Government Level

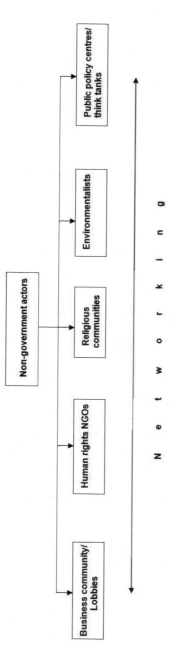

At the same time, Russian energy companies (that are strictly controlled by the government) were concerned about their over-dependence on the Baltic States and Poland in case of oil and gas transit. For example, they were unsatisfied with high transit fees: Russian companies had to pay $700 million a year to Latvia for oil transit. In 1992–1999, these companies lost more than $5 billion because of transit fees (http://www.nefte.ru/projekt/r20.htm). In addition, Russia disliked EU political demands to break its energy sector and split oil, gas and electricity giants into smaller companies. This is why instead of developing cooperative projects with the EU in the sphere of energy infrastructure, the Russian business community (with the full support of the government) has opted for unilateral actions or bilateral (country-to-country) projects.

The construction of the Baltic Pipeline System (BPS) was the first large-scale project of that sort. The BPS, operational since 2002, ships oil from the Russian High North and Urals to the coastal terminal in the Leningrad Region (150 km north of St. Petersburg). It brings 65 million ton of crude oil to European countries and in terms of capacity is comparable with the terminals on the Black Sea coast (Novorossiysk, Tuapse). According to a representative of Transneft (a member of the consortium that runs the BPS), Russia saves $200 million bypassing Latvia via the Russian Baltic ports.

Another project was the North European Gas Pipeline (NEGP). This pipeline is designed to bring gas from Russia's Arctic sector to Germany and potentially to some other European countries (Denmark and U.K.) *via* the Russian territory and then the bottom of the Baltic Sea. This project ignores earlier proposals by Finland, the Baltic States and Poland to construct a land-based version of this pipeline *via* their territories. Gazprom and its German partners also ignored environmental concerns related to potential disasters involving the underwater pipeline or the risk to damage German chemical weapons buried in the Baltic Sea after World War II. The members of the NEGP consortium point out that this pipeline frees them from transit fees, political blackmailing from the transit countries and makes gas shipment to Europe more reliable. This issue, however, has become a bone of contention between EU countries as well as between the EU and Russia. Those EU countries that have perceived themselves as losers obstructed both the energy dialogue between Brussels and Moscow as well as the EU-Russia negotiations on a new cooperative agreement that should replace the existing PCA.

To sum up, the influence of the Russian energy sector plays a rather contradictory role in the EU-Russia relations. On the one hand, it is interested in expanding energy dialogue and cooperation with Europe but on the other hand, it presses the Russian government to opt in favor of unilateral or bilateral (country-to-country, company-to-company) rather than multilateral projects, complementary to the logic of the EU. With the introduction of the Western sanctions against Russia in 2014 the energy lobby put pressure on the Russian government to diversify its export policies, particularly to find new partners in Asia.

Other business groups are less influential in Russian foreign policy making. For example, in the 1990s, the Russian timber industry put pressure on Moscow to increase quotas for exporting timber to European countries (Neva News 1996, 6; Deinichenko 1996, 10). However, the federal government preferred to develop timber processing in the country so that it could produce furniture, paper, cardboard, building-materials, etc. For this reason, both central and regional authorities favored foreign investment and foreign know-how in this sector of the Russian economy. Some Russian regions, such as Novgorod Oblast and Karelia were quite successful in establishing joint ventures with foreign partners and promoting their local products on the domestic and international markets.

Russian transport companies enthusiastically supported EU-Russian plans to upgrade and develop the existing transport infrastructure in Western and North-Western Russia. They were particularly interested in developing two pan-European transport corridors: (1) Berlin-Warsaw-Moscow-Nizhny Novgorod-Yekaterinburg and (2) Helsinki-St. Petersburg-Moscow-Kiev-Crete. Kaliningrad's business community was especially interested in developing two branches of the second corridor—*via Baltica* and *via Hanseatica*.

For the first corridor, the renovation of the highway from Europe to Moscow and Nizhny Novgorod is complete. The other Helsinki-Crete corridor is still under construction. The Kaliningrad sectors of *via Baltica* and *via Hanseatica* are almost complete but the Baltic States and Poland for various reasons (mainly political) block construction works on their territories.

Russian tourist companies are also very keen on establishing stable and dynamic relations with foreign partners. In some regions they succeeded in establishing special associations to lobby local and federal authorities as well as foreign embassies to ease visa and border control regimes. For example, in the late 1990s the Kaliningrad tourist association concluded a series of agreements with the local representative offices of the Russian Foreign Ministry, State Customs Committee and Federal Border Service to simplify visa, customs and border control formalities for tourists. This scheme was quite efficient until both Lithuania and Poland introduced a new visa regime with Russia in 2003.

In other words, the influence of the business community is growing concerning Russian foreign policy making.

Human rights NGOs. These organizations have focused their activities on two areas:

- Domestic issues. Russian human rights activists tried to mobilize international support for solving Russian domestic problems, such as introduction of an alternative military service, protection of young soldiers from bullying in the armed forces, ensuring sexual minorities' rights and the right of political protests / demonstrations. The leading international human rights organizations (Amnesty International, Transparency International, etc.) cooperate with Russian NGOs and even establish local representative offices to monitor the situation from inside the country. Human rights-oriented European organizations (the Council of Europe, OSCE, European Parliament, NATO Parliamentary Assembly, etc.) also help Russian NGOs and send fact-finding missions to the most problematic regions. The situation, however, has become rather complicated for the Russian domestically-oriented NGOs and international organizations' branches with adoption of a foreign agents registration act of 2012. The NGOs are obliged to register as foreign agents if they get foreign funds and participate in Russian politics or involved in the lobbying activities.

- International issues. Human rights' NGOs are mostly interested in protection of the Russia-speaking minorities in the post-Soviet republics (the Baltic States, Trans-Caucasus, Moldova, Central Asia). The Association for Cooperation with Compatriots Abroad "Motherland" (est. in 1992) is the leading organization that tried to help ethnic Russians either to migrate to the Motherland or protect their rights in the country of the residence from the early 1990s.

In the first half of the 1990s, when the Yeltsin government did not pay a proper attention to its 27 million compatriots various radical (rightist and leftist) organizations tried to take a lead in this field. At that time both nationalists (e.g., the Liberal Democratic Party of Vladimir Zhirinovsky) and neo-Marxists (the Communist Party of the Russian Federation) criticised the Yeltsin administration (and its pro-Western leaders) for the lack of any sound strategy on the future of compatriots in the 'near abroad'. Although this criticism often was a product for domestic consumption rather than a serious alternative to government policies, the radicals succeeded in attracting public attention to the problem and forced the Yeltsin administration to develop a special strategy on the Russian-speaking minorities abroad and charge Russian diplomatic, trade and other missions with protection of their rights. Since the late 1990s, many Russian centrist / liberal NGOs and political parties have also joined the campaign to protect compatriots in the 'near abroad'. Now the "Motherland" Association coordinates its activities with the Kremlin's soft power instruments such as *Rossotrudnichestvo* and "Russian World".

Environmentalists. The environmental movement has rapidly spread in post-Communist Russia and for a while became influential in domestic politics. Indeed, a great number of post-perestroika leaders started their political careers as environmentalists (Van Buren 1995, 127–135). The Russian 'greens', for example, succeeded in promoting Academician Alexei Yablokov to the post of State Counsellor of the Russian Federation on Ecology and Health Care, thus becoming their major voice in the government.

The environmentalist NGOs were indispensable in identifying major ecological problems of the Russian North-West and High North as well as in encouraging Russian local, regional and federal governments to cooperate with neighboring states and international organizations—UN Environment Program, CBSS, Helsinki Commission, BEAC, Arctic Council and Nordic institutions. Particularly, the Russian "greens" played a visible role in designing a Multilateral Nuclear Environmental Program in the Russian Federation (MNEPR) which was signed in 2003 by several OECD countries. MNEPR aimed to facilitate cooperation and assistance to Russia in the field of spent nuclear fuel safety and radioactive waste management. Projects covered by MNEPR included securing and cleaning up spent nuclear fuel storage sites and dismantling old decommissioned nuclear submarines. The ecologists also convinced Moscow to participate in the Northern Dimension's Environmental Partnership (NDEP) which was launched in 2001 and remains to date one of the most efficient EU-Russian cooperative programs.

Religious organizations. Depending on the nature of their confession, different religious groups had various foreign policy interests. Yet the main religious influence, the Russian Orthodox Church (ROC) had (and still has) two major priorities as regards foreign policies:

- The ROC was one of the first protectors of Russian national minorities in the post-Soviet countries. The Church's concern with minority rights may be explained not only by religious doctrine or historical traditions, but also by the personal background of the then Patriarch Aleksii II. Aleksii II (Ridiger), the son of a Russified Baltic German father and Russian mother, was born in Estonia in 1929. After ordination to the priesthood, he spent eight and a half years serving in the Russian city of Kokhtla-Yarve in north-eastern Estonia, a hotbed of anti-secessionist sentiment from 1989 to 1991. In the period 1961–64 he was Bishop of Tallinn and Estonia, before acquiring the key position of chancellor of the Moscow Patriarchate. From 1988 through 1990, he served as the Metropolitan of Leningrad and Novgorod, before being elected Patriarch on 7 June 1990 (Dunlop 1993, 158–159). Hence, the Patriarch knew from personal experience how complex the problem of inter-ethnic and inter-religious relations in the ex-Soviet republics.

The Church has specifically ruled out the use of force to protect Russians living in the 'near abroad'. It has proposed that the Russian government should conclude bilateral agreements on national minorities' status within the ex-Soviet republics. The government should also use the law-enforcement mechanisms of the UN, OSCE and other international organisations dealing with human rights. The Church itself has tried to influence those governments involved in human rights violations through its numerous international contacts, especially by participating in the work of the World Council of Churches, the Conference of European Churches and other ecumenical bodies (Petlyuchenko 1993, 65).

The new Patriarch Kirill (elected in 2009) also pays great attention to the protection of ethnic Russians abroad since he was the head of the ROC's department of external affairs (1989–2008) and deputy President of the World Russian People's Council (1995–2008). He regularly meets with the Russian diaspora's representatives during his foreign trips and attends congresses of the Russian compatriots (http://www.patriarchia.ru/db/text/4265245.html).

- One more issue for the ROC's concern is the aggressive infiltration of different foreign confessions (Catholicism, Protestantism, etc.) and sects (including totalitarian ones). The Church has charged these missionaries with dishonest behavior: They have used Orthodoxy's financial difficulties of the 1990s to undermine its influence in Russia. By distributing humanitarian aid and free literature, buying newspaper space and broadcasting time they have tried to divert potential Orthodox believers from their religion. Particularly alarming for the Church is that some of those missionaries / sects have tried to persuade people that the Orthodox religion supports them. They have borrowed components of Orthodox doctrine and used Orthodox religious symbols, a practice which the Church has seen as outright sacrilege (Petlyuchenko, [1993]: 69–70).

The ROC has even called for the Russian law enforcement agencies to stop anti-Orthodox activities. The Church insisted that the Russian Foreign Ministry and security services should pay more attention to the 'subversive' activities of various foreign sects in Russia.

It is interesting to note that the ROC has often served as Moscow's soft power instrument in its relations with foreign countries. In addition to the close contacts with the Russian communities abroad, the Moscow Patriarchate has successfully initiated the process of unification with the Russian Orthodox Church Abroad (ROCA) which ended up with the 2007 agreement between the two Orthodox churches. The ROCA has 409 parishes and 39 monasteries with several million Orthodox believers (most of them live in North America). Altogether the ROC and ROCA have 829 parishes and 52 monasteries that unite around 30 million Russian Orthodox believers (Patriarch Kirill 2013, 19).

The ROC sometimes serves as a "back channel" for the Kremlin's delicate diplomatic communications with foreign countries. For example, through the ROC's connections with the Georgian Orthodox Church Moscow has managed to maintain its relations with the Georgian society and some local elites even in the aftermath of the "five-day war" with Tbilisi in August 2008. The same informal channel is used by Moscow to communicate with the Ukrainian society because around 21 per cent of the local respondents (with exception of the Donbass region) belong to the Ukrainian Orthodox Church which is subordinated to the Moscow Patriarchate (http://dif.org.ua/ua/publications/press-relizy/bilshist-naselgo-patr iarhatu.htm).

Other Russian religious groups have been interested in Russian foreign policies as well. The Russian Muslim community is active in developing cooperation with Islamic countries. For example, Tatarstan regularly organizes the World Tatar Congress in Kazan to work with numerous Tatar diasporas throughout the world and bring foreign investment to the regional economy. The Jewish community serves as an efficient channel of communications with Israel and the Jewish diasporas around the world.

Conclusions

The following broad conclusions emerge from the above analysis.

Several IR theories are helpful in explaining Russia's present-day international course, although some of them should be further developed (PTT and soft power concept) or updated (peaceful coexistence doctrine). It should be noted that these theories are complimentary rather than mutually exclusive.

As far as the Russian post-Soviet IR debate is concerned the following generalizations can be made:

First, Russian international studies have experienced a very quick and dramatic transformation from a discipline dominated by the Marxist ideology to multiparadigmatic discourse. This transition process was not easy and for some years Russian IR has experienced numerous problems of methodological / theoretical and financial / institutional nature.

Second, although the realist / geopolitical school currently dominates the discipline, other perspectives (such as idealism / liberalism, globalism and post-positivism) do exist and produce some alternatives to the prevailing paradigm. It appears that in the foreseeable future the Russian foreign policy discourse will look like a polyphony rather than monophony.

Third, the mainstream of Russian IR has managed to avoid xenophobic / extremist views on international affairs and develop more or less moderate and well-balanced concepts.

Fourth, the Russian authors have taken great strides in exploring international problems such as diplomatic history and present-day Russian foreign policy. However, Russian scholarship still lacks profound theoretical works in this field. Russian specialists often copy foreign methodological and theoretical approaches without adapting them to the local reality.

Fifth, international studies have changed its status by being transformed from an elitist discipline (as was the case in the Soviet period) to a "normal" one. Now many people have an access both to studying IR and developing their own theories.

Sixth, the "democratization", "demonopolization" and "normalization" of International Relations have had many implications at the institutional level: the number of research centers dealing with international studies has dramatically increased, new regional centres have emerged. This made Russian IR scholarship even more diverse and interesting.

There were also a number of serious changes in Russian threat perceptions and doctrinal basis of Moscow's policies in Europe:

First, over the last twenty five years Russia has managed to formulate its national interests, threat perceptions and a more or less coherent national security strategy.

Second, Russian national security doctrines defined both national interests and security threats quite realistically. They are based on the assumption that there are no major external threats to its security and that internal sources of threats should be given more attention. Logically, Russian security concerns have shifted from the 'hard' to the 'soft' security domain.

Third, Russian national security doctrines are based on a broader understanding of the notion of security in which the non-military issues such as economy, social problems, environment, demography, information, culture and religion are included.

Fourth, in line with the democratic principles, these concepts acknowledged the need for ensuring national security at three levels (the individual, society and the state) albeit the state 'bias' still remains (particularly in the field of implementation of national security strategy). The Russian civil society still remains rather passive in the decision-making process and foreign policy and security debates.

Fifth, with the adoption of a non-aggressive military strategy and clarification of Russia's national security interests, Moscow became a more attractive and predictable international partner. Although some Russia's international partners in North America (Canada, the U.S.) and Europe (e.g. the Baltic States, Poland, U.K., etc.) are still quite cautious about Moscow's international intentions and plans (some of them believe that Russia conducts neo-imperialist policy) but most of them expressed their interest in developing stable and mutually beneficial relations with Moscow.

Sixth, it appears that the national security debate has been a rather effective way of nation-building and constructing a new Russian identity. The national security concepts claim that they are based on national values and traditions and aim at the search for a national consensus and a unifying national idea. Of course, this process is far from an end (or perhaps it's a never-ending process) and Russia needs regular revisions of its threat perceptions and national security doctrines in order to keep them in line with domestic and international realities.At the same time, first steps in a positive direction were made. Russia is transparent in terms of public debate on foreign and national security issues and open to dialogue both domestically and internationally.

The Russian decision-making system on Europe has also evolved rapidly over the last quarter of century. One can make the case for both positive and negative / problematic changes. Looking at the bright side of this dynamic process the following promising trends can be identified:

Russia's foreign policy has become less ideological and more pragmatic, oriented to national interests.

The chaos of the early 1990s has been overcome and a more-or-less stable decision-making machinery on foreign policy has been created within the executive branch of government.

A more-or-less reliable civilian control over the military and other so-called 'power' agencies has been established. The Defense Ministry and the Russian intelligence community are of secondary importance as regards the decision-making process. They are guided by the political structures (Presidential Administration and Cabinet) rather than play a role of key or independent actors.

Elements of parliamentary control over the decision-making process have been created. The Russian legislature (although it is much weaker than its U.S. or European counterparts) has some important functions, such as the "power of the purse", parliamentary investigations and diplomacy.

An executive-legislative liaison / consultative mechanism has been established and it facilitated the dialogue between the Kremlin and the legislature on foreign policies.

The role of the Russian regional and local governments became more salient in foreign policy-making. The federal center had to take into account regional interests and preferences as regards their relations with international partners. Moscow has also had to allow some sort of horizontal / networking type of relations of regional and local governments with corresponding equals in foreign countries. Cross- and trans-border cooperation brought about a number of success stories in the case of several Europe-oriented Russian regions—Kaliningrad, Karelia, Novgorod, Murmansk, etc.

Non-governmental actors have got some say in foreign policy-making. The Russian business community (especially the energy sector) has become an influential player in Moscow's foreign policy-making. Relatively new political actors, such as human rights and environmental NGOs, religious communities and independent think tanks became an integral part of the decision-making process. In contrast with the Soviet period when foreign policy-making was a purely elitist business the current Russian political leadership has to take into account various interests of different segments of an emerging Russian civil society.

At the same time, numerous problems in organizing and practical functioning of the Russian foreign policy decision-making mechanism can be found:

First, the decision-making system of the government is still far from an ideal. There is a lack of a proper division of labor between different executive agencies regarding foreign policy making. These agencies differ by their conceptual approaches to Russia's international strategies. There is sometimes an unhealthy competition between them for influence, funds, resources, personnel and access to information.

Russia's Parliament has too few powers to take an active part in the shaping of Moscow's foreign and national security policies. It is also unable to provide proper public scrutiny and accountability. This makes the Kremlin too independent in its foreign policy initiatives.

The role of Russian regional and local governments in foreign policy-making is still ambivalent. The federal center is too jealous of its foreign policy activities. A number of promising international region-in-the building projects (Northern Dimension, Euroregions) have found themselves in a bind because of the lack of federal support. It is a long way to go to revive these projects and put them in line with international standards (albeit the potential and resources are still there).

Although civil society and its institutions have came into the picture and now have some minor say in foreign policy-making it should be noticed that a lot has to be done to transform non-governmental actors into a full-fledged policy players. There is still discrepancy between the interests of Russian foreign policy elites and the civil society that often wants a different international strategy from the government. What is especially important is that the Russian government actors should treat expertise with respect due to policy information from independent think tanks. In sum, a more reliable feed-back system from civil society is needed.

As far as the implications of the Ukrainian crisis for the future of Moscow's foreign policy are concerned the main change that it has brought about was not territorial (e.g., reintegration of Crimea to Russia and turmoil in Ukraine's south-east), but rather strategic and mental one. Russia has finally down with the project to integrate into the West and become part of the Euro-Atlantic economic and security systems. It has retreated to its 'home base' / Heartland in Eurasia and has prioritized cooperation with non-Western countries (especially with China). In a certain sense, the answer to one of the Russian perennial questions "What should be done?" has been partially found: Russia turned its back to the West and looks forward to cooperation with the East.

This dramatic shift in Moscow's foreign policy priorities has been reflected in Russia's new military, maritime and national security doctrines. Conceptually, Moscow tries to integrate its soft and hard power policies into a 'smart power' strategy to adequately meet internal and external challenges. One more conceptual shift in Russian foreign policy thinking is returning a peaceful coexistence principle (albeit on a different, non-Marxist-Leninist, philosophical basis).

In seeking for realignment of its foreign policies the Kremlin is trying to play different games with international institutions such as BRICS, SCO, EEU and CSTO. From the Russian point of view, these players can have partly competitive, partly complimentary roles. Sometimes they can draw resources from the same pools (for instance, BRICS development bank vs. a prospective SCO development bank) but they also have somewhat different agendas.

As far as the 'Western dimension' of Russian foreign policy strategy is concerned Moscow, on the one hand, plans to reduce its dependence on exports of energy products to Europe and import of Western technologies and consumer goods as well as to limit its cooperation with the U.S. and EU to certain areas.

However, on the other hand, the Russian strategists believe that Russia should share with the West an interest in halting and reversing the slide toward confrontation, bridging the gap that divides them, enhancing predictability, and developing effective channels for cooperation (or at least minimizing confrontation). Particularly, they believe that cooperation is possible in selected areas, such as:

- measures to avoid military escalation in south-east Ukraine;

- support for Ukraine to avoid an economic collapse;

- humanitarian assistance and reconstruction support for war-damaged areas in Ukraine;

- dialogue on the future of the European security order (with the OSCE as a backbone of a new security architecture);

- cooperation on a number of global and regional challenges (non-proliferation of weapons of mass destruction, fighting international terrorism, transnational organized crime, illegal migration, piracy, global climate change mitigation, etc.).

Some Russian experts suggest to change the level and focus of cooperation with European countries, particularly, to move it from government-to-government to the subnational and non-governmental tiers, from the hierarchical / vertical to horizontal / networking type of interaction. This could be helpful for securing and further development of the interdependency mechanism that emerged over the last two decades and now is being under the stress.

The expert / academic community also recommends not to focus on formalized multilateral institutions; rather, a priority should be given to flexible international regimes that are designed better to survive turbulent times.

In general, both the Russian IR mainstream and policy-makers are (cautiously) optimistic with regard to the future of Russia's international standing. They believe that the Western sanctions will be counterproductive to those intentions, which they initially pursued, and that the Russian economy will eventually grow stronger as a result of self-reliance and import-substitute policies. They also believe that Moscow can avoid international isolation by developing its links to the non-Western countries and institutions. In sum, the Ukrainian crisis did not destroyed completely but just delayed Moscow's geopolitical project of building a multipolar world where Russia could take its "rightful place".

References

Achkasov, Valery and Sergei Lantsov. 2011. Mirovaya Politika i Mezhdunarodnye Otnosheniya [World Politics and International Relations]. Moscow: Aspect Press (in Russian).

Adarchev, O.V. 1998. Zapadnoevropeiskiy Soyuz v Sisteme Evropeiskoi Bezopasnosti [West European Union in the European Security System]. Moscow: General Staff Academy Press (in Russian).

Ahunov, Viktor. 2000. The Speech of Mr Viktor Ahunov, Deputy Director General, Ministry for Atomic Energy. In Nissinen, Marja (ed.). Foreign Ministers' Conference on the Northern Dimension, Helsinki, 11–12 November 1999. A Compilation of Speeches. Helsinki: Unit for the Northern Dimension in the Ministry for Foreign Affairs, pp. 73–74.

Akhtamzyan, Abdulkhan A. 1994. Obyedinenie Germanii, ili Anshlyus GDR k FRG [German Unification or Anschlus of the GDR]. Moscow: MGIMO (in Russian).

Alexeeva, Tatyana. 2001. Sovremennye Politicheskie Teorii [Contemporary Political Theories]. Moscow: ROSSPEN (in Russian).

Andreev, Andrei and Vladimir Petukhov. 2015. Rossiya i Okruzhayushiy Mir [Russia and the World]. Svobodnaya Mysl' 3. http://svom.info/entry/560-rossiya-i-okruzhayushij-mir-kak-menyaetsya-otnoshe/ (in Russian).

Andrusenko, Lydia and Olga Tropkina. 2002. Mezalyans s Amerikoi [Misalliance with America]. Nezavisimaya Gazeta, 11 September, p. 1 (in Russian).

2006. Antiglobalizm i Global'noe Upravlenie [Anti-Globalism and Global Governance]. Moscow: MGIMO Press (in Russian).

Antonenko, Oksana. 1996. New Russian Analytical Centers and Their Role in Political Decisionmaking. Cambridge, Mass.: John F. Kennedy School of Government, Harvard University.

Antyukhina-Moskovchenko, V.I., Zlobin, A.A. and M.A. Khrustalev. 1988. Osnovy Teorii Mezhdunarodnykh Otnosheniy [Basics of International Relations Theory]. Moscow: MGIMO Press (in Russian).

Arbatov, Alexei. 1992. Imperya ili Velikaya Derzhava? [Empire or Great Power?]. Novoye Vremya 42: 49, pp. 16–18; and 50, pp 20–23 (in Russian).

Arbatov, Alexei. 1993. Russia's Foreign Policy Alternatives. International Security 18: 2, pp. 5–43.

Arbatov, Alexei. 1994. Russian National Interests. In Blackwill, Robert D. and Sergei A. Karaganov (eds.). Damage Limitation or Crisis? Russia and the Outside World. Washington / London: Brassey's, Inc., pp. 55–76.

Arbatov, Alexei. 1995a. NATO and Russia. Security Dialogue 26: 2, pp. 135–141.

Arbatov, Alexei. 1995b. Rossiya i NATO [Russia and NATO). Nezavisimaya Gazeta, 9 June (in Russian).

Arbatov, Alexei. 1996. The Future of European Security: Split or Unity? In Visions of European Security—Focal Point: Sweden and Northern Europe. Stockholm: The Olof Palme International Center, pp. 234–250.

Arbatov, Alexei. 1999. NATO – Glavnaya Problema dlya Evropeiskoi Bezopasnosti [NATO Is the Main Problem for European Security]. Nezavisimaya Gazeta, 16 April, p. 8 (in Russian).

Arbatov, Georgy. 1970. Ideologicheskaya Bor'ba v Sovremennykh Mezhdunarodnykh Otnosheniyakh [Ideological Struggle in Contemporary International Relations]. Moscow: Politizdat (in Russian).

Arbatova, Nadezhda. 1999. Samiy Tyagostniy Urok Poslednego Vremeni [The Most Painful Lesson of Recent Times]. Nezavisimaya Gazeta, 6 April, p. 3 (in Russian).

Artemov, V.A. (ed.). 1999. Germaniya i Rossiya. Sobytiya, Obrazy, Lyudi [Germany and Russia. Events, Images, People]. Voronezh: Voronezh State University Press (in Russian).

Avtotor. 2014. Nadezhnoe Partnerstvo Avtotor–BMW [A Solid Partnership Between Avtotor and BMW]. www.avtotor.ru/index.php?option=com_content&view =article&id=117&Itemid=519 (in Russian).

Baev, Pavel. 1996. The Russian Debate about the Near Abroad. In Godzimirski, Jakub (ed.). Conference Proceedings: Russia and Europe. Oslo: NUPI (NUPI Report No. 210).

Bakushev, V.V. 1997. Integratsionnye Tendentsii Politiki Vedushikh Mezhdunarodnykh Organizatsiy i Novoi Rossii [Integrationist Policies of Leading International Organizations and New Russia], Moscow: Russian Academy of Public Service (in Russian).

Ball, Deborah. 1999. How Kosovo Empowers the Russian Military. Cambridge, MA: Davis Center for Russian Studies, Harvard University (PONARS Policy Memo Series, No. 61).

Baltinfo. 2012. Politolog: Litve Povezlo Chto Osnovnoi Problemoi Rossii Yavlyaetsya Korruptsiya [Political Scientist: Lithuania Is Lucky That Corruption Is Russia's Main Problem]. http://www.baltinfo.ru/2012/10/13/Politolog-Li tve-povezlo-chto-osnovnoi-problemoi-Rossii-yavlyaetsya-korruptciya-310256 (in Russian).

Baluev, Dmitry. 2001. Informatsionnaya Revolutsiya i Sovremennye Mezhdunarodnye Otnosheniya [Information Revolution and Contemporary International Relations]. Nizhny Novgorod: Nizhny Novgorod State University Press (in Russian).

Baluev, Dmitry. 2002. Sovremennaya Mirovaya Politika i Problemy Lichnostnoi Bezopasnosti [Contemporary World Policy and Problems of Human Security]. Nizhny Novgorod: Nizhny Novgorod State University Press (in Russian).

Baluev, Dmitry. 2003. Rol' Gosudarstva v Sovremennoi Mirovoi Politike [The Role of State in Contemporary World Politics]. Nizhny Novgorod: Nizhny Novgorod State University Press (in Russian).

Baranovsky, Vladimir. 1996. Russia. In Krohn, A. (ed.). The Baltic Sea Area: National and International Security Perspectives. Baden-Baden: Nomos Verlagsgesellschaft, pp. 164–182.

Baranovsky, Vladimir. (ed.). 1997. Russia and Europe: The Emerging Security Agenda. New York: Oxford University Press.

Baranovsky, Vladimir. 2002. Russia's Attitudes Towards the EU: Political Aspects. Helsinki: UPI.

Barry, Ellen. 2009. A Wild Cossack Rides Into a Cultural Battle. Kyiv Post, 12 April.

Barygin, Igor. 2007. Regionovedenie [Area Studies]. Moscow: Aspect Press (in Russian).

1994. The Basic Provisions of the Military Doctrine of the Russian Federation. June's Intelligence Review, Special Report, January, pp. 3–12.

Bausin, Alexei. 2003. Druzhby s Vashingtonom Moskve ne Izbezhat' [Moscow Cannot Avoid Friendship with Washington]. Nezavisimaya Gazeta, 29 May, p. 2 (in Russian).

Belkin, Viktor and Vyacheslav Storozhenko. 1995. Ot Vyzhyvaniya k Ustoichivomu Razvitiyu [From Survival to Sustainable Development]. Svobodnaya Mysl' 5, pp. 32–41.

Berzins, Indulis. 2000. The speech of Mr. Indulis Berzins, Minister of Foreign Affairs of Latvia. In: Nissinen, Marja. (ed.). Foreign Ministers' Conference on the Northern Dimension, Helsinki, 11–12 November 1999. A Compilation of Speeches. Helsinki: Unit for the Northern Dimension in the Ministry for Foreign Affairs, pp. 21–22.

Bikbulatova, A. 2009. Obshaya Teoriya Konflikta [General Theory of Conflict]. Ufa: Bashkir State University Press (in Russian).

Bisk, Israel (ed.). 2001. Veimarsjaya Respublika: Istoriya i Istochnikovedenie [The Weimar Republic: History and Sources]. Ivanovo: Ivanovo State University Press (in Russian).

Blackwill, Robert D. and Sergei A. Karaganov (eds.). 1994. Damage Limitation or Crisis? Russia and the Outside World. Washington, DC and London: Brassey's, Inc.

Blishenko, Igor. 1990. Diplomaticheskoe Pravo [Diplomatic Law]. Moscow: Vyshaya Shkola (in Russian).

Blishenko, Igor, Fisenko, I.V. 1998. Mezhdunarodny Ugolovny Sud [International Criminal Court]. Moscow: Zakon i Pravo (in Russian).

Bogaturov, Alexei. 1997. Velikiye Derzhavy na Tikhom Okeane [Great Powers in the Pacific Ocean]. Moscow: Konvert-MONF (in Russian).

Bogaturov, Alexei (ed.). 2000. Sistemnaya Istoriya Mezhdunarodnykh Otnosheniy [Systemic History of International Relations]. Moscow: Moskovskiy Rabochiy, Vol. 1–4 (in Russian).

Bogaturov, Alexei (ed.). 2010. Sovremennye Global'nye Problemy [Contemporary Global Problems]. Moscow: Aspect Press.

Bogaturov, Alexei, Kosolapov, Nikolai and Mark Khrustalev. 2002. Ocherki Teorii i Politicheskogo Analiza Mezhdunarodnykh Otnoshenoy [Essays on Theory and Policy Analysis of International Relations]. Moscow: NOFMO (in Russian).

Bogaturov, Alexei, Mikhail Kozhokin and Konstantin V. Pleshakov. 1992. Vneshnyaya Politika Rossii [Russia's Foreign Policy]. USA: Economics, Politics, Ideology 15: 10, pp. 28–37 (in Russian).

Bogomolov, Oleg. 1994. Russia and Eastern Europe. In Robert D. Blackwill and Sergei A. Karaganov (eds.). Damage Limitation or Crisis? Russia and the Outside World. Washington, DC and London: Brassey's, Inc., pp. 158–46.

Borko, Yuri. 2000. Chto Takoe Evropeiskiy Soyuz? [What Is the European Union About?]. Moscow (in Russian).

Borko, Yuri. 2003. Ot Evropeiskoi Idei – k Edinoi Evrope [From European Idea to United Europe]. Moscow: Delovaya Literatura (in Russian).

Branitski, Andrei. 2006. Erit una Europa? Istoriya Objedineniya Evropy: Protivorechiya, Proekty, Perspectivy [Erit una Europa? History of the European Integration: Contradictions, Projects, Prospects]. Nizhny Novgorod: Nizhny Novgorod State University Press (in Russian).

Branitski, Andrei and G.V. Kamenskaya. 2003. Istoriya Evropeiskoi Integratsii [History of European Integration]. Nizhny Novgorod: Nizhny Novgorod State University Press (in Russian).

Brutents, Karen. 2014. Velikaya Geopoliticheskaya Revolyutsiya [The Great Geopolitical Revolution]. Moscow: Mezhdunarodnye Otnosheniya (in Russian).

Buren, van L. 1995. Citizen Participation and the Environment in Russia. In DeBardeleben J. and J. Hannigan (eds.). Environmental Security and Quality after Communism: Eastern Europe and the Soviet Successor States. Boulder: Westview Press, pp. 127–137.

Burlak, V. 1992. Humankind Needs a Program for Survival. International Affairs (Moscow) 38: 1, pp. 16–24.

Busygina, Irina M. 1995. Postmodernism v Moskve [Postmodernism in Moscow]. Polis 6, pp. 5–9 (in Russian).

Busygina, Irina M. 2006. Politicheskaya Regionalistika [Area Political Studies]. Moscow: ROSSPEN (in Russian).

Butorina, Olga and Yuri Borko (eds.). 2006. Rasshirenie Evropeiskogo Souyza i Rossiya [EU Enlargement and Russia]. Moscow: Delovaya Literatura (in Russian).

Butorina, Olga, Borko, Yuri and Ivan Ivanov (eds.). 2003. Evropeiskiy Soyuz: Spravochnik-Putevoditel' [The European Union: A Guide]. Moscow: Delovaya Literatura (in Russian).

Carafano, James Jay (ed). 2015. U.S. Comprehensive Strategy Toward Russia. Washington, DC: The Heritage Foundation. http://thf-reports.s3.amazo naws.com2015/SR173.pdf

Casula, Philipp. 2010. "Primacy of Your Face": Changing Discourses of National Identity and National Interest in the United States and Russia after the Cold War. Ab Imperio 3, pp. 245–271.

Charap, Samuel and Jeremy Shapiro. 2014a. A New European Security Order: The Ukraine Crisis and the Missing Post-Cold War Bargain. Paris: FRS.

Charap, Samuel and Jeremy Shapiro. 2014b. How to Avoid a New Cold War. Current History 113: 765, pp. 265–271.

Chossudovsky, Evgeny. 1972. Genoa Revisited: Russia and Coexistence. Foreign Affairs 50: 3, pp. 554–77.

Chubarian, Alexander. 1976. Mirnoe Sosushestvovanie: Teoriya i Praktika [Peaceful Coexistence: Theory and Practice]. Moscow: Politizdat (in Russian).

Chugayev, Sergei, 1997: "Sostoyanie Ekonomiki i Obshesyva—Glavnaya Ugroza Rossii—Govoritsya v Rossiyskoi Kontseptsii Natsionalnoi Bezopasnosti" [State of the Economy and Society Is the Main Threat for Russia, Says the Russian National Security Concept], in: Izvestiya, 19 December 1997 (in Russian).

Churkin, Vitaly (1995) 'U Rossii s NATO Nikogda ne Bylo Konfliktov' [Russia and NATO Never Had Conflicts], Segodnya (13 April): 3 (in Russian).

Clinton, Hillary. 2009. Foreign Policy Address at the Council for Foreign Relations. Washington DC, 15 June. http://www.state.gov/secretary/rm/2009a/july/1 26071.htm

Clunan, Anne L. 2009. The Social Construction of Russia's Resurgence: Aspirations, Identity, and Security Interests. Baltimore: Johns Hopkins University Press.

Cohen, Saul (1963) Geography and Politics in a World Divided, New York: Random House.

Collins, James F. 2015. Daunting Challenges and Glimmers of Hope in Ukraine. 20 November. Washington, DC: Carnegie Endowment for International Peace. http://carnegieendowment.org/2015/11/20/dauntingchallengesandglimmersof hopeinukraine/im6s

Commission of the European Communities. 1998. Communication: A Northern Dimension for the Policies of the Union (13768/98). Brussels: Commission of the European Communities.

Commission of the European Communities. 2000. Action Plan for the Northern Dimension in the External and Cross-Border Policies of the European Union 2000–2003. Commission Working Document: Draft, 28 February. Brussels: Commission of the European Communities.

Commission of the European Communities. 2001a. Communication on Kaliningrad, Brussels, 17 January. http://europa.eu.int/comm/external_relations/north _dim/doc/com2001_0026en01.pdf

Commission of the European Communities. 2001b. A Northern Dimension for the Policies of the Union: An Inventory of Current Activities, April. http://euro pa.eu.int/comm/external_relations/north_dim/conf/formin2/invent_01.pdf

Commission of the European Communities. 2003. The Second Northern Dimension Action Plan, 2004–06. Brussels, 10 June. http://europa.eu.int/comm/external_relations/north_dim/ndap/com03_343.pdf

Communist Party of the Russian Federation. 2011. Predvybornaya Programma KPRF [CPRF Election Program]. 12 October. http://kprf.ru/crisis/ offer/97653.html (in Russian).

Communist Party of the Soviet Union. 1961. Programma KPSS [CPSU Program]. http://leftinmsu.narod.ru/polit_files/books/III_program_KPSS_files/III_progra m_KPSS.htm (in Russian).

Communist Party of the Soviet Union. 1986. Programma KPSS. Novaya Redaktsiya [CPSU Program. New Edition]. In XXVII S'ezd Kommunisticheskoy Partii Sovetskogo Soyuza. Stenografichesky Otchet [XXVIIth Congress of the Communist Party of the Soviet Union. Verbatim Report]. Moscow: Polizdat, vol. 1, pp. 554–623. http://soveticus5.narod.ru/85/xxviit1.htm (in Russian).

Conley, H., Gerber, T., Moore L. And M. David. 2011. Russian Soft Power in the 21st Century. An Examination of Russian Compatriots in Estonia. Washington, DC: CSIS.

Council of the European Union. 2000. Action Plan for the Northern Dimension with External and Cross-Border Policies of the European Union 2000–2003. 9401/00. June 14. http://europa.eu.int/comm/external_relations/north_d im/ndap/06_00_fr.pdf

Council of the European Union. 2001. Full Report on Northern Dimension Policies, 9804/01, 12 June. http://europa.eu.int/comm/external_relations/ north_im/doc/full_report.pdf

Cox, Ramsey. 2014. Reid: Putin Is 'Homesick' for Soviet Union. 26 March. http://thehill.com/blogs/floor-action/senate/201779-reid-putin-is-homesick-for-soviet-union

Crow, Suzanne. 1993. The Making of Foreign Policy in Russia under Yeltsin, Munich and Washington, DC: Radio Free Europe/Radio Liberty Research Institute.

Ćwiek-Karpowicz, J. 2012. Limits to Russian Soft Power in the Post-Soviet Area. DGAP Analyse 8.

Dakhin, Vladimir. 1995. Kontury Novogo Mira' [The Contours of a New World]. Svobodnaya Mysl' 4, pp. 78–86 (in Russian).

Davydov, Yuri. 1993. Russia and Eastern Europe. Providence: Brown University Press.

Dawisha, Karen and Bruce Parrott. 1994. Russia and the States of Eurasia: The Politics of Upheaval. New York: Cambridge University Press.

De Coning, Cedric, Mandrup, Thomas and Liselotte Odgaard (eds.). 2014. The BRICS and Coexistence: An Alternative Vision of World Order. Abingdon: Routledge Taylor & Francis Group.

Deinichenko, P. 1996. Karel Culture and Forest Go Together. Moscow News, 28 March-3 April, p. 10.

Delany, Max and Kevin O'Flynn. 2007. As Sochi Gets Olympics, a Gold Medal for Putin. International Herald Tribune, 5 July.

Delyagin, Mikhail. 2006. Rossiya i Krizisy Globalizatsii. [Russia and the Crisis of Globalization]. Political Class 14 (in Russian).

Deryabin, Yuri. 2000. Severnoye Izmerenie Politiki Evropeiskogo Soyuza i Interesy Rossii [The EU Northern Dimension and Russia's Interests]. Moscow: Institute of Europe, RAS (in Russian).

Dick, C. 1994. The Military Doctrine of the Russian Federation. Jane's Intelligence Review (Special Report) 1, pp. 3–5.

Dmitriev, Anatoly. 2000. Konfliktologiya [Conflict Studies]. Moscow: Gardariki (in Russian).

Dmitrieva, Olga. 2003a. Plyusy Odnogo Polyusa [Pluses of a Single Pole]. Rossiyskaya Gazeta, 20 May, p. 6 (in Russian).

Dmitrieva, Olga. 2003b. Vosmyerka Budet Pravit' Mirom? [Will the G-8 Rule the World?]. Rossiyskaya gazeta, 31 May, pp. 1, 4 (in Russian).

Donaldson, Robert and Joseph Nogee. 2009. The Foreign Policy of Russia: Changing Systems, Enduring Interests. Armonk, NY: M.E. Sharpe.

Dugin, Alexander. 2002. Metafizika i Geopolitika Prirodnykh Resursov. Kakoi Byt' Energeticheskoy Strategii Rossii. [Metaphysics and Geopolitics of Natural Resources. How Russia's Energy Strategy Should Look Like]. 14 December. http://www.centrasia.ru/newsA.php?st=1039816440 (in Russian).

Dugin, Alexander. 2012. Teoriya Mnogopolyarnogo Mira [Multipolar World Theory]. Moscow: Eurasian Movement (in Russian).

Dunlop, J.B. 1993. The Rise of Russia and the Fall of the Soviet Empire. Princeton: Princeton University Press.

East, M.A., 1972. Status Discrepancy and Violence in the International System: an Empirical Analysis. In Rosenau, J.H., Davis, V. and M.A. East (eds.). The Analysis of International Politics: Essays in Honor of Harold and Margaret Sprout. New York: Free Press, pp. 299–319.

Elections. 1995. Parties' Foreign Policy Views. International Affairs (Moscow) 41: 11–12, pp. 3–13.

Eliasson, Jan. 2000. The Speech of Mr. Jan Eliasson, State Secretary for Foreign Affairs, Sweden. In Nissinen, Marja (ed.). Foreign Ministers' Conference on the Northern Dimension, Helsinki, 11–12 November 1999. A Compilation of Speeches. Helsinki: Unit for the Northern Dimension in the Ministry for Foreign Affairs, pp. 68–70.

Emerson, Michael (ed.). 2007. The Elephant and the Bear Try Again: Options for a New Agreement Between the EU and Russia. Brussels: Center for Eurpean Policy Studies.

Engelbrekt, Kjell and Bertil Nygren (eds.). 2010. Russia and Europe. Building Bridges, Digging Trenches. London: Routledge.

Ennis, Stephen. 2014. Russian TV sees US plot behind Ukraine and IS militants. 25 September. http://www.bbc.com/news/world-europe-29368707

Ernst and Young. 2012. Rapid-Growth Markets Soft Power Index. http://www.ey.com/Publication/vwLUAssets/Rapid-growth_markets:_Soft_po wer_index/$FILE/Rapid-growth_markets-Soft_Power_Index-Spring_2012.pdf

Eurostat. 2015. Natural gas consumption statistics. July. http://ec.europa.eu/eur ostat/statistics-explained/index.php/Natural_gas_consumption_statistics

Fadeev, D.A. and V. Razuvayev. 1994. Russia and the Western Post-Soviet Republics. In Blackwill, Robert D. and Sergei A. Karaganov (eds). Damage Limitation or Crisis? Russia and the Outside World. Washington / London: Brassey's, Inc., pp. 106–122.

2001. Federalism i Publichnaya Sfera v Rossii i Kanade [Federalism and Public Policy in Russia and Canada]. Moscow: The Gorbachev Foundation (in Russian).

Fel'dman, Dmitry. 1998. Politologiya Konflikta [Political Analysis of Conflict]. Moscow: Strategy (in Russian).

Flockhart, Trine (ed.). 2014. Cooperative Security: NATO's Partnership Policy in a Changing World. Copenhagen: Danish Institute for International Studies.

Forsberg, Tuomas, Heller, Regina and Reinhard Wolf. 2014. Introduction. Communist and Post-Communist Studies 47, pp. 261–268.

Fukuyama, Francis. 1992. The End of History and the Last Man. Harmonsworth: Penguin.

Gaddy, Clifford and Michael O'Hanlon. 2015. Toward a "Reaganov" Russia: Russian Security Policy After Putin. The Washington Quarterly 38:2, pp. 205–221.

Gadzhiev, Kamaludin S. 1997. Geopolitika [Geopolitics]. Moscow: Mezhdunarodnye Otnosheniya (in Russian).

Galtung, Johan. 1964. A Structural Theory of Aggression. Journal of Peace Research 11: 2, pp. 95–119.

Galtung, Johan. 1969. Violence, Peace and Peace Research. Journal of Peace Research 6: 3, pp. 167–191.

Galtung, Johan and Carl Jacobsen. 2000. Searching for Peace: The Road to TRANSCEND. London: Pluto Press.

Gantman, V.I. (ed.). 1984. Sistema, Struktura I Protsess Razvitiya Sovremennykh Mezdunarodnykh Otnosheniy [System, Structure and Process of Development of Contemporary International Relations]. Moscow: Nauka (in Russian).

Gertchikova, Irina N. 1994 / 1995. Management. Moscow: Mezhdunarodnye Otnosheniya (in Russian).

Gizewski, P. 1995. Military Activity and Environmental Security: The Case of Radioactivity in the Arctic. DeBardeleben, J. and J. Hannigan (eds.). Environmental Security and Quality after Communism: Eastern Europe and the Soviet Successor States. Boulder: Westview Press, pp. 25–41.

1987. Globalnye Problemy Sovremennosti i Sotrudnichestva v Khode ikh Resheniya [Present-Day Global Problems and Cooperation in the Process of Problem-Solving]. Berlin: MISON (in Russian).

Glukhova, A.V. 1997. Tipologiya Politicheskikh Konfliktov [Political Conflict Typology]. Voronezh: Voronezh State University Press (in Russian).

Goncharov, Sergei. 1992. Osobye Interesy Rossii—Cho Eto Takoye? [Special Interests of Russia —What Are They?]. Izvestiya, 25 February, p. 3 (in Russian).

Goodby, James E. and Benoit Morel (eds). 1993. The Limited Partnership: Building a Russian-US Security Community. New York: Oxford University Press.

Gorbachev, Mikhail. 1987. Perestroyka dlya Strany i Vsego Mira [Perestroyka for the Country and the Whole World]. Moscow: Politizdat (in Russian).

Gorbachev, Mikhail. 1991. Epilogue. In Bremeh, Bento (ed.). Europe by Nature. Assen: Van Gorcum, pp. 230–231.

Gordon, M.R. 1996. Officer Charged as Spy is Treated Soviet-Style. International Herald Tribune, 29 November, p. 6.

Gorny, Mikhail (ed.). 2004. Publichnaya Politika: Voprosy Myagkoi Bezopasnosti v Baltiyskom Regione [Public Policy: Soft Security Issues in the Baltic Sea Region]. St. Petersburg: Norma (in Russian).

Government of the Russian Federation. 2012. Soveschanie Rukovoditelei Predstavitel'stv Rossotrudnichestva za Rubezhom [The Meeting of the Heads of the Rossotrudnichestvo's Representative Offices Abroad]. http://www.government.ru/stens/20531/ (in Russian).

Grabovski, V. et al. (eds.). 2005. Evropeiskie Strany SNG: Mesto v Bol'shoi Evrope [CIS European Countries: the Role on the Wider Europe]. Moscow: Mezhdunarodnye Otnoshenie (in Russian).

Granholm, Niklas, Malminen Johannes and Gudrun Persson (eds). 2014. A Rude Awakening. Ramifications of Russian Aggression Towards Ukraine. Stockholm: FOI

Gressel, Gustav. 2015. Russia's Quiet Military Revolution, and What It Means for Europe. London: The European Council on Foreign Relations.

Griffiths, Franklyn. 1964. Origins of Peaceful Coexistence: A Historical Note. Survey 50, pp. 195–201.

Grigoriev, Sergei. 1995. Neo-Imperialism: The Underlying Factors. In Ra'anan, Uri and Kevin Martin (eds.). Russia: A Return to Imperialism? New York: St. Martin's Press, pp. 3–16.

Grigoryev, Yevgeny. 2003. Peterburg ne Stanet Mestom Pokayaniya [St Petersburg Will not be a Place for Repentance]. Nezavisimaya Gazeta, 30–31 May, p. 6 (in Russian).

Gromov, Felix. 1995. Znachenie Kaliningradskogo Osobogo Rayona dlya Oboronosposobnosti Rossiyskoi Federatsii [The Role of the Kaliningard Special District for the Russian Federation's Defense]. Voennaya Mysl July-August, pp. 9–13 (in Russian).

Gromyko, Andrey and Vladimir B. Lomeiko. 1984. Novoye Myshlenie v Yaderny Vek [New Thinking in the Nuclear Age]. Moscow: Politizdat (in Russian).

Gronskaya, Natalya and Andrei Makarychev. 2010. Ideya Imperii i "Myagkaya Sila": Mirovoy Opyt i Rossiyskie Perspectivy [The Idea of Empire and "Soft Power": World Experience and Russian Prospects]. Voprosy Upravleniya 10, pp. 22–27 (in Russian).

Grygas, A. 2012. Legacies, Coercion and Soft Power: Russian Influence in the Baltic States. Chatham House Briefing Paper. August. http://www.chathamhouse.org/sites/files/chathamhouse/public/Research/Russia%20and%20Eurasia/0812bp_grigas.pdf

Guschin, A.V., Markedonov, S.M. and A.N. Tsibulina. 2015. The Ukrainian Challenge for Russia. Moscow: Spetskniga. http://russiancouncil.ru/common/upload/WP-Ukraine-Russia-24-eng.pdf

Guseinov, Vladimir. 1999. Obnovlenie NATO i Bezopasnost Rossii [NATO's Renaissance and Russia's Security]. Nezavisimoye Voennoe Obozrenie, 16–21 April, p. 4 (in Russian).

Gvosdev, Nikolas K. and Christopher Marsh. 2013. Russian Foreign Policy: Interests, Vectors, and Sectors. Washington: Congressional Quarterly Press.

Haass, Richard N. 2008. The Palmerstonian Moment. The National Interest. January-February. http://nationalinterest.org/article/the-palmerstonian-moment-1918

Hansen, Flemming Splidsboel. 2013. Integration in the Post-Soviet Space. International Area Studies Review 16: 2, pp. 142–159.

Hansen, Flemming Splidsboel and Alexander Sergunin. 2014. Russia, BRICS, and peaceful coexistence: between idealism to instrumentalism. In De Coning, Cedric, Mandrup, Thomas and Liselotte Odgaard (eds.). The BRICS and Co-existence: An Alternative Vision of World Order. Abingdon: Routledge Taylor & Francis Group, pp. 75–99.

Heininen, Lassi and Jyrki Käkönen (eds.). 1991. Arctic Complexity: Essays on Arctic Interdependence. Tampere: Tampere Peace Research Institute (TA-PRI Occasional Papers; No.44).

Horak, Stephan. 1964. Lenin on Coexistence: A Chapter in Soviet Foreign Policy. Studies on the Soviet Union 3, pp. 20–30;

Ilyin, Mikhail. 1995. Ocherki Khronopoliticheskoi Tipologii [Essays on Chronopoliti-cal Typology]. Moscow: MGIMO (in Russian).

Institute of Europe. 1995. Geopoliticheskie Peremeny v Evrope, Politika Zapada i Alternativy dlya Rossii [Geopolitical Changes in Europe, Western Policy and Alternatives for Russia]. Moscow: Institute of Europe (in Russian).

Ivanenko, V.S. et al. 2003. Entsiklopedia Mezhdunarodnykh Organizatsiy [Ency-clopedia of International Organizations]. St. Petersburg: St. Petersburg State University (in Russian).

Ivanov, Igor. 2003. Irakskiy Vopros Snova v OON [The Iraqi Question is Again in UN]. Nezavisimaya Gazeta, 30–31 May, pp. 1, 6 (in Russian).

Jacobson, Jon. 1994. When the Soviet Union Entered World Politics. Berkeley: University of California Press.

Joenniemi, Pertti and Alexander Sergunin. 2003. Russia and European Union's Northern Dimension: Clash or Encounter of Civilizations? Nizhny Novgorod: Nizhny Novgorod State Linguistic University Press.

Joenniemi, Pertti and Alexander Sergunin. 2012. Laboratories of European Integra-tion: City-Twinning in Northern Europe. Tartu: Peipsi Center for Transbound-ary Cooperation.

Joenniemi, Pertti and Alexander Sergunin. 2013. Another Face of Glocalization: Cities Going International (the Case of North-Western Russia). In Russia's Changing Economic and Political Regimes. Ed. by Andre Mommen and An-drei Makarychev. New York: Routledge, pp. 229–58.

Joenniemi, Pertti and Alexander Sergunin. 2014. Paradiplomacy as a Capacity-Building Strategy: The Case of Russia's Northwestern Subnational Actors, Problems of Post-Communism 61: 6, pp. 18–33.

2009. Joint Declaration of the Prague Eastern Partnership Summit, 7 May 2009, Prague. http://www.consilium.europa.eu/uedocs/cms_data/docs/pressdata/en/er/10758.pdf.

Kachanov, Y. 1995. Politicheskaya Topologiya: Strukturirovaniye Politicheskoi Realnosti [Political Topology: Structuring Political Reality]. Moscow: Nauka (in Russian).

Kamenskaya, Galina et al. (eds.). 2007. Istoriya Mezhdunarodnykh Otnosheniy [International Relations History]. Moscow: Logos (in Russian).

Kanet, Roger E. (ed.). 2007. Russia: Re-emerging Great Power. Basingstoke: Palgrave Macmillan.

Kanet, Roger E. 2010. Russian Foreign Policy in the 21st Century. London / New York: Palgrave Macmillan.

Kant, Immanuel. 1795 / 1957. Perpetual Peace. Indianapolis and New York: Bobbs-Merill.

Kapustin, Boris. 1996. Natsionalnyi Interes kak Konservativnaya Utopiya. [National Interest as a Conservative Utopia]. Svobodnaya Mysl 6, pp. 13–28 (in Russian).

Karaganov, Sergei. 1995. Fifty Years After Victory. International Affairs (Moscow) 41: 4–5, pp. 59–64.

Karaganov, Sergei. 2003. U Rossii Est' Unikalny Vneshnepolitichesky Resurs [Russia Has a Unique Foreign Policy Resource]. Nezavisimaya Gazeta, 12 May, pp. 9, 15 (in Russian).

Katsy, Dmitry (ed.). 2007. International Relations: From Local Challenges to Global Shifts. St. Petersburg: St. Petersburg State University Press.

Kharitonovich, D.E. 1995. Poisk Novykh Metodov v Istoricheskoi Nauke. [The Search for New Methods in the Historical Science]. Novaya i Noveishaya Istoriya 15: 4, pp. 248–250 (in Russian).

Khokhlysheva, Olga. 1999. Praktikum po Istorii Mezhdunarodnykh Otnosheniy [Reader on International Relations History]. Nizhny Novgorod: Nizhny Novgorod State University Press, Vol. 1–3 (in Russian).

Khokhlysheva, Olga. 2000. Razoruzhenie, Bezopasnost', Mirotvorchestvo: Global'noe Izmerenie [Disarmament, Security, Peace-Keeping: the Global Dimension]. Nizhny Novgorod: Nizhny Novgorod State University Press (in Russian).

Khokhlysheva, Olga. 2002. Miroponimanie, Mirotvorchestvo, Mirosokhranenie: Opyt XX Stoletiya [Peace-Understanding, Peace-Making and Peace-Keeping: 20th Century's Experience]. Nizhny Novgorod: Nizhny Novgorod State University Press (in Russian).

Khokhlysheva, Olga. 2005. Mirovaya Politika i Mezhdunarodnoe Pravo. Zakonomernosti, Tendentsii, Perspectivy [World Politics and International Law. Regularities, Trends, Perspectives]. Nizhny Novgorod: Nizhny Novgorod State University Press, Vol. 1–2 (in Russian).

Khrustalev, Mark A. 1991. Teoriya Politiki i Politicheskiy Analiz [Political Theory and Political Analysis]. Moscow: MGIMO (in Russian).

Khrustalev, Mark A. 1992. After the Disintegration of the Soviet Union: Russia in a New World. Moscow: MGIMO.

Khudolei, Konstantin (ed.). 2004. Rossiya i NATO: Novye Sfery Partnerstva [Russia and NATO: New Spheres of Partnership]. St. Petersburg: St. Petersburg State University Press (in Russian).

Khudolei, Konstantin (ed.). 2006. Post-Cold War Challenges to International Relations. St. Petersburg: St. Petersburg State University Press.

Kokoshin, Andrei and Alexei Bogaturov (eds.). 2005. Mirovaya Politika. Teoriya, Metodologiya, Prikladnoi Analiz [World Politics. Theory, Methodology, Applied Analysis]. Moscow: KomKniga (in Russian).

Kolikov, Nikolai. 1994. Rossiya v Kontekste Globalnykh Peremen [Russia in the Context of Global Transition]. Svobodnaya Mysl' 2–3, pp. 3–18 (in Russian).

Kolobov, Oleg (ed.). 2001. Istoriya Mezhdunarodnykh Otnosheniy [International Relations History]. Nizhny Novgorod: Nizhny Novgorod State University Press, Vol. 1–2 (in Russian).

Kolobov, Oleg (ed.). 2004. Teoriya Mezhdunarodnykh Otnosheniy [International Relations Theory]. Nizhny Novgorod: Nizhny Novgorod State University Press, Vol. 1–2 (in Russian).

Kolobov, Oleg (ed.). 2005. NATO i Rossiya v Global'nom Grazhdanskom Obshestve [NATO and Russia in the Global Civil Society]. Nizhny Novgorod: Nizhny Novgorod State University Press (in Russian).

Kolobov, Oleg et al. 1997. Zapad: Novye Izmereniya Natsional'noi i Mezhdunarodnoi Bezopasnosti [The West: New Dimensions of National and International Security]. Nizhny Novgorod: Nizhny Novgorod State University Press (in Russian).

Kolobov, Oleg A., Kornilov, Alexander and Irina Luneva. 2005. Problemy Voiny i Mira v XX Veke [Problems of War and Peace in the 20th Century]. Nizhny Novgorod: Nizhny Novgorod State University Press (in Russian).

Kolobov, Oleg and Andrei Makarychev (eds.). 1998. Russia, NATO and a New European Security Architecture. Nizhny Novgorod: Nizhny Novgorod State University Press (in Russian).

Kolobov, Oleg and V.N. Yasenev. 2001. Informatsionnaya Bezopasnost' i Antiterroristicheskaya Deyatel'nost' Sovremennogo Gosudarstva [Information Security and Anti-Terrorist Activities of the Present-Day State]. Nizhny Novgorod: Nizhny Novgorod State University Press (in Russian).

Kolobov, Oleg A., Kornilov, Alexander A., Makarychev, Andrei S. and Alexander A. Sergunin. 1992. Protsess Prinyatiya Vneshnepoliticheskikh Resheniy: Istoricheskiy Opyt SShA, Gosudarstva Israil' i Zapadnoi Evropy [Foreign Policy Decision-Making: Historical Experiences of the United States, Israel, and West Europe]. Nizhny Novgorod: Nizhny Novgorod State University Press (in Russian).

Kolosov, Yuri, Krivtchikova, Emilia S. et al. 1994. Mezhdunarodnoye Pravo [International Law]. Moscow: Mezhdunarodnye Otnosheniya (in Russian).

Konovalov, Alexander. 1997. The Generals' 'Circular Defense' and National Security Interests. RIA-Novosti, January.

Karaganov, Sergey. 2006. Rossiya – SshA: Obratno k Mirnomu Sosushestvovaniyu? [Russia-USA: Back to Peaceful Coexistence?]. Rossiiskaya Gazeta 24 March (in Russian).

1977. Konstitutsiya (Osnovnoy Zakon) Soyuza Sovetskikh Sotsialisticheskikh Respublik [Constitution (Organic Law) of the Union of the Soviet Socialist Republics]. Moscow: Politizdat. http://www.hist.msu.ru/ER/Etext/cnst1977.htm#4 (in Russian).

1993. Kontseptsiya Vneshney Politiki Rossiyskoi Federatsii [Foreign Policy Concept of the Russian Federation]. Diplomaticheskiy Vestnik (Special Issue), January, pp. 3–23 (in Russian).

Konyshev, Valery. 2001. Neorealizm v Sovremennoi Politicheskoi Mysli SshA [Neorealism in Contemporary U.S. Political Thought]. St. Petersburg: The Library of the RAS Press (in Russian).

Konyshev, Valery. 2004. Amerikansky Neorealizm o Prirode Voiny: Evolutsiya Politicheskoi Teorii [American Neorealism on the Nature of War: Evolution of Political Theory]. St. Petersburg: Nauka (in Russian).

Konyshev, Valery. 2006. Sovremennaya Amerikanskaya Politicheskaya Mysl': Istoriografiya Neorealizma [Contemporary American Political Thought: Historiography of Neorealism]. St. Petersburg: St. Petersburg State University Press (in Russian).

Konyshev, Valery and Alexander Sergunin. 2012. Novaya Voennaya Doktrina Baraka Obamy i Natzional'nye Interesy Rossii [Barak Obama's New Military Doctrine and Russia's National Interests]. Natzional'nye interesy: prioritety i bezopasnost' [National Interests: Priorities and Security] 14, pp. 2–9 (in Russian).

Konyshev, Valery and Alexander Sergunin (eds.). 2013. Sovremennye Teorii Mezhdunarodnykh Otnosheniy [Contemporary International Relations Theories]. Moscow: Prospekt (in Russian).

Konyshev, Valery and Alexander Sergunin. 2014. Mezdunarodnaya Bezopasnost: Podkhody i Kontsepty [International Security: Approaches and Concepts]. In Ivanov, Oleg (ed.). 21 Vek: Perekrestki Mirovoy Politiki [21st Century: At the Crossroads of World Politics]. Moscow: Kanon-Plus, pp. 39–61 In Russian).

Kortunov, Andrei. 1996. NATO Enlargement and Russia: In Search of an Adequate Response. In Haglund, David G. (ed.). Will NATO Go East? The Debate Over Enlarging the Atlantic Alliance. Kingstone: Queen's University, pp. 71–82.

Kosachev, Konstantin. 2012a. The Specifics of Russian Soft Power. Russia in Global Affairs. 7 October. http://eng.globalaffairs.ru/number/The-Specifics-of-Russian-Soft-Power-15683.

Kosachev, Konstantin. 2012b. V Mire Slozhilas Prezumptsiya Vinovnosti Rossii [Presumption of Russia's Culpability Exists in the World]. Kommersant, 1 September (in Russian).

Kosolapov, Nikolai. 1992. Sila, Nasilie, Bezopasnost': Sovremennaya Dialektika Vzaimosvyazei [Force, Violence, Security: the Present-Day Dialectics of Interdependency]. Mirovaya Economika i Mezhdunarodnye Otnosheniya 11, pp. 1–7 (in Russian).

Kosolapov, Nikolai. 1999. Analiz Vneshnei Politiki: Osnovnye Napravleniya Issledovaniy [Foreign Policy Analysis: Main Research Topics]. Mirovaya Economika i Mezhdunarodnye Otnosheniya 2, pp. 75–81 (in Russian).

Kozin, Vladimir. 1994. Moskva Dolzhna Prisoedinitsya k Partnerstvu vo Imya Mira [Moscow Should Join "Partnership for Peace"]. Nezavisimaya Gazeta, 15 February, p. 4 (in Russian).

Kozyrev, Andrei. 1994. Statement of the Russian Foreign Minister. Nezavisimaya Gazeta, 19 January (in Russian).

Krasin, Yuri. 1996. Natsionalnye Interesy: Mif ili Realnost'? [National Interests: Myth or Reality?]. Svobodnaya Mysl' 3, pp. 3–29 (in Russian).

Kremenyuk, Viktor. 1994. Conflicts In and Around Russia: Nation-Building in Difficult Times. Westport, Conn. / London: Greenwood Press.

Krutikov, Yevgeny. 2014. Ne Tol'ko Ukraina [Not Just Ukraine]. Vzglyad, 25 March. http://www.vz.ru/politics/2014/3/25/678423.html (in Russian).

Kubálková, V. and A. Cruickshank. 1978. The Soviet Concept of Peaceful Coexistence: Some Theoretical and Semantic Problems. Australian Journal of Politics and History 24, pp. 184–98.

Kubyshkin, Alexander and Alexander Sergunin. 2012. The Problem of the "Special Path" in Russian Foreign Policy (From the 1990s to the Early Twenty-First Century). Russian Politics and Law 50: 6, pp. 7–18.

Kubyshkin, Alexander and Natalya Tzvetkova. 2013. Publichnaya Diplomatiya SShA [U.S. Public Diplomacy]. Moscow: Aspect-Press.

Kudors, A. 2010. Russian World—Russia's Soft Power Approach to Compatriots Policy. Russian Analytical Digest 81, June 6, pp. 1–4.

Kudryavtsev, V.N. (ed.). 1994. Yuridicheskiy Konflikt: Sfery i Mekhanizmy [Legal Conflict: Spheres and Mechanisms]. Moscow: Institute of Government and Law, RAS (in Russian).

Kudryavtsev, V.N. (ed.). 1995. Yuridicheskaya Konfliktologiya [Legal Conflict Studies]. Moscow: Institute of Government and Law, RAS (in Russian).

Kühn, Ulrich. 2015. Understanding Russia. Russian Analytical Digest 162, 10 February, pp. 5–8.

Kukk, Mare, Jervell, Sverre and Pertti Joenniemi. The Baltic Sea Area: A Region in the Making. Oslo: Europa-Programmet.

Kukulka, Yuri. 1980. Problemy Teorii Mezhdunarodnykh Otnosheniy [International Relations Theory Problems]. Moscow: Progress (in Russian).

Kulagin, Vladimir. 2006. Mezhdunarodnaya Bezopasnost' [International Security]. Moscow: Aspect Press (in Russian).

Kulagin, V.A. and T.A. Mitrova (eds.). 2015. Gazovy Rynok Evropy: Utrachennye Illyuzii i Robkie Nadezhdy [European Gas Market: Lost Illusions and Faint Hopes]. Moscow: Higher School of Economics / Institute for Energy Studies, Russian Academy of Sciences. http://www.eriras.ru/files/gazovyy_ry nok_evropy.pdf

Kuznetsov, Arthur. 1995. A New Model for Traditional Civilizations. International Affairs (Moscow) 41: 4–5, pp. 95–100.

Lantsov, Sergei and Valery Achkasov. 2007. Mirovaya Politika i Mezhdunarodnye Otnosheniya [World Politics and International Relations]. St. Petersburg: Piter (in Russian).

Lapin, G.E. (2002) Konsul'skaya Sluzhba [Consular Service], Moscow: Mezhdunarodnye Otnosheniya (in Russian).

Larson, Deborah Welch and Alexei Shevchenko. 2003. Shortcut to Greatness: The New Thinking and the Revolution in Soviet Foreign Policy. International Organization 57: 1, pp. 77–109.

Larson, Deborah Welch and Alexei Shevchenko. 2010. Status Seekers. Chinese and Russian Responses to U.S. Primacy. International Security 34: 4, 63–95.

Laruelle, Marlene. 2008. Russian Eurasianism, an Ideology of Empire. Baltimore: John Hopkins University Press.

Lebedeva, Marina. 1997. Politicheskoye Uregulirovanie Konfliktov: Podkhody, Reshenya, Technologii [Conflict Resolution: Approaches, Solutions, Techniques]. Moscow: Aspect Press (in Russian).

Lebedeva, Marina (ed.). 2000. Mirovaya Politika i Mezhdunarodnye Otnosheniya: Kluychevye Slova i Ponyatiya [World Politics and International Relations: Kew Words and Notions]. Nizhny Novgorod: Nizhny Novgorod State University Press (in Russian).

Lebedeva, Marina. 2003/2006. Mirovaya Politika [World Politics]. Moscow: Aspect Press (in Russian).

Lebedeva, Marina and Pavel Tsygankov (eds.). 2001. Mirovaya Politika i Mezhdunarodnye Otnosheniya v 1990-e Gody: Vzglyady Amerikanskikh i Frantsuzskikh Issledovatelei [World Politics and International Relations in the 1990s: Views of American and French Scholars]. Moscow: MONF (in Russian).

Legvold, Robert (ed.). 2007. Russian Foreign Policy in the 21st Century and the Shadow of the Past. New York: Columbia University Press.

Lenin, Vladimir. 1970a. Amerikanskim Rabochim [To American Workers]. Polnoye Sobranie Sochineniy, 5-e Izdanie [Complete Works, 5th Ed.]. Moscow: Politizdat 39, pp. 196–197 (in Russian).

Lenin, Vladimir. 1970b. Sobranie Aktiva Moscovskoy Organizatsii RKP (b). 6 Dek-abrya 1920 g. Doklad o Kontsessiyakh [Meeting of the RCP (b) Moscow Or-ganization Activists. 6 December 1920. Report on Concessions]. Polnoye Sobranie Sochineniy, 5-e Izdanie [Complete Works, 5th Ed.]. Moscow: Politizdat 42, pp. 55–78 (in Russian).

Lerner, Warren. 1964. The Historical Origins of the Soviet Doctrine of Peaceful Coexistence. Law and Contemporary Society 29, pp. 865–870

Leshukov, Igor (ed.). 1999. Desyatiletie Sotrudnichestva (1988–1998): Evropeiskiy Soyuz i Rossiya v Perspective [The Decade of Cooperation (1988–1998): the European Union and Russia in the Perspective]. St. Petersburg: Nadezhda (in Russian).

Leshukov, Igor. 2000. Rossiya i Evropeiskiy Soyuz: Strategiya Vzaimootnosheniy [Russia and the European Union: a Strategy of Interaction]. Trenin, Dmitri (ed.). Rossiya i Osnovnye Instituty Bezopasnosti v Evrope: Vstupaya v XXI Vek [Russia and the Main European Security Institutions: Approaching the 21st century]. Moscow: Moscow Carnegie Center, pp. 23–48 (in Russian).

Libert, U., Logunov, L. et al. (eds.). 2005. Rossiysko-Evropeiskie Sravnitel'nye Issledovaniya [Russian-European Comparative Studies]. Moscow: Russian State University of Humanities (in Russian).

Light, Margot. 1988. The Soviet Theory of International Relations. Brighton: Wheatsheaf.

Litera, Bohuslav. 1994 / 1995. The Kozyrev Doctrine—A Russian Variation on the Monroe Doctrine. Perspectives 4, pp. 45–52.

Lockwood, David. 1994. Nuclear Arms Control. In SIPRI Yearbook 1994. Oxford: Oxford University Press, pp. 639–672.

Lomagin, Nikita (ed.). 2001. Vvedenie v Teoriyu Mezhdunarodnykh Otnosheniy i Analiz Vneshnei Politiki [Introduction to International Relations Theory and Foreign Policy Analysis]. St. Petersburg: St. Petersburg State University Press (in Russian).

Lucas, Edward. 2009. The New Cold War: Putin's Russia and the Threat to the West. Rev. ed. New York: Palgrave Macmillan.

Lukin, Vladimir P. 1994. Russia and its Interests. In Sestanovich, Stephen (ed.). Rethinking Russia's National Interests. Washington, DC: Center for Strategic and International Studies, pp. 106–15.

Lukin, Vladimir P. 2003. Prishla Pora Igrat v Komandnuyu Igru [It's Time Now to Play Team Game]. Nezavisimaya Gazeta, 24 March, p. 15 (in Russian).

Lukov, Vadim. 1995. Russia's Security: The Foreign Policy Dimension. Internation-al Affairs (Moscow) 41: 5, pp. 3–8.

Lukyanov, Fyodor. 2009. Poiski Myagkoy Sily [In search of Soft Power]. Forbes Online, 2 November. http://www.forbes.ru/column/23084-poiski-%C2%ABmy agkoi%C2%BB-sily (in Russian).

Lukyanov, Fyodor. 2010. Russian Dilemmas in a Multipolar World. Journal of International Affairs 63: 2. http://jia.sipa.columbia.edu/russian-dilemmas-multipolar-world/

Lukyanov, Fyodor. 2011. BRICS Goes from Fantasy to Reality. Russia in Global Affairs, 17 April. http://www.globalaffairs.ru/redcol/BRICS-goes-from-fantasy-to-reality-15169.

Lukyanov, Fyodor. 2013. Depardye Protiv Progressa [Depardieu Is Against Progress]. Gazeta.ru, 17 January. http://www.gazeta.ru/column/lukyano v/4929549.shtml (in Russian).

Lukyanov, Fyodor. 2014. Russia and the BRICS. Moscow: Observo.

Lukyanov, Fyodor and Ivan Krastev (eds.). 2015. New Rules or No Rules? Moscow: International Discussion Club "Valdai". http://ru.scribd.com/d oc/258588112/The-World-Order-New-Rules-or-No-Rules

Lyasko, A. 1995. Doktrina Noven'kaya, a Vyglyadit Staren'koi [Doctrine Is New but Looks Old], Komsomolskaya Pravda, 29 September, p. 2 (in Russian).

Mackinder, Halford J. 1904. The Geographical Pivot of History. Geographical Journal, 13: 4, pp. 421–444.

Mackinder, Halford J. 1919. Democratic Ideals and Reality: A Study in the Politics of Reconstruction. New York: Henry Holt.

Magomedov, Arbakhan. 2000. Misteriya Regionalizma [Mistery of Regionalism]. Moscow: MONF (in Russian).

Makarov, Dmitry. 1997. Rasshirenie NATO Podtolknet Rossiyu k Reformam [NATO Expansion Will Further Russian Reforms]. Argumenty i Facty 22, p. 9 (in Russian).

Makarychev, Andrei (ed.). 2000. Mezdunarodnye Otnosheniya v 21-m Veke: Regional'noe v Global'nom, Global'nke v Regional'nom [International Relations in the 21st Century: Regional in Global, Global in Regional]. Nizhny Novgorod: Nizhny Novgorod State Linguistic University Press (in Russian).

Makarychev, Andrei (ed.). 2002. Rossiya Pered Global'nymi Vyzovami: Panorama Regional'nykh Strategiy [Russia Faces Global Challenges: the Panorama of Regional Strategies]. Nizhny Novgorod: Nizhny Novgorod State Linguistic University Press (in Russian).

Makarychev, Andrei (ed.). 2002. Rossiyskie Regiony v Mirovoi Politike: Mezhdu Globalizmom i Protektsionizmom [Russian Regions in the World Politics: Between Globalism and Protectionism]. Nizhny Novgorod: Nizhny Novgorod State Linguistic University Press (in Russian).

Makarychev, Andrei. 2003. Globalizm, Globalizatsiya, Globalisty: Regional'niy Vzglyad na Problemu [Globalism, Globalization, Globalists: A Regional Perspective]. In Makarychev, Andrei (ed.). Globalisty i Antiglobalisty [Globalists and Anti-Globalists]. Nizhny Novgorod: Nizhny Novgorod State Linguistic University Press, pp. 12–52 (in Russian).

Makarychev, Andrei. 2005. Russia as Seen from its Edges. Discursive Strategies of Russia's Western Borderlands. In Makarychev, Andrei (ed.). Russia's North West and the European Union: A Playground for Innovations, Nizhny Novgorod: Nizhny Novgorod State Linguistic University Press, pp. 7–54.

Makarychev, Andrei. 2006. Russia's Discursive Construction of Europe and Herself: Towards New Spatial Imaginery. In EU-Russia: the Four Common Spaces (Working Paper Series, N 1). Nizhny Novgorod: Nizhny Novgorod State Linguistic University Press, pp. 5–29.

Makarychev, Andrei. 2007. Terrorism: Encyclopedia, Arkheologiya, Grammatika [Terrorism: Encyclopedia, Archeology and Grammar]. Index Bezopasnosti 13: 2, pp. 133–142 (in Russian).

Makarychev, Andrei and Alexander Sergunin. 1996. Postmodernism i Zapadnaya Politicheskaya Nauka [Postmodernism and Western Political Science]. Sotsialno-politichesky Zhurnal 15: 3, pp. 151–168 (in Russian).

Makarychev, Andrei and Alexander Sergunin. 1999. Sovremennaya Zapadnaya Politicheskaya Mysl': Postpsitivistskaya Revolutsiya [Contemporary Western Political Thought: a Post-positivist Revolution]. Nizhny Novgorod: Nizhny Novgorod State Linguistic University Press (in Russian).

Makarychev, Andrei and Alexander Sergunin. 2013a. The EU, Russia and Models of International Society in a Wider Europe. Journal of Contemporary European Research 9: 2, pp. 313-329.

Makarychev, Andrei and Alexander Sergunin. 2013b. Russian military reform: institutional, political and security implications, Defense & Security Analysis 29: 4, pp. 320–328.

Maksimychev, Igor. 1994. Nuzhna li Evrope NATO? [Does Europe Need NATO?]. Nezavisimaya Gazeta, 8 April, p. 3 (in Russian).

Malcolm, Neil. 1994. New Thinking and After: Debate in Moscow about Europe. In Malcolm, Neil (ed.). Russia and Europe: An End to Confrontation. London and New York: Pinter Publishers, 151–181.

Malcolm, Neil and Alex Pravda. 1996. Democratization and Russian Foreign Policy. International Affairs 72: 3, pp. 537–552.

Malcolm, Neil, Pravda, Alex, Allison, Roy and Margo Light. 1996. Internal Factors in Russian Foreign Policy. New York: Oxford University Press.

Malhotra, Vinay Kumar and Alexander Sergunin. 1998. Theories and Approaches to International Relations. New Delhi: Anmol Publications Pvt. Ltd.

Malinova, Olga. 2014. Obsession with Status and Ressentiment: Historical Backgrounds of the Russian Discursive Identity Construction. Communist and Post-Communist Studies 47, pp. 291–303.

Mankoff, Jeffrey. 2009. Russian Foreign Policy: The Return of Great Power Politics. New York: Rowman and Littlefield.

Manykin, Alexander (ed.). 2001. Vvedenie v Teoriyu Mezhdunarodnykh Otnosheniy [Introduction into International Relations Theory]. Moscow: Moscow State University Press (in Russian).

Manykin, Alexander (ed.). 2009. Osnovy Obshei Teorii Mezhdunarodnykh Otnosheniy [Basics of General International Relations Theory]. Moscow: Moscow State University Press (in Russian).

Markov, Sergei. 2014. After Kiev Coup, the West Will Focus on Moscow. The Moscow Times, 27 March. http://www.themoscowtimes.com/opinion/article/after-kiev-coup-the-west-will-focus-on-moscow/496915.html

Mearsheimer, John. 2014. Why the Ukraine Crisis Is the West's Fault. Foreign Affairs September-October, pp. 1–12.

Medvedev, Dmitry. 2008. Kontseptsiya Vneshney Politiki Rossiyskoi Federatsii [Foreign Policy Concept of the Russian Federation]. http://www.mid.ru/bdomp/ns-osndoc.nsf/4e5fa867101effb4432569fa003a705a/d48737161a0bc944c32574870048d8f7!OpenDocument (in Russian).

Medvedev, Dmitry. 2009. European Security Treaty. Draft. 29 November 2009. http://eng.kremlin.ru/text/docs/2009/11/223072.shtml

Medvedev, Dmitry. 2009. Strategia Natsionalnoi Bezopasnosti Rossiyskoi Federatsii do 2020 goda [National Security Strategy of the Russian Federation up to 2020]. 12 May. http://www.scrf.gov.ru/documents/99.html (in Russian).

Medvedev, Dmitry. 2010. Voennaya Doktrina Rossiyskoy Federatsii [The Military Doctrine of the Russian Federation]. http://prezident.rf/ref_notes/461 (in Russian).

Medvedev, Sergei. 1998. Riding into the Sunset: Russia's Long Journey into Europe. In Huru, Jouko Jalonen, Olli-Pekka and Michael Sheehan (eds.). New Dimensions of Security. Tampere Peace Research Institute (Research Report № 83).

Medvedev, Sergei. 2006. EU–Russian Relations: Alternative Futures. Helsinki: The Finnish Institute of International Affairs.

Meister, Stefan. 2014. Reframing Germany's Russia Policy—An Opportunity for the EU. London: The European Council on Foreign Relations.

Melville, Andrei (ed.). 1997. Global'nye Sotsial'nye i Politicheskie Peremeny v Mire [Global Social and Political Changes in the World]. Moscow: Polis (in Russian).

Mezhevich, Nikolai. 2002. Globalism i Regionalism – Tendentsii Mirovogo Razvitiya i Factor Sotsial'no-Ekonomicheskogo Razvitiya Rossii [Globalism and Regionalism—Tendencies of the World Development and Factor of Russia's Socio-Economic Development]. St. Petersburg: St. Petersburg State University Press (in Russian).

Miasnikov, Vladimir. 1994. Russia and China. In Robert Blackwill and Sergei Karaganov (eds.). Damage Limitation or Crisis? Russia and the Outside World. Washington, DC and London: Brassey's, pp. 227–240.

Michel, Casey. 2014. How Significant Is the Eurasian Economic Union? The Diplomat, 4 June. http://thediplomat.com/2014/06/how-significant-is-the-euras ian-economic-union/

Midlarsky, M. 1969. Status Inconsistency and the Onset of International Warfare. PhD Disseration. Northwestern University.

Migranyan, Andronik. 1999. Nuzhno li nam Pomogat' Yugoslavii? [Should We Help Yugoslavia?]. Nezavisimaya Gazeta, 28 April, pp. 1, 6 (in Russian).

De Miguel, Ramon. 2000. The answer to Europe's important challenges in transborder matters: cooperation in Justice and Home Affairs. In Nissinen, Marja (ed.). Foreign Ministers' Conference on the Northern Dimension, Helsinki, 11–12 November 1999. A Compilation of Speeches. Helsinki: Unit for the Northern Dimension in the Ministry for Foreign Affairs, pp. 65–67.

Mikhailenko, Valery. 1998. Teoriya Mezdunarodnykh Otnosheniy. Filosofskoe Vvedenie [International Relations Theory. A Philosophic Introduction]. Yekaterinburg: Ural State University Press (in Russian).

Mikhailenko, Valery. 2008. Globalizatsiya i Global'noe Upravlenie [Globalization and Global Governance]. Yekaterinburg: Ural State University Press (in Russian).

Mikhailova, Yekaterina. 2013. Russia and Cross-Border Cooperation. In Tüür, Karmo and Viacheslav Morozov (eds.). Russian Federation 2013: Short Term Prognosis. Tartu: CEURUS, pp. 73–77.

Ministry of Defense of the Russian Federation. 1992. Osnovy Voennoy Doktriny Rossii [Basic Provisions of Russia's Military Doctrine]. Voennaya Mysl' (Special Issue) 5, pp. 3–9 (in Russian).

Ministry of Foreign Affairs of the Russian Federation. 1993. Kontseptsiya Vneshney Politiki Rossiyskoy Federatsii [The Foreign Policy Concept of the Russian Federation]. Diplomaticheskiy Vestnik (Special Issue) 1, pp. 3–23 (in Russian).

Ministry of Foreign Affairs of the Russian Federation. 2012. The Russian Presidency of the Council of the Baltic Sea States (July 2012–June 2013). http://www.cbss-russia.ru/sbgm_eng.pdf

The Ministry of Higher Education of the Russian Federation. 1997. Polozheniye ob Uchebno-Metodicheskom Obyedinenii Vyshykh Uchebnykh Zavedeniy Rossiyskoi Federatsii po Obrazovaniyu v Oblasti Mezhdunarodnykh Otnosheniy pri MGIMO MID RF [A Charter of the Association of the Russian Higher Education Institutes on Teaching International Relations Based in the MGIMO, Ministry of Foreign Affairs of the Russian Federation]. Moscow: MGIMO (in Russian).

Minzarari, D. 2012. Soft Power with an Iron Fist: Putin Administration to Change the Face of Russia's Foreign Policy Toward Its Neighbors. Eurasia Daily Monitor 9: 163, 10 September. http://www.jamestown.org/single/?no_cac he=1&tx_ttnews%5Btt_news%5D=39821

Modestov, Sergei. 1992. Voennaya Politika Russkogo Natsionalnogo Sobora [Military Policy of the Russian National Convention]. Nezavisimaya Gazeta, 27 August, p. 6 (in Russian).

Monaghan, Andrew. 2013. The New Russian Foreign Policy Concept: Evolving Continuity. London: Chatham House. www.chathamhouse.org/sites/default /files/public/Research/Russia%20and%20Eurasia/0413pp_monaghan.pdf.

Morozov, Vyacheslav. 2002. Vvedenie v Evropeiskie Issledovaniya [Introduction to European Studies]. St. Petersburg: St. Petersburg State University Press (in Russian).

Morozov, Vyacheslav. 2005. New Borderlands in a United Europe: Democracy, Imperialism, and the Copenhagen Criteria. In EU-Russia: the Four Common Spaces (Working Paper Series, N 1), Nizhny Novgorod: Nizhny Novgorod State Linguistic University Press, pp. 74–84.

Morozov, Vyacheslav. 2006. Teoriya Sekyuritizatsii [Securitization Theory]. St. Petersburg: St. Petersburg State University Press (in Russian).

Morozov, Vyacheslav. 2009. Rossia i Drugie. Identichnost' i Granitsy Politicheskogo Soobschestva [Russia and Others. Identity and the Limits of Political Community]. Moscow: NLO.

Morrison, James W. 1994. Vladimir Zhirinovskiy: An Assessment of a Russian Ultra-Nationalist. Washington, DC: National Defense University.

Mouritzen, Hans (ed.). 1998. Bordering Russia: Theory and Prospects for Europe's Baltic Rim. Aldershot: Ashgate.

Mshvenieradze, V.V. (ed.). 1987. Sotsialno-filosofskie Aspecty Sovremennykh Mezdunarodnykh Otnosheniy [Social-philosophical Aspects of Contemporary International Relations]. Moscow (in Russian).

Nadkarni, Vidya and Norma Noonan (eds.). 2013. Emerging Powers in a Comparative Perspective: The Political and Economic Rise of the BRIC countries. New York: Bloomsbury.

Narinsky, Mikhail M. 1995. Kholodnaya Voina: Novye Documenty [The Cold War: New Documents]. Mocow: Pamyatniki Istoricheskoi Mysli (in Russian).

1996. National Interests in Russian Foreign Policy. International Affairs (Moscow) 42: 2, pp. 1–24.

NATO. 2010. Strategic Concept for the Defense and Security of the Members of the North Atlantic Treaty Organization: Active Engagement, Modern Defense. Lisbon, 19 November. http://www.nato.int/cps/en/natolive/official_texts _68580.htm

NATO. 2011. Active Engagement in Cooperative Security: A More Efficient and Flexible Partnership Policy. http://www.nato.int/nato_static/assets/pdf/ pdf_2011_04/20110415_110415-Partnership-Policy.pdf

Nechipurenko, V. 1999. Sibirskoe Soglashenie s Belorussiey [The Siberian Accord with Belorussia]. Rossiyskaya Gazeta. 16 October, p. 4 (in Russian).

Neumann, Iver. 2007. Russia as a Great Power. Journal of International Relations Development 11: 2, pp. 128–151.

Neumann, Iver. 2005. Russia as a Great Power. In Hendeskog, J., Konnander, V., Nygren, B., Oldberg, I. and C. Pursiainen (eds.). Russia as a Great Power. Dimensions of Security Under Putin. Abingdon: Routledge, pp. 13–28.

Nezhinsky, Leonid N. et al. 1995. Sovetskaya Vneshnaya Politika v Gody "Kholodnoi Voiny' [Soviet Foreign Policy in the Cold war Period]. Moscow: Mezdunarodnye Otnosheniya (in Russian).

Nikolaev, Andrei. 2003. Staraya Strategiya na Noviy Lad [A New Strategy in an Old Shape]. Nezavisimaya Gazeta, 12 May, pp. 9, 14 (in Russian).

Nissinen, Marja (ed.). 2000. Foreign Ministers' Conference on the Northern Dimension, Helsinki, 11–12 November 1999. A Compilation of Speeches. Helsinki: Unit for the Northern Dimension in the Ministry for Foreign Affairs.

Novikov, Gennady. 1996. Teorii Mezhdunarodnykh Otnosheniy [International Relations Theories]. Irkutsk: Irkutsk State University Press (in Russian).

Nye, Joseph. 2004. Soft Power: The Means to Success in World Politics. New York: Public Affairs.

Nye, Joseph. 2013. What China and Russia Don't Get About Soft Power, 29 April. http://www.foreignpolicy.com/articles/2013/04/29/what_china_and_russia_do n_t_get_about_soft_power

1999. O Voine NATO Protiv Yugoslavii: Zayavlenie Soveta po Vneshnei i Oboronnoi Politike [On the War of NATO Against Yugoslavia: The Statement of the Council on Foreign and Defense Policy]. Nezavisimaya Gazeta, 16 April, 1, 8 (in Russian).

Odgaard, Liselotte. 2012. China and Coexistence: Beijing's National Security Strategy for the 21st Century. Washington, D.C: Woodrow Wilson Center Press/Johns Hopkins University Press.

Okuneva, L.S. 2012. BRIKS: Problemy i perspektivy [BRICS: Problems and Perspectives]. Moscow: MGIMO (in Russian).

Onuf, Nicholas. 2013. Making Sense, Making Worlds. Constructivism in Social Theory and International Relations. Abingdon: Routledge.

Organski, A.F.K. 1958. World Politics. New York: Alfred and Knopf.

Orlov, Boris. 1999. Pochemu Nezavisimaya Gazeta Protiv NATO? [Why is Nezavisimaya Gazeta Against NATO?]. Nezavisimaya Gazeta, 23 April, p. 15 (in Russian).

Orlov, Vladimir. 1993. Head of Security Council Forced to Resign. In Moscow News, May 14, p. 9.

Orlov, Vladimir (ed.). 2002. Yadernoe Nerasprostranenie [Nuclear Non-Proliferation]. Moscow: PIR-Center, Vol. 1–2 (in Russian).

Orlyanski, V.S. 2007. Konfliktologiya [Conflict Studies]. Kiev: Tzentr Uchobovoi Literatury.

Osherenko, Gail and Oran Young. The Age of the Arctic. Hot Conflicts and Cold Realities. Cambridge: Cambridge University Press, 1989.

Panarin, Alexander S. 1997. Politologiya [Political Science]. Moscow: Prospect (in Russian).

Panarin, Alexander S. 2003. Strategicheskaya Nestabil'nost' v XXI-m Veke [Strategic Instability in the 21st Century]. Moscow: Algoritm-Kniga (in Russian).

Panova, Victoria. 2013. BRIKS: Problemy Vzaimodeystviya i Potentsial Sotrudnichestva [BRICS: Problems of Interaction and Cooperative Potential]. Obozrevatel'-Observer 1, pp. 39–53 (in Russian).

Patriarch Kirill. 2013. Doklad na Arkhiereyskom Sobore Russkoy Pravoslavnoy Tserkvi [Report to the Episcopal Congress of the Russian Orthodox Church]. 2 February. Zhurnal Moskovskoy Patriarkhii [The Journal of the Moscow Patriarchate] 3, pp. 12–45 (in Russian).

Patrushev, Nikolai. 2015. Velikaya Pobeda v Velikoi Voine [The Great Victory in a Great War]. Krasnaya Zvezda, 6 May. http://www.redstar.ru/index.php/newspaper/itemlist/category/7968 (in Russian).

Patten, Chris. 2000. A Northern Dimension for the Policies of the European Union: Current and Future Activities. In Nissinen, Marja (ed.). Foreign Ministers' Conference on the Northern Dimension, Helsinki, 11–12 November 1999. A Compilation of Speeches. Helsinki: Unit for the Northern Dimension in the Ministry for Foreign Affairs, pp. 10–13.

Payne, Keith B. and Mark B. Schneider. 2016. Russia's New National Security Strategy. Stark Realities Confronting the West. 12 February. http://www.realcleardefense.com/articles/2016/02/12/russias_new_national_security_strategy_109016.html.

Petlyuchenko, V. 1993. The Orthodox Church and Foreign Policy. International Affairs 39: 3, pp. 62–71.

Petrovsky, Vladimir. 1982. Razoruzhenie: Kontseptsiya, Problemy, Mekhanizm [Disarmament: Concept, Problems, Mechanism]. Moscow: Progress (in Russian).

Pharamazyan, R. 1982. Razoruzhenie i Ekonomika [Disarmament and Economy]. Moscow: Progress (in Russian).

Pichugin, Boris. 1996. Russia and the European Union's Eastward Expansion. International Affairs (Moscow) 42: 1, pp. 90–96.

Pierre, Andrew J. and Dmitry Trenin. 1997. Developing NATO-Russian Relations. Survival 39: 1, pp. 5–18.

Pipes, Richard. 2009. Craving to Be a Great Power. Moscow Times, 15 July. http://www.themoscowtimes.com/opinion/article/tmt/379522.html

Piskulov, Yuri. 1999. Initsiativa Finlandii Dayet Rossii Unikalny Shans [The Finnish Initiative Provides Russia with a Unique Chance]. Euro (Moscow) 11, pp. 25–29 (in Russian).

Pleshakov, Konstantin. 1993. Russia's Mission: the Third Epoch. International Affairs (Moscow) 39: 12, pp. 17–26.

Pleshakov, Konstantin. 1994. Komponenty Geopoliticheskogo Myshleniya [Components of Geopolitical Thinking]. Mezhdunarodnaya Zhizn 40: 10, pp. 29–37 (in Russian).

Pleshakov, Konstantin. 1995. The Geoideological Paradigm. International Affairs (Moscow) 41: 4–5, pp. 101–107.

Plimak, Yuri. 1996. Glavnye Alternativy Sovremennosti [Main Alternatives of Our Time]. Svobodnaya Mysl' 8, pp. 42–52 (in Russian).

Podberezkin, Alexei. 1995. Cherez Dukhovnost—k Vozrozhdeniyu Otechestva [Restoring Motherland Through Spirituality]. Svobodnaya Mysl' 5, pp. 87–99 (in Russian).

Podberezkin, Alexei. 1996. Geostrategicheskoe Polozhenie i Bezopasnost Rossii [Russia's Geostrategic Position and Security]. Svobodnaya Mysl' 7, pp. 86–99 (in Russian).

1989. Politika Sily ili Sila Razuma? Gonka Vooruzheniy i Mezhdunarodnye Otnosheniya [Power Politics or Power of Ratio? Arms Race and International Relations]. Moscow: Politizdat (in Russian).

Polyakov, Leonid. 2016. Promezhutochnye Itogi [Interim Results]. Rossiyskaya Gazeta, 3 March. http://rg.ru/2016/03/03/chetyre-goda-nazad-vladimir-putin-byl-izbran-na-novyj-prezidentskij-srok.html (in Russian).

Polyviannyi, Dmitry. 2003. Considering the EU Enlargement to the East and its Consequences for Russia: Are the Generalizations Really Productive? In Goldthau, Andreas and Pavel Onokhine (eds.). Russia-the European Union: Interaction without Strategy? Yekaterinburg: Civic Education Project, pp. 70–77.

Popov, Vladimir I. 2004. Sovremennaya Diplomatiya: Teoriya i Praktika [Modern Diplomacy: Theory and Praxis]. Moscow: Mezhdunarodnye Otnosheniya (in Russian).

Potemkina, Olga. 2002. Evropeiskoe Prostranstvo Svobody, Bezopasnosti i Pravoporyadka: Granitsy, Soderzhanie, Mekhanizmy [European Space of Freedom, Security and Justice: Limits, Contents, Mechanisms]. Moscow: Institute of Europe (in Russian).

Pozdnyakov, Elgiz. 1976. Sistemniy Podkhod i Mezhdunarodnye Otnosheniya [System Approach and International Relations]. Moscow: Nauka (in Russian).

Pozdnyakov, Elgiz. 1992. The Geopolitical Collapse and Russia. International Affairs (Moscow) 38: 9, pp. 3–12.

Pozdnyakov, Elgiz. 1993a. Russia is a Great Power. International Affairs (Moscow) 39: 1, pp. 3–13.

Pozdnyakov, Elgiz. 1993b. Russia Today and Tomorrow. International Affairs (Moscow) 39: 2, pp. 22–31.

Pozdnyakov, Elgiz. (ed.). 1993c. Geopolitika: Teoriya i Praktika [Geopolitics: Theory and Practice]. Moscow: IMEMO (in Russian).

Pozdnyakov, Elgiz. 1994. Filosofya Politiki [Philosophy of Politics]. Vol. 2. Moscow: Paleya (in Russian).

2009. Predstavitelstvo Kaliningradskoi Oblasti v Litve Okonchatelno Prodano [Kaliningrad Oblast's Representative Office in Lithuania Is Finally Sold]. APN Severo-Zapad. 27 February. www.apn-spb.ru/news/article4949.htm (in Russian).

Proskuryakova, Liliana. 2005. Russian Foreign Policy and the EU: from Bilateral Dialogue to Misperception of a 25-Big Europe. In Makarychev, Andrei (ed.). Russia's North West and the European Union: A Playground for Innovations. Nizhny Novgorod: Nizhny Novgorod State Linguistic University Press, pp. 85–93.

Pushkov, Alexei. 1995. Chinese Mirage. Moscow News, 6–12 June, p. 4.

Putin, Vladimir. 2000a. Kontseptsiya Natsionalnoy Bezopasnosti Rossiyskoi Federatsii [The National Security Concept of the Russian Federation]. Nezavisimaya Gazeta, 14 January, pp. 4–5 (in Russian).

Putin, Vladimir. 2000b. Kontseptsiya Vneshney Politiki Rossiyskoi Federatsii [Foreign Policy Concept of the Russian Federation]. 28 June. http://www.scrf.gov.ru/documents/25.html (in Russian).

Putin, Vladimir. 2000c. Voennaya Doktrina Rossiyskoi Federatsii [The Military Doctrine of the Russian Federation]. Available at: http://www.ipmb.ru/1_3.html (in Russian).

Putin, Vladimir. 2007. Vystuplenie i Discussiya na Munhenskoi Konferentsii po Politike Bezopasnosti [Presentation and Remarks at the Munich Conference on Security Policy]. 10 February. http://www.kremlin.ru/appears/2007/02/10/1737_type63374type63376type63377type63381type82634_118109.shtml (in Russian).

Putin, Vladimir. 2012a. Rossiya i Menyauschiysya Mir [Russia and the Changing World]. Moscow News, 27 February (in Russian).

Putin, Vladimir. 2012b. Ukaz Prezidenta RF ot 7 Maya 2012 No. 605 'O Merakh po Realizatsii Vneshnepoliticheskogo Kursa Rossiyskoi Federatsii' [Decree of the President of the RF, 7 May 2012, No. 605 'On the Measures on the Implementation of the Russian Federation's Foreign Policy Course']. http://text.document.kremlin.ru/SESSION/PILOT/main.htm (in Russian).

Putin, Vladimir. 2012c. Vystuplenie na Soveschanii Poslov i Postoyannykh Predstavitelei Rossii, 9 Iulya 2012 [Speech at the Meeting of Russian Ambassadors and Permanent Representatives]. http://www.kremlin.ru/news/15902 (in Russian).

Putin, Vladimir. 2013a. Kontseptsiya Vneshney Politiki Rossiyskoi Federatsii [Foreign Policy Concept of the Russian Federation]. 12 February. http://archive.mid.ru//brp_4.nsf/0/6D84DDEDEDBF7DA644257B160051BF7F (in Russian).

Putin, Vladimir. 2013b. Osnovy Gosudarstvennoi Politiki Rossiyskoi Federatsii v Oblasti Mezdunarodnoi Informatsionnoy Bezopasnosti na Period do 2020 Goda [Fundamentals of the State Polic of the Russian Federation in the Field of International Information Security for the Period up to 2020]. 24 July. http://www.scrf.gov.ru/documents/6/114.html (in Russian).

Putin, Vladimir. 2014. Voennaya Doktrina Rossiyskoy Federatsii [The Military Doctrine of the Russian Federation]. http://static.kremlin.ru/media/events/files/41d527556bec8deb3530.pdf (in Russian).

Putin, Vladimir. 2015a. Morskaya Doktrina Rossiyskoy Federatsii [Maritime Doctrine of the Russian Federation]. http://statc.kremlin.ru/media/events/files/ru/uAFi5nvux2twaqjftS5yrIZUVTJan77L.pdf (in Russian).

Putin, Vladimir (2015b). O Strategii Natsional'noi Bezopasnosti Rossiyskoi Federatsii [On the National Security Strategy of the Russian Federation]. http://www.scrf.gov.ru/documents/1/133.html (in Russian).

Pyadyshev, Boris. 1999. Novy Tsentr Mirovoi Vlasti [A New Center of the World Power]. Nezavisimaya Gazeta, 5 November, p. 2 (in Russian).

Ra'anan, Uri. 1995. Imperial Elements in Russia's Doctrines and Operations. In Ra'anan, Uri and Kevin Martin (eds.). Russia: A Return to Imperialism? New York: St. Martin's Press, pp. 19–31.

Ranieri, Umberto. 2000. The speech of Mr Umberto Ranieri, Under Secretary of State, Italy. In Nissinen, Marja (ed.). Foreign Ministers' Conference on the Northern Dimension, Helsinki, 11–12 November 1999. A Compilation of Speeches. Helsinki: Unit for the Northern Dimension in the Ministry for Foreign Affairs, pp. 61–64.

Razuvayev, Vladimir. 1993a. Geopolitika Postsovetskogo Perioda [The Geopolitics of the Post-Soviet Period]. Moscow: Institute of Europe, RAS (in Russian).

Razuvayev, Vladimir. 1993b. Russia and the Post-Soviet Geopolitical Area. International Affairs (Moscow) 39: 8, pp. 109–116.

Reddaway, Peter and Robert W. Orttung (eds.). 2005. Dynamics of Russian Politics: Putin's Reform of Federal–Regional Relations. Lanham: Rowman and Littlefield.

2011. Reiting Regionov Rossii po Ob'emu Inostrannykh Investitsii [The Rating of Russian Regions in Terms of Foreign Investment]. Investitsii, Innovatsii, Biznes [Investments, Innovations, Business]. 22 February 2011. http://spb-venchur.ru/news/6027.htm (in Russian).

Reut, Oleg. 2000. Republic of Karelia: A Double Asymmetry or North-Eastern Dimensionalism. Copenhagen: Copenhagen Peace Research Institute (COPRI Working Paper No. 13).

Richter, Jim. 1996. Russian Foreign Policy and the Politics of National Identity. In Celeste A. Wallander (ed.). The Sources of Russian Foreign Policy After the Cold War. Boulder, Colorado: Westview Press, pp. 69–93.

Roberts, Sean P. 2013. Russia as an International Actor: The View from Europe and the US. Helsinki: The Finnish Institute of International Affairs.

Rogov, Sergei. 1993. A National Security Policy for Russia. In Goodby, James E. and Benoit Morel (eds.). The Limited Partnership: Building a Russian-US Security Community. New York: Oxford University Press, pp. 75–80.

Rogov, Sergei. 1995. Russia and the United States: A Partnership or Another Disengagement. International Affairs (Moscow) 41: 7, pp. 3–11.

Rogov, Sergei. 1997. Dogovor Podpisan, Problemy Ostayutsya [Agreement is Signed but Problems Remain]. Literaturnaya Gazeta, 28 May, p. 9 (in Russian).

Rusakova, O.F. 2010. Kontsept "Myagkoy" Sily v Sovremennoy Politicheskoy Philosophii. In Yearbook of the Institute of Philosophy and Law. Ural Section. Russian Academy of Science 10, pp. 173–192 (in Russian).

2014. Russia Says BRICS Development Bank Ready to Launch. The Moscow Times, 9 July. http://www.themoscowtimes.com/business/article/russia-says-brics-development-bank-ready-to-launch/503183.html.

2015. Russia Revises Navy Doctrine Over NATO's 'Inadmissible' Expansion. 26 July. http://news.yahoo.com/russia-revises-navy-doctrine-over-natos-inadmissible-expansion-191235893.html

Russian Foreign Ministry. 2013. Concept of Participation of the Russian Federation in BRICS. http://eng.news.kremlin.ru/media/events/eng/files/41d452b13d9c2624d228.pdf

Russian International Affairs Council. 2015a. Kazakh Experts on the Eurasian Economic Union: Aligned Competition or Aligned Stagnation? http://russiancouncil.ru/en/inner/?id_4=5830#top-content.

2015. Russian Military Doctrine. Global Security. http://www.globalsecurity.org/military/world/russia/doctrine.htm.

1992. Russia's National Interests. International Affairs (Moscow) 38: 8, pp. 134–43.

Ryabov, Andrei. 2003. Khoronit' NATO Poka Prezhdevremenno [It Is Premature to Bury NATO]. Nezavisimaya Gazeta, 12 May, p. 14 (in Russian).

Rybkin, Ivan. 1995. The State Duma and Russia's External Interests. International Affairs (Moscow) 41: 11–12, pp. 28–33.

Safronova, Olga. 2001. Teoriya Mezhdunarodnykh Otnosheniy [International Relations Theories]. Nizhny Novgorod: Nizhny Novgorod State University (in Russian).

Sakwa, Richard. 1993. Russian Politics and Society. London and New York: Routledge.

Samarin, A. 2008. Kul'tura Mira' kak Otkryty Mezdisciplinarny Project [Peace Culture as an Open Inter-Disciplinary Project]. http://www.confstud.ru/content/view/28/2/ (in Russian).

Sanakoev, Shalva and Nikolai Kapchenko. 1977. O Teorii Vneshnei Politiki Sotsi-alizma [On the Socialist Foreign Policy Theory]. Moscow: Mezhdunarodnye Otnosheniya (in Russian).

Satanovsky, Yevgeny. 2003. Nastupaet Ocherednoi Peredel Mira. [The New Re-division of the World Is Coming]. Nezavisimaya Gazeta, 24 March, p. 1 (in Russian).

Satarov, Georgy. 2003. Pragmatichny Romantizm [Pragmatic Romanticism]. Ros-siyskaya Gazeta, 18 March, p. 7 (in Russian).

Savitsky, Pyotr. 2003. Geograficheskie i Geopoliticheskie Osnovy Evraziystva [Geographic and Geopolitical Foundations of Eurasianism]. In Korolev, K. (ed.). Klassika Geopolitiki, XX Vek [Classics of Geopolitics]. Moscow: Iz-datel'stvo AST, pp. 677–687 (in Russian).

Selyaninov, O.P. 1998. Tetradi po Diplomaticheskoi Sluzhbe Gosudarstv [Notes on Foreign Services of States]. Moscow: MGIMO Press (in Russian).

Sergunin, Alexander. 1993. The Russian Dimension of Nordic Security: Challenges and Opportunities, Copenhagen: Center for Peace & Conflict Research (Working Papers, no. 13).

Sergunin, Alexander. 1996. The Russian Dimension of Nordic Security—Hard Choices and Opportunities. In Lassinanti, Gunnar (ed.). Visions of European Security—Focal Point Sweden and Northern Europe. Stockholm: The Olof Palme International Center, pp. 104–116.

Sergunin, Alexander. 1997. Post-Communist Security Thinking in Russia: Chang-ing Paradigms. Copenhagen: Copenhagen Peace Research Institute (COPRI Working Papers, no. 4).

Sergunin, Alexander. 1998. Russia: A Long Way to the National Security Doctrine. Copenhagen: Copenhagen Peace Research Institute (COPRI Working Pa-per, no. 10).

Sergunin, Alexander. 1999a. Executive-Legislative Liaison Mechanism in Russia and the West: Comparative Analysis. Nizhny Novgorod: Nizhny Novgorod State University Press.

Sergunin, Alexander. 1999b. The Process of Regionalization and the Future of the Russian Federation. Copenhagen: Copenhagen Peace Research Institute (COPRI Working Papers, no. 9).

Sergunin, Alexander. 2001. External Determinants of Russia's Regionalization. Zurich: Center for Security and Conflict Studies.

Sergunin, Alexander. 2003. Rossiyskaya Vneshnepoliticheskaya Mysl: Problemy Natsional'noi i Mezhdunarodnoi Bezopasnosti [Russian Foreign Policy Thought: Problems of National and International Security]. Nizhny Novgorod: Nizhny Novgorod State Linguistic University Press (in Russian).

Sergunin, Alexander. 2004. International Relations Discussions in Post-Communist Russia. Communism and Post-Communism Studies 37, pp. 19–35.

Sergunin, Alexander. 2005. Global Challenges to Russia's National Security: Any Chances for Resisting / Bandwagoning / Adapting / Contributing to an Emerging World Order? In Aydinli, Ersel and James Rosenau (eds.). Globalization, Security, and the Nation State: Paradigms in Transition. Albany: SUNY Press, pp. 117–134.

Sergunin, Alexander. 2006. Kaliningrad, Euroregions and 4Fs (Freedoms) in the Baltic Sea Region. INTAS Working Paper Series 3.

Sergunin, Alexander. 2007a. International Relations in Post-Soviet Russia: Trends and Problems. Nizhny Novgorod: Nizhny Novgorod Linguistic University Press.

Sergunin, Alexander. 2007b. Russia's Decision-Making on Europe: Decision-Making Mechanism. Nizhny Novgorod: Nizhny Novgorod Linguistic University Press.

Sergunin, Alexander. 2008. Russian Foreign-Policy Decision Making on Europe. In Hopf, Ted (ed.). Russia's European Choice. New York: Palgrave Macmillan, pp. 59–96.

Sergunin, Alexander. 2010. Towards a Pan-European Security System? Notions on the Russian Draft of the European Security Treaty. In Freedom, Security, Justice—Common Interests in the Baltic Sea Region. Helsinki: STETE, pp. 33–40.

Sergunin, Alexander. 2013. Bridging a (mis)perceptional gap: the EU's Eastern Partnership and Russian policies in the Trans-Caucasus. Bilge Strateji 5: 8, pp. 17–37.

Sergunin, Alexander. 2014a. Has Putin the Pragmatist Turned into Putin the Ideologue? Vlaams Marxistisch Tijdschrift 48: 2, pp. 68–69.

Sergunin, Alexander. 2014b. Russian views on the Ukrainian crisis: from confrontation to damage limitation. Vlaams Marxistisch Tijdschrift 48: 2, pp. 80–92.

Sergunin, Alexander. 2015. The Russian Academic Debate on Conflict Resolution and Mediation. Joenniemi, Pertti (ed.). Russia's Approach to Arms Control, Peace Mediation and National Dialogues. Tampere: University of Tampere Press, pp. 33–76.

Sergunin, Alexander and Leonid Karabeshkin. 2015. Understanding Russia's Soft Power Strategy. Politics 35: 3–4, pp. 347–363.

Sergunin, Alexander and Andrei Makarychev. 1999. Sovremennaya Zapadnaya Politicheskaya Mysl': Postpositivistskaya Revolutsiya [Contemporary Western Political Thought: Postpositivist Revolution]. Nizhny Novgorod: Nizhny Novgorod State Linguistic University Press (in Russian).

Sergunin, Alexander and Sergei Subbotin. 1996a. Indo-Russian Military Cooperation: Russian Perspective. Asian Profile, February, pp. 23–34.

Sergunin, Alexander and Sergei Subbotin. 1996b. Sino-Russian Military Cooperation and Evolving Security System in East Asia. Nizhny Novgorod: Nizhny Novgorod State University Press.

Sergunin, Alexander and Sergei Subbotin. 1999. Russian Arms Transfers to East Asia in the 1990s. New York: Oxford University Press.

Shakhnazarov, Georgi. 1995. Vostok i Zapad: Samoidentifikatsiya na Perelome Vekov [East and West: In Search for Identity on the Turn of the Century]. Svobodnaya Mysl' 8, pp. 73–79 (in Russian).

Shakleina, Tatyana. 2002a. Rossiya i SShA v Novom Mirovom Poryadke. Diskussiya v Politiko-Akademicheskikh Soobshestvakh Rossii i SshA (1991–2002) [Russia and the U.S. in the New World Order. Discussion in the Russian and U.S. Politico-Academic Communities (1991–2002)]. Moscow: Institute of the USA and Canada, RAS (in Russian).

Shakleina, Tatyana. 2002b. Vneshnyaya Politika i Bezopasnost' Sovremennoi Rossii [Russia's Foreign Policy and Security]. Moscow: ROSSPEN, Vol. 1–4 (in Russian).

Shannon, V., Kowert, P. (eds.). 2012. Psychology and Constructivism in International Relations. Ann Arbor: The University of Michigan Press.

Shaposhnikov, Yevgeny. 1993. A Security Concept for Russia. International Affairs 39: 10, pp. 10–19.

Shapovalov, Alexei (2014). 'Tamozhenny Soyuz ne Srastaetsya Torgovley' [The Customs Union is not Tied up by Mutual Trade], Kommersant, May 19, http://www.kommersant.ru/doc/2474260 (Access: 26.07.2015) (in Russian).

Shedrovitsky, Pyotr. 2000. Russkij Mir i Transnatsionalnoe Russkoe [Russian World and Transnational Russian]. Russkij Zhurnal 2, March. http://old.russ.ru/politics/meta/20000302_schedr.html (in Russian).

Simha, Rakesh Krishnan. 2013. Why Russia Prefers BRICS to Europe. Russia beyond the Headlines, 8 October. http://in.rbth.com/blogs/2013/10/08/why_russia_prefers_brics_to_europe_29979.html

Simons, Greg. 2013. Nation Branding and Russian Foreign Policy. Stockholm: The Swedish Institute of International Affairs. http://www.ui.se/eng/upl/files/96881.pdf.

SIPRI. 1996. SIPRI Yearbook 1996. New York: Oxford University Press.

SIPRI. 1997. SIPRI Yearbook 1997. New York: Oxford University Press.

Smirnov, V. 2012. Russia's 'Soft Power' in the Baltic, 12 May. http://russiancouncil.ru/en/inner/?id_4=367

Smith, Hanna (ed.). 2005. Russia and its Foreign Policy: Influences, Interests and Issues. Helsinki: Aleksanteri Institute.

Smith, Hanna. 2014. Russia as a great power: Status inconsistency and the two Chechen wars. Communist and Post-Communist Studies 47, pp. 355–363.

Snetkov, Aglaya. 2015. From Crisis to Crisis: Russia's Security Policy Under Putin. Russian Analytical Digest 173, 12 October, pp. 2–5.

2002. Sodruzhestvo Nezavisimykh Gosudarstv: Uroki i Vyzovy Sovremennosti [The Commonwealth of Independent States: Lessons and Challenges of Modernity]. St. Petersburg: The Baltic Research Center (in Russian).

Solodovnik, Sergei. 1995. Crisis Management in the CIS: Whither Russia? Baden-Baden: Nomos Verlagsgesellschaft.

Sorokin, Konstantin. 1995. Geopolitika Sovremennogo Mira i Rossiya [Contemporary Geopolitics and Russia]. Politicheskie Issledovaniya 3: 1, pp. 3–12 (in Russian).

St. Petersburg Committee on External Relations. 2014. St. Petersburg Information Business Centers. www.kvs.spb.ru/informatcionnie_delovie_tcentri_sankt-peterburga_za_rubezhom18 (in Russian).

St. Petersburg Committee on Investment. 2014. Investment in St. Petersburg. http://gov.spb.ru/gov/otrasl/invest/statistic/development (in Russian).

Stankevich, Sergei. 1992. A Transformed Russia in a New World. International Affairs (Moscow) 38: 4–5, pp. 81–104.

Stankevich, Sergei. 1992. Derzhava v Poiskakh Sebya [The Power in Search of Itself]. Nezavisimaya Gazeta, 28 March, p. 4 (in Russian).

Stankevich, Sergei. 1994. Toward a New National Idea. In Sestanovich, Stephen (ed.). Rethinking Russia's National Interests. Washington, DC: Center for Strategic and International Studies, pp. 24–31.

Stent, Angela E. 2014. The Limits of Partnership: U.S. Russian Relations in the Twenty-First Century. Princeton: Princeton University Press.

Stepanov, Y. 2014. Obespechenie Processa Modernizatssii v Usloviyakh Sovremennoy Globalizatsii [Ensuring Modernization in the Context of the On-Going Globalization]. Konfliktologiya 9: pp. 9–27 (in Russian).

Stepanov Y., Aksentyev V., Golovin Y., Kukonkov P. 2007. Monitoring Sotsial'nykh Napryazheniy i Konflictov v Krupnykh Regional'nykh Tsentrakh Rossii' [Monitoring of Social Tensions and Conflicts in Large Regional Centers of Russia]. In Gorshkov, M. (ed.). Rossiya Reformiruyushayasya [Russia Reformed]. Moscow: Institute of Sociology, Russian Academy of Sciences, pp. 235–252 (in Russian).

Stepanova, Yekaterina (ed.). 2003. Anti-terrorism and Peace-Building During and After Conflict. Stockholm: SIPRI.

Stoner, Kathryn and Michael McFaul. 2015. Who Lost Russia (This Time)? Vladimir Putin. The Washington Quarterly 38: 2, pp. 167–187.

Stranga, A. 1996. Russia and the Security of the Baltic States: 1991–1996. In Lejins, A. and D. Bleiere (eds.). The Baltic States: Search for Security. Riga: Latvian Institute of International Affairs.

1992. Strategiya dlya Rossii: Doklad Soveta po Vneshney i Oboronnoy Politike [Strategy for Russia: Report of the Council for Foreign and Defense Policy]. Nezavisimaya Gazeta, 19 August, p. 5 (in Russian).

1999. Stroitel'stvo Novogo Mirovogo Poryadka [Building a New World Order]. Rossiiskaya Gazeta. 4 September. http://www.rg.ru/prilog/es/0904/1.htm

Stuenkel, Oliver. 2014. Emerging Powers and Status: The Case of the First BRICS Summit. Asian Perspective 38: 1. http://kr.vlex.com/vid/emerging-powers-status-brics-summit-494287502

Stupavsky, Peter. 1996. Zahranicna Politika Ruska v Ere Jel'cina' [Russia's Foreign Policy in the Yeltsin Era]. Mezdunarodni Vstahy 3, pp. 5–10 (in Czech).

Sushko, Alexander. 2009–2010. How to Make Secure a New European Security System. Vlast 51: 26. http://www.zn.ua/1000/1600/68160/ (in Russian).

Suslov, Dmitry. 2003. Voina v Irake ne Povliyala na Polozhenie Rossii v Mire [The Iraq War Did Not Affect Russia's Position in the World]. Nezavisimaya Gazeta, 21 April, pp. 9, 14 (in Russian).

Sutyrin, S.F. and N.A. Lomagin (eds.). 2001. Sotrudnichestvo i Konflikt v Mezhdunarodnykh Otnosheniyakh [Cooperation and Conflict in International Relations]. St. Petersburg: Sentyabr (in Russian).

Tammen, Ronald L. et al. 2000. Power Transitions: Strategies for the 21st Century. New York: Seven Bridges Press.

TASS. 2015. Russian Security Council preparing new Doctrine of Russia's Information Security. 7 April. http://tass.ru/en/russia/787625.

Tauscher, Ellen and Igor Ivanov (eds.). 2015. Managing Differences on European Security in 2015. U.S., Russian, and European Perspectives. Washington, DC: The Atlantic Council of the United States. http://www.atlanticcouncil.org/images/publications/ACUS_Managing_Differences_Report.pdf.

Tereshkin, V. 1996. Environmentalist or Spy? Moscow News, 4–10 April, p. 6.

2012. Tezisy po Vneshnej Politike Rossii (2012–2018) [Theses on Russia's Foreign Policy (2012–2018)]. Moscow: Russian International Affairs Council (in Russian).

Torkunov, Anatoly V. 1995. Koreyskaya Problema: Noviy Vzglyad [The Korean Problem: A New Outlook]. Moscow: ANKIL (in Russian).

Torkunov, Anatoly V. (ed.). 1997, 1999, 2001. Sovremennye Mezhdunarodnye Otnosheniya [Contemporary International Relations]. Moscow: ROSSPEN (in Russian).

Torkunov, Anatoly V. (ed.). 2005. Sovremennye Mezhdunarodnye Otnosheniya i Mirovaya Politika [Contemporary International Relations and World Politics]. Moscow: Prosveshenie (in Russian).

Torkunov, A.V. and A.V. Mal'gin (eds.). 2012. Sovremennye Mezhdunarodnye Otnosheniya [Contemporary International Relations]. Moscow: Aspect-Press (in Russian).

1992. A Transformed Russia in a New World. International Affairs (Moscow) 38: April-May, pp. 81–104.

Travkin, Nikolai. 1994. Russia, Ukraine, and Eastern Europe. In Sestanovich, Stephen (ed.). Rethinking Russia's National Interests. Washington, DC: Center for Strategic and International Studies, pp. 33–41.

Trenin, Dmitry. 1994. Budet li NATO Rasshiryatsya na Vostok? [Will NATO Expand Eastwards?]. Novoye Vremya, 2 December (in Russian).

Trenin, Dmitry. 1995. NATO: How to Avoid Confrontation. International Affairs (Moscow) 41: 7, pp. 20–6.

Trenin, Dmitry. 1997. Rossiya i Novaya Evropeyskaya Sistema' [Russia and a New European System]. Rubezhy 1 (in Russian).

Trenin, Dmitry. 1999. Realpolitik i Realnyaya Politika [Realpolitik and Realist Policy]. Nezavisimoye Voene Obozrenie, 1–7 October, pp. 1–4 (in Russian).

Trenin, Dmitry. 2000. Rossiya i Osnovnye Instituty Bezopasnosti v Evrope: Vstupaya v XXI Vek [Russia and the Main European Security Institutions: Entering the XXIst Century]. Moscow: The Moscow Carnegie Center (in Russian).

Trenin, Dmitri. 2009. From a "Treaty to Replace All Treaties" to Addressing Europe's Core Security Issues. Carnegie Moscow Center. 30 November. http://www.carnegie.ru/en/pubs/media/83465.htm

Trenin, Dmitry. 2015. Ukraine Crisis Causes Strategic, Mental Shift in Global Order, Global Times. 17 May. http://carnegie.ru/2015/05/17/ukrainecrisisca usesstrategicmentalshiftinglobalorder/i8q4

Troitsky, Mikhail. 2004. Transatlanticheskiy Soyuz (1991–2004) [Trans-Atlantic Alliance (1991–2004)]. Moscow: NOFMO (in Russian).

Troitsky, Mikhail. 2011. Russian Soft Power in the European Union. Conference on 'Russian Soft Power: Perspectives and Prospects. Center for Polish-Russian Dialogue and Understanding, Warsaw, 20 December. http://mikhailtroitski.livejournal.com/2099.html.

Trubetskoi, Nikolai. 2003. My i Drugie [We and Others]. In Korolev, K. (ed.). Klassika Geopolitiki, XX Vek [Classics of Geopolitics]. Moscow: Izdatel'stvo AST, pp. 106–125.

Trush, Sergei. 1996. Prodazha Rossiyskogo Oruzhiya Pekinu: Rezony i Opaseniya [Russian Arms Sales to Beijing: Pro and Contra]. Nezavisimaya Gazeta, 25 April, p. 4 (in Russian).

Trynkov, Anatoly A. 1995. O Nekotorykh Realiyakh Politiko-ekonomicheskoi Karty Evropy [On Some Realities Following from the Politico-Economic Map of Europe]. In Zapadnaya Evropa na Poroge Tretyego Tysyacheletiya [Western Europe on the Threshhold of the Third Millenium]. Moscow: Russian Institute for Strategic Studies / Institute of World Economy and International Relations, pp. 65–68 (in Russian).

Tsygankov, Andrei P. 2012. Russia and the West from Alexander to Putin: Honor in International Relations. Cambridge: Cambridge University Press.

Tsygankov, Andrei. 2013a. Moscow's Soft Power Strategy. Current History 112: 756, pp. 259–264.

Tsygankov, Andrei. 2013b. Vsesil'no Potomuchto Verno? [Omnipotent Because True?]. Russia in Global Affairs. December. http://www.globalaffairs.ru/number/Vsesilno-ibo-verno-16251 (in Russian).

Tsygankov, Andrei P. 2014. The Frustrating Partnership: Honor, Status, and Emotions in Russia's Discourses of the West. Communist and Post-Communist Studies 47, pp. 345–354.

Tsygankov, Andrei P. 2016. Russia's Foreign Policy: Change and Continuity in National Identity. 4th ed. New York: Rowman and Littlefield.

Tsygankov, Andrei and Pavel Tsygankov (eds.). 2005. Rossiskaya Nauka Mezhdunarodnykh Otnosheniy: Novye Napravleniya [Russian International Relations: New Perspectives]. Moscow: PER SE (in Russian).

Tsygankov, Andrei and Pavel Tsygankov. 2006. Sotsiologiya Mezhdunarodnykh Otnosheniy: Analiz Rossiyskikh i Zapadnykh Teoriy [Sociology of International Relations: Analysis of Russian and Western Theories]. Moscow: Aspekt Press (in Russian).

Tsygankov, Pavel A. 1995. Mirovaya Politika: Problemy Teorii i Praktiki [World Politics: Problems of Theory and Practice]. Moscow: Moscow State University Press (in Russian).

Tsygankov, Pavel A. 1996. Mezhdunarodnye Otnosheniya [International Relations]. Moscow: Novaya Shkola (in Russian).

Tsygankov, Pavel A. (ed.). 1998. Mezhdunarodnye Otnosheniya: Sotsiologicheskie Podkhody [International Relations: Sociological Approaches]. Moscow: Gardariki (in Russian).

Tsygankov, Pavel A. 2002. Teoriya Mezhdunarodnykh Otnosheniy [International Relations Theory]. Moscow: Gardariki (in Russian).

Tsygankov, Pavel A. (ed.). 2007. Mezhdunarodnye Otnosheniya: Teorii, Konflikty, Dvizheniya, Organizatsii [International Relations: Theories, Conflicts, Movements, Organizations]. Moscow: Alfa-M / INFRA-M (in Russian).

Tsypkin, Mikhail. 1994. Military Power in Russian National Security Policy. In Lieberman, S.R., Powell, D.E., Saivetz, C.R. and S.M. Terry (eds.). The Soviet Empire Reconsidered: Essays in Honour of Adam B. Ulam. Boulder, Co.: Westview Press.

Tsypkin, Mikhail. 2009. Moscow's European Security Gambit. SperoNews. 10 December 10. http://www.speroforum.com/a/24078/Moscows-European-Security-Gambit

Tyulin, Ivan G. 1991. Politicheskaya Nauka: Vozmozhnosti i Perspectivy Mezhdistsiplinarnogo Podhoda [Political Science: Opportunities and Prospects on Inter-Disciplinary Approach]. Moscow: MGIMO (in Russian).

Tyulin, Ivan G. 1994. Theory and Practice in Foreign Policy Making: National Perspectives on Academics and Professionals in International Relations. London: Pinter Publishers Ltd.

Tyulin, Ivan G. 1997. Between the Past and the Future: International Studies in Russia. Zeitschrift fur Internationale Beobahtung 4: 1, pp. 181–194.

Uspensky, Nikolai and Sergei Komissarov. 1993. New Stage in Cooperation in the Baltic Region. International Affairs (Moscow) 39: 2, pp. 79–85.

Utkin, Anatoly. 1995a. Natsionalizm i Buduschee Mirovogo Soobschestva [Nationalism and the Future of the World Community]. Svobodnaya Mysl' 3, pp. 78–86 (in Russian).

Utkin, Anatoly. 1995b. Rossiya i Zapad: Problemy Vzaimnogo Vospriyatiya i Perspektivy Stroitelstva Otnosheniy [Russia and the West: Mutual Perceptions and Prospects for Building Partnership]. Moscow: Russian Research Foundation (in Russian).

Utkin, Anatoly. 2000. Amerikanskaya Strategiya dlya 21 Veka [American Strategy for the 21st Century]. Moscow: Logos (in Russian).

Utkin, Anatoly. 2003. Edinstvennaya Sverkhderzava [The Only Superpower]. Moscow: Algoritm (in Russian).

Vaz, Keith. 2000. The Speech of Mr Keith Vaz, Minister for Europe, United Kingdom. In Nissinen, Marja (ed.). Foreign Ministers' Conference on the Northern Dimension, Helsinki, 11–12 November 1999. A Compilation of Speeches. Helsinki: Unit for the Northern Dimension in the Ministry for Foreign Affairs, pp. 55–57.

Vestnik MGU. 1994. Series No. 12: Social-Political Studies. Moscow: Moscow State University Press (in Russian).

Vizgin, V.P. 1995. Mishel Fuko—Teoretik Tsivilizatsii Znaniya [Michael Foucault is a Theorist of the Civilization of Knowledge]. Voprosy Filosofii 30: 6, pp. 116–126 (in Russian).

Vladimirov, Alexander. 1992. Eta Systema Mogucha i Dostatochno Zla [This System is Powerful and Angry Enough]. In Rossiyskaya Gazeta, 22 September, p. 3 (in Russian).

Vladislavlev, Alexander and Sergey A. Karaganov. 1992. The Idea of Russia. International Affairs (Moscow) 38: 12, pp. 30–6.

Vlassov, Evgueny A. and Stanislav V. Vasiliev. 1997. All about MGIMO: Academic Yearbook. Moscow: MGIMO.

2000. Voennaya Doktrina Rossiyskoi Federatsii [The Military Doctrine of the Russian Federation]. Rossiyskaya Gazeta, 25 April, pp. 5–6 (in Russian).

Volkov, Alexander. 2003. Bez Suda i Sledstviya [Without Justice and Investigation]. Rossiyskaya Gazeta, 18 March, p. 7 (in Russian).

Vollebaek, Knut. 2000. On the Conference of Ministers of Energy in the Baltic Sea Region, Helsinki, 24–25 October 1999. In Nissinen, Marja (ed.). Foreign Ministers' Conference on the Northern Dimension, Helsinki, 11–12 November 1999. A Compilation of Speeches. Helsinki: Unit for the Northern Dimension in the Ministry for Foreign Affairs, pp. 19–20.

Von Riekhoff, H. 1973. Status Inconsistency and the War Behaviour of Major Powers, 1815–1965. Paper presented at the International Conference on International Relations Theory, York University (Canada).

Vorkunova, Olga. 2008. Regional Security in Russia and the Near Abroad. In Solomon, Hussein (ed.). Challenges to Global Security: Geopolitics and Power in an Age of Transition. London: I.B.Tauris & Co. Ltd., pp. 166–187.

Vorkunova, Olga. 2009. Nauka Mira [Science of Peace]. http://unce.pww.ru/page2.html (in Russian).

Vorkunova, Olga. 2012. Path to Peace in the Trinity Sea System. In Fabian, Attila (ed.). A Peaceful World is Possible. Sopron: University of West Hungary Press, pp. 325–341.

Voskresensky, Alexei. 1996. Veter s Zapada ili Veter s Vostoka? Rossiya, SShA, Kitai i Mirovoe Liderstvo [Is There Wind From the West or East? Russia, the USA, China, and World Leadership]. Svobodnaya Mysl' 10, pp. 89–100 (in Russian).

Voskresensky, Alexei (ed.). 2002. Vostok / Zapad: Regional'nye Podsistemy i Regional'nye Problemy Mezhdunarodnykh Otnosheniy [East-West: Regional Sub-Systems and Regional Problems of International Relations]. Moscow: ROSSPEN (in Russian).

Wallace, M.D. 1971. Power, Status and International War. Journal of Peace Research 8: 1, pp. 23–35.

Wallace, M.D. 1973. Alliance Polarization, Cross-Cutting and International War, 1815–1964: a Measurement Procedure and Some Preliminary Evidence. Journal of Conflict Resolution 17: 4, 575–604.

Wallander, Celeste. 1999. Russia, Kosovo and Security Cooperation. Cambridge, MA: Davis Center for Russian Studies, Harvard University (PONARS Policy Memo Series, No. 58).

Wallander, Celeste. 2000. Institutional Assets and Adaptability: NATO after the Cold War. International Organization 54: 4, pp. 705–735.

Wittkopf, Eugene R. 1997. World Politics: Trend and Transformation. New York: St. Martin's Press.

Yeltsin, Boris. 1992a. Zakon Rossiyskoi Federatsii o Bezopasnosti [The Law on Security of the Russian Federation]. Rossiyskaya Gazeta, 6 May, p. 5 (in Russian).

Yeltsin, Boris. 1992b. Zakon Rossiyskoi Federatsii ob Oborone [The Law on Defense of the Russian Federation]. Krasnaya Zvezda, 10 October.

Yeltsin, Boris. 1994. The Basic Provisions of the Military Doctrine of the Russian Federation. Jane's Intelligence Review (Special Report) 1, pp. 6–12.

Yeltsin, Boris. 1997. Kontseptsiya Natsionalnoy Bezopasnosti Rossiyskoi Federatsii [The National Security Concept of the Russian Federation]. Rossiyskaya Gazeta, 26 December, pp. 4–5 (in Russian).

Zagorski, Andrei. 1994. SNG: Ot Dezintegratsii k Integratsii [From Disintegration to Integration]. Moscow: MGIMO (in Russian).

Zagorski, Andrei. 1995a. Geopolitik versus Geowirtschaft. Wostok 6, pp. 3–10 (in German).

Zagorski, Andrei. 1995b. Was für eine GUS erfüllt ihren Zweck. Aussenpolitik 46: 3, pp. 263–270 (in German).

Zagorski, Andrei. 1996. Russia and Europe. Romanian Journal of International Affairs 2: 1–2, pp. 52–69.

Zagorski, Andrei and Michael Lucas. 1993. Rossiya Pered Evropeyskim Vyzovom [The European Challenge to Russia]. Moscow: Moscow State Institute of International Relations (in Russian).

Zagorski, Andrey, Zlobin, Anatoly A. et al. 1992. Sodruzhestvo Nezavisimykh Gosudarstv: Protsessy i Perstectivy [The Commonwealth of Independent States: Developments and Prospects]. Moscow: MGIMO (in Russian).

Zagorski, Andrei, Anatoly Zlobin, Sergei Solodovnik and Mark Khrustalev. 1992. Russia in a New World. International Affairs (Moscow) 38: 7, pp. 3–11.

Zaitsev, Vladimir. 1999. Tainye Plany SShA Stanovyatsaya Yavnymi [The US Secret Plans to Become Explicit]. Nezavisimaya Gazeta, 13 April, p. 3 (in Russian).

Zamyatin, D.N. 2004. Vlast' Prostranstva i Prostranstvo Vlasti: Geograficheskie Obrazy v Politike i Mezhdunarodnykh Otnosheniyakh [Power of Space and Space of Power: Geographic Images in Politics and International Relations]. Moscow: ROSSPEN (in Russian).

Zagorski, Andrei. 2014. Strengthening the OSCE. Building a Common Space for Economic and Humanitarian Cooperation, an Indivisible Security Community from the Atlantic to the Pacific. Moscow: Spetskniga.

Zhirinovskiy, Vladimir. 1993. Poslednyi Brosok na Yug [Last Dash to the South]. Moscow: Liberal Democratic Party of Russia (in Russian).

Zhurkin, Vitaly. 1998. Evropeisky Soyuz: Vneshnyaya Politika, Bezopasnost, Oborona [The European Union: Foreign Policy, Security, Defense]. Institute of Europe's Reports, no. 47 (in Russian).

Zonova, Tatyana. 2003. Sovremennaya Model Diplomatii: Istoki Stanovleniya i Perspectivy Razvitiya [The Modern Model of Diplomacy: Origins and Prospects for Development]. Moscow: ROSSPEN (in Russian).

Zonova, Tatyana (ed.). 2004. Diplomatiya Inostrannykh Gosudarstv [Diplomacy of Foreign Countries]. Moscow: ROSSPEN (in Russian).

Zöpel, Christoph. 2000. The speech of Mr. Christoph Zöpel, the Minister of State, Germany. In Nissinen, Marja (ed.). Foreign Ministers' Conference on the Northern Dimension, Helsinki, 11–12 November 1999. A Compilation of Speeches. Helsinki: Unit for the Northern Dimension in the Ministry for Foreign Affairs, pp. 23–26.

Zyuganov, Gennady. 1995. Za Gorizontom [Over the Horizon]. Orel: Veshnie Vody (in Russian).

Zyuganov, Gennady (ed.). 1997. Voyennaya Reforma: Otsenka Ugroz Natsionalnoy Bezopasnosti Rossii [Military Reform: Assessment of the Threats to the National Security of Russia]. Moscow: RAU-Universitet (in Russian).

SOVIET AND POST-SOVIET POLITICS AND SOCIETY

Edited by Dr. Andreas Umland

ISSN 1614-3515

ibidem-Verlag / *ibidem* Press
Melchiorstr. 15
70439 Stuttgart
Germany

ibidem@ibidem.eu
ibidem.eu